57600

THE MAN WHO
REALLY LOVED WOMEN

Casanova

THE MAN WHO
REALLY LOVED WOMEN

Lydia Flem

TRANSLATED BY
CATHERINE TEMERSON

FARRAR · STRAUS · GIROUX

NEW YORK

Farrar, Straus and Giroux
19 Union Square West, New York 10003

Copyright © Editions du Seuil, May 1995
Translation copyright © 1997 by Farrar, Straus and Giroux, Inc.
All rights reserved
Distributed in Canada by Douglas & McIntyre Ltd.
Printed in the United States of America
Designed by Jonathan D. Lippincott
First published in 1995 by Editions du Seuil, France,
in "La Librairie du XXe siècle," edited by Maurice Olender,
as *Casanova ou l'exercice du bonheur*
First Farrar, Straus and Giroux edition, 1997

Library of Congress Cataloging-in-Publication Data
Flem, Lydia.
[Casanova, ou, L'exercice du bonheur.   English]
Casanova : the man who really loved women / Lydia Flem :
translated by Catherine Temerson.
p.   cm.
Includes index.
ISBN 0-374-11957-0 (alk. paper)
1. Casanova, Giacomo, 1725–1798.   2. Europe—Biography.
I. Title.
D285.8.C4F5913   1997
940.2'53'092—dc21
[B]   97-20644

Contents

THREE

The Curtain Rises

FOUR

The Stratagems of Voluptuousness

FIVE

Gardens of Love

SIX

On the World's Stage

SEVEN

The Backstage of the Body

EIGHT

Happiness Regained

Some Landmarks in the Life of Casanova

1724   27 February. Marriage of Giovanna Maria (Zanetta) Farussi (1708–76) and Gaetano Giuseppe Casanova (Parma 1697–Venice 1733) in the Church of San Samuele in Venice. The Patriarch of Venice who married them is Pietro Barbarigo.

1725   2 April. Birth of Giacomo Girolamo Casanova, their first son, in Venice on the Calle della Commedia. In his novel *Ne amori ne donne*, Casanova will suggest that he may have been the illegitimate son of the patrician Michele Grimani. He is brought up by his maternal grandmother, Marzia Farussi, on the Calle delle Monache.

    5 May. Giacomo's baptism in the Church of San Samuele.

1727   His parents go for two years to London, where Zanetta makes her theatrical debut.

    June. Birth of Francesco Casanova in London.

1730   Birth of Jean (Giovanni Battista) Casanova in Venice.

1731   Birth of Faustina Maddalena. (She dies in 1736.)

1732   Birth of Maria Maddalena. (She will marry Peter August, a musician at the court of the Elector of Saxony. Their daughter, Marianne, will marry Carlo Angioloni in 1787. Maria Maddalena dies in Dresden in 1800.)

1733   August. Giacomo's hemorrhage, and the scene with the witch and the fairy.

Mid-November. Scene with the stolen optical crystal.

December. Death of Giacomo's father.

1734   April. Giacomo is sent to live with Doctor Gozzi in Padua, where he stays until 1737.

First spasms of love with Bettina.

1735–37   Zanetta, his mother, is in St. Petersburg.

1737   28 November. Giacomo enrolls at the University of Padua.

1738   Zanetta leaves for Dresden.

1738–41   Casanova studies in Padua and returns to Venice to work for the lawyer Manzoni.

1740   14 February. He is tonsured. He studies science and philosophy with old Senator Malipiero.

Teresa Imer, Nanetta and Marton, Juliette.

1741   22 January. Casanova receives the four minor orders.

19 March. The bungled sermon in Venice.

Spring. First departure for Corfu and, possibly, Constantinople.

1742   Work in Venice for a lawyer. Scientific studies at Santa Maria della Salute. He lives in the Calle della Commedia.

June. Casanova obtains his doctorate from the University of Padua.

1743   18 March. Death of his grandmother, Marzia Farussi.

Brief stay at the house of Tintoretta, then at the seminary in Murano.

April–July. Sojourn at Fort Sant'Andrea.

26 August. Arrival of Bernardo da Bernardis in Venice.

August–October. Casanova works for the lawyer Marco Leze.

10 October. He leaves Venice. Chioggia.

November. He stays about a month with Father Steffano, in Ancona.

December. Travels to Rome, on foot, then leaves for Martorano.

1744   January. Naples. Don Lelio Caraffa, Antonio Casanova.

Casanova leaves for Rome with Donna Lucrezia, her husband, and her sister, Angelica.

January–March. He stays in Rome in the service of Cardinal Acquaviva, meets Pope Benedict XIV, takes French lessons with

Barbarucci, has to leave Rome because, although he is innocent, he is implicated in a kidnapping. Late February–March. He meets Teresa-Bellino (the false castrato) in Ancona and creates a fantasy costume in Bologna. Second trip to Corfu, in the service of Giacomo da Riva.

1745   Carnival, theater in Corfu. Love affair with Mme F., until May. June. Sojourn (second?) in Constantinople.

1746   Casanova is violinist in the San Samuele theater in Venice. 18–20 April. The Corner–Soranzo marriage. Casanova comes to know Senator Matteo Bragadin.

7 August. A document indicates Casanova as a practicing notary's clerk with Manzoni. End of the year. Venice. Countess A.S. Sojourns in Padua.

1749   Fearing the State Inquisitors who overhear him discussing cabalistic practices with Bragadin, Casanova flees Venice. Milan, Cremona.

Zanetta, at the Saxon court in Dresden, plays Rosaura in *Amor non ha riguardi*.

Summer. At Cesena, the magical episode of the hidden treasure, with Genoveffa.

Autumn. Henriette. Parma, Milan, Geneva.

1750   February. Henriette leaves.

June. Casanova goes to Lyons, where he is received as a Freemason, then on to Paris. The Balletti family.

1752   7 February. Dresden. Zanetta plays Erinice in the opera *Zoroastre*, which Casanova has translated into Italian.

1753   29 May. On his return to Venice, Casanova—until 25 July 1755—shares with the Abbé Bernis the favors of two nuns, M.M. and C.C. A spy, Manuzzi, sends reports to the Inquisitors.

1755   26 July. Casanova is arrested and sent to the Leads Prison.

1756   26 February. Zanetta makes her last stage appearance before her involuntary retirement (because of the Seven Years' War), in Goldoni's *La Vedova Scaltra*.

31 October–1 November. During the night, Casanova escapes

from the Leads Prison; he will live in exile from Venice for eighteen years.

1757   5 January. Casanova arrives in Paris on the day of Damiens' attempt on the life of King Louis XV. Becomes a millionaire by participating in the founding of the state lottery of the Ecole Militaire. Mme d'Urfé, Manon Balletti.

August. Reconnaisance mission in Dunkirk (as a spy for Louis XV?).

1758   16 September. Death of Silvia Balletti.

October. Casanova goes to Holland on a business trip. Esther, Lucie.

1759   January. Returning to Paris, he is implicated in being involved in an abortion. Establishes a workshop for manufacturing printed silks. Lives in his "folly" in the Little Poland district.

August. He is arrested for being involved in an abortion. Released after the intervention of Mme d'Urfé, he goes again to Holland on an official mission, then for the next four years travels all over Europe.

1760   April–August. In Switzerland, Casanova thinks of becoming a monk at the abbey in Einsiedeln. Zurich. Baroness von Roll, Soleure, La Dubois.

24 April. He uses the name "Chevalier de Seingalt" on a document for the first time.

6 July. Casanova's first visit to Voltaire at Les Délices.

December. Rome. Mengs, Winckelmann, Mariuccia, Pope Clement XIII. In Florence, he sees Teresa-Bellino again.

1761   January. Naples. The Duke of Matalona, Leonilda, Lucrezia.

1762   Travels with Mme d'Urfé and La Corticelli.

1763   May. The non-encounter with Henriette when he is at the Croix d'Or with Marcolina.

14 June. London. Pauline, then La Charpillon. Thinks of suicide.

1764   March. Casanova leaves England, fearing he will be hanged over a matter of a false bill of exchange.

April–May. In Germany. Very ill, he is looked after by Doctor Peipers, in Wesel.

May–June. At the Wolfenbüttel library. Zanetta retires and receives a pension of 400 thalers. Her son Giovanni comes back to Dresden.

July. Casanova meets Frederick the Great. The dancer La Denis.

December. Casanova goes to St. Petersburg.

1765   January–September. Empress Catherine II, Zaïre, La Valville.

10 October. Casanova arrives in Warsaw.

1766   5 March. Duel with Branicki.

1767   Summer. In Spa. Charlotte.

September. Casanova returns to Paris.

14 October. Death of Bragadin.

November. Casanova is arrested by *lettre de cachet*. He goes to Spain.

1768   Casanova works on projects for the colonization of the Sierra Morena, lets himself be seduced by the wife of a captain-general. Sent to prison, he writes a refutation of a French work criticizing Venetian policy.

December. After his release, he narrowly escapes assassination.

1769   February–May. Ill, he is discreetly watched over by Henriette.

1770   Salerno. Leonilda, Lucrezia.

1772   Publication of *Lana Caprina*.

November. Trieste. Casanova renders various services for his country and awaits a pardon. He writes, in Italian, his vast, well-documented *History of Unrest in Poland*. His *Story of My Life* breaks off abruptly in the middle of its account of this sojourn in Trieste.

1774   3 September. The Inquisitors' pardon comes, after eighteen years.

15 November. Casanova returns to his native Venice, where he will live for eight years, before a final disgrace.

1775–76   Casanova writes a great deal. Volumes II and III of his Polish history are published. He translates the *Iliad* into Italian verse.

1776   29 November. Casanova's mother dies in Dresden.

1776–82   Casanova files secret reports for the Inquisition. His literary efforts do not meet with success: seven issues of *Opuscoli miscellanei*, ten of *Messager de Thalie*, one of *Talia*, an adaptation of a novel by Mme de Tencin, *The Siege of Calais*. He lives with the dressmaker Francesca Buschini. Organizes a theater troupe.

1782   August. Casanova, after a financial dispute with the Marchese Spinola and the Grimani brothers, avenges himself with a novel, *Ne amori ne donne, ovvero la stalla ripulita*, which sends him into a second exile. From now on, he will write in French. At the age of fifty-seven, he is distressed by the idea of a life of wandering.

1783   Paris, Dresden, Berlin, Prague.

1784   February. He settles in Vienna, where he becomes secretary to the Venetian ambassador. At a dinner he meets Count Waldstein, a Freemason with a taste for the occult.

1785   April. With the ambassador's death, Casanova must set forth again. He thinks of asking for a position at the Academy in Berlin. Waldstein suggest that he become librarian at his castle at Dux, in Bohemia (today Duchkov, in the Czech Republic).

September. Casanova goes to Dux.

1786–98   For thirteen years Casanova writes. He publishes only some of his manuscripts; the many unpublished ones are in the state archives in Prague.

1786   Publication in Prague of *Soliloque d'un penseur*, a brief denunciation of Cagliostro and Saint-Germain.

1787   Publication in Prague of his *Story of My Flight*, the only episode from his memoirs that appears during his lifetime, with an account of his duel in Warsaw.

October. Prague. Encounter with Mozart; the premiere of *Don Giovanni*.

1788–89   Casanova works on various philosophical treatises and publishes pamphlets on mathematics and his novel *Icosaméron*.

1789   Birth of Camilla Angiolini, Casanova's grand-niece, who will become a singer.

Casanova works on the first version of his *Story of My Life*, revising and correcting his manuscript several times.

1793   He undertakes *Raisonnement d'un spectateur sur la Révolution française*, which he will not finish.

1794   He revises the manuscript of *Story of My Life* so that the Prince de Ligne may read it.

1797   Final revision of the text. Casanova notes on the cover page, "Story of My Life until the Year 1797," but he will not have time to recount the last twenty-six years.

His last publication: *Lettre à Léonard Snetlage.*

1798   April. He falls ill.

29 April. His admirer Elise von der Recke sends him soups and wine. She promises him crayfish soup, which he especially likes, but he gets none, since the rivers, with the spring floods, are too high for catching crayfish.

27 May. His nephew-in-law, Carlo Angiolini, comes from Dresden to be with him.

4 June. Death of Giacomo Casanova, at Dux, in Bohemia. Angiolini takes away the manuscript of *Story of My Life* and will bequeath it to his son.

1821   Carlo Angiolini *fils* sells the manuscript to Brockhaus, a publisher in Leipzig, for 200 thalers.

1822–28 Schütz translates and adapts it into German.

1826–38 First French translation—with the text cut, rewritten, and changed by Laforgue.

1945   The manuscript escapes destruction and is transferred to Wiesbaden.

1960–62 First edition of the true text of the original French manuscript, published by Brockhaus and Plon.

THE MAN WHO

REALLY LOVED WOMEN

The Last Castle

THE PRESENT MOMENT AND MEMORY

In a castle in Bohemia, an exiled old man spends thirteen hours a day writing the history of his life. He has no possessions; he has thrown away or squandered everything he once owned. He has no woman, no fortune, no house, no homeland. He gave and received freely, without calculation. He has enjoyed life as few men—and even fewer women—have dared enjoy it. He threw himself into life and required nothing in return except that most insolent, most scandalous of rewards: pleasure.

Unreservedly he surrenders to the present moment, heedless of the past or future. It is the perfect moment—pure present, pure loss. Suspended between yesterday and tomorrow, he gives of himself generously and devotes himself to today. Since he has no fear of displeasure, his daring knows no bounds. Since he has nothing to lose, everything is his. His spectacular escape decades ago from the prison in Venice is the emblem of his life, and he could never imagine telling the story of it in less than two hours, a narrative in which he is both hero and bard; it is his best letter of introduction into society. He speaks, and doors open.

I have always believed, he reflects with a certain delight, *that when a man takes it into his head to see some project through and attends to it exclusively, he will inevitably be successful, whatever the difficulties; this man will become grand vizier, he will become Pope, he will overturn a monarchy—provided he starts early.*

The sentence appeals to him, he writes it down. With his notes scattered around him, pens and sheets of paper strewn across the table, the old man, brought from Venice to Bohemia by peculiar twists of fate, is gripped by the compulsion to write. In celebrating his past, he makes up for his daily life. Not a day goes by when the servants of the castle do not torment him in some odious fashion. Everything is cause for a quarrel: the coffee, the milk, the dish of macaroni which must be prepared in the Italian way. The cook spoils the polenta or serves him scalding soup out of malice. The dogs bark in the night, and the shrill, off-key sounds of a hunting horn are ear-splitting. He shuts himself in his room, sits down at his writing desk, and lets all the seasons of his life flow out from his lively pen. His last project— the most audacious, craziest, but also most joyful one, the one for which he feels a firm, unqualified determination—is to treat himself to the happiness of living his experiences a second time and reveling in them until sated.

He is surrounded by death. The French Revolution is rumbling beyond the mountains; his best friends are dying; the women he loved are departing from this life; the old world, to which he feels he still belongs, is being mocked, insulted, guillotined. The new values he holds dear—individual freedom, the power of the Enlightenment and Reason, atheism—are not yet widely accepted. The Venetian feels lonely. The young Count Waldstein who welcomed him as librarian in his castle in Dux is all too often absent. How can one live without talking, dancing, playing cards, or amusing people? How can one bear the boredom of having no audience, no intrigue to pursue, no new adventures to engage in? For the first time in his life he turns away from the present, withdraws, plunges into the days of his memories. One by one, he summons them before his eyes, and he is elated, in writing, at the thought that he may be bestowing the gift of immortality on himself. Like Voltaire, his implacable model and enemy. He dreams of literary glory. He fantasizes that the pages he is hastily covering with ink will be translated into every language. He expects that countries where people feel strongly about accepted morals will ban his writings. These two ideas amuse him. He is glad to be defying his oppressive daily life and even, possibly, death, the cold monster against which he juxtaposes the splendor and excesses of his adventures. Life, for him, is an entertainment, a joyful drama: a *dramma giocoso.*

He admits to being intrepid, thoughtless, avid in his pursuit of sensual or intellectual enjoyment, and ready to violate all the laws that would curb his unfettered pleasure. He sees himself as king of his own life but his self-love encompasses the pleasure of the men and women he loves. He hates suffering and is loath to inflict it or endure it. Death is cruel since it expels the attentive spectator from this great theater too soon, before the end of the play in which he is so deeply absorbed. For him, life must be a party, a ball, an endless carnival. Each person must invent a role for himself and play it with brio. Disguises and masks offer pleasure incognito, freedom in the present moment, joyful and unbridled invention with impunity. He loves being center stage. He has the volubility, cheek, daring, and liveliness of someone who seizes the day. He embroiders, composes, invents on all canvases. He immediately takes on whatever persona is expected of him according to the situation or the desire of others. He is a man of impromptus. Luck is often on his side, but mostly he is brimming with self-confidence. He feels ready to embark on any adventure. *Jump, Marquis!* is his command-ment to himself.

This is how God prepared what I needed for a flight that was to be admirable, even wondrous. I admit I am proud of it, but my pride stems not from having succeeded, for luck played a great part, but from the fact that I considered it feasible and had the courage to undertake it.

The pluck to imagine, a conquering energy, and, in precarious equilibrium—like a tightrope walker on the lead roofs of the Ducal Palace, dressed uncannily in taffeta, torn lace, and a hat with Spanish trimming and a white plume—the impudence to succeed, with a verse from Dante on his lips: *"E quindi uscimmo a riveder le stelle."* "And then we came forth to contemplate the stars."

Thereafter, he could do what he pleased. He could even take refuge in the house of the chief of police who had pursued him, where he finds the kindest hospitality: that of a young child playing with a top in the courtyard, a pregnant woman, an at-tentive grandmother who dresses his wounds, feeds him, puts him to sleep as though he were her own son—a triple image of good fortune, innocence, and unconditional love. Then he reaches Paris, the only city in the universe where, according to him, the blind goddess dispenses her favors to those who sur-render to her.

The Venetian journeys from place to place but not for the sake of travel; he belongs in the place where he happens to be. He speaks vivaciously on all subjects, and very learned people credit him with enormous knowledge and reading. He squanders his gifts, touches on everything with equal elegance, equal ease, equal cheek. He scatters things to the winds and never plows or reaps anything durable. With the suggestion of a dance step he piques people's interest, then vanishes backstage with a last pirouette. He adores being talked about and has such wonderful stage presence that throughout Europe his name and reputation precede him. He amuses, astonishes, and arouses curiosity in a century that celebrates variety and entertainment above all. He also annoys, disturbs, and upsets the established order; his pride and haughtiness are inordinate, yet he always seduces through his irresistible mastery of the art of conversation. What more is required of a gentleman in the eighteenth century?

Since his earliest youth, people have liked him. Whatever the scene of action, he gains admittance among princes, archbishops, and ambassadors whose privileges and wealth he does not share. He pulls the wool over their eyes. He is welcomed; sometimes he is sent packing for a trifle or much worse. Guilty, he gets off; innocent, he is punished! Fortune is sometimes unpredictably moody. He is both an insider and an outsider. By birth, he will always be a pariah, a déclassé, but in terms of talents, charm, and savoir faire, he belongs right at the center of aristocratic society.

Eager, impatient, desirous of variety, he anticipates events, new actions, and new developments. His soul is tyrannized by novelty. Sometimes fortune elevates him to great heights, sometimes knocks him way down; he climbs back up, falls, and quickly scales the wheel of fortune again. He has gone around several times. Having reached the pinnacles of success, wealth, and fame, he lets himself be dragged to ruin, even causes it. Happy days intoxicate and exhilarate him; unhappy ones he mocks, proudly avoiding their pitfalls. He insists on being his own man. He acknowledges that he himself is the main cause of the unfortunate and fortunate things that happen to him. He takes full responsibility for his errors, misdeeds, and crimes, and feels neither shame nor remorse. He neither confesses nor repents. He does not expect forgiveness. Nothing stops him, for he knows no fear and fears no suffering. To the end he has the courage to assert himself as voluptuously free and fickle.

Now he is isolated from salon mirrors and intrigues, forgotten in games of chance and love, an adventurer without adventures, a stationary traveler. He treats himself to the ultimate, most desirable enjoyment, which, he believes, accompanies and justifies all other pleasures, the enjoyment of words. By an unexpected conjuring trick, just as the seducer's stage show seems over, here, in Dux, in Count Waldstein's castle, time suddenly ceases to run out. Memory takes revenge on old age and exile, dispelling melancholy and society's persecutions. As a final insolence, thumbing his nose, for the last time, at his contemporaries, at posterity, and at public morals, the Venetian revels in his reminiscences.

Thirteen hours a day seem to go by like thirteen minutes, as he recounts his life to himself, as though he were not limited, as everyone else is, to living it only once. Such is the privilege of the artist: by the magic of his narrative, he summons the living and the dead, converses with those who are gone, and assigns meaning to impulses and scattered moments of passion from the past. As the memoirist assembles, unifies, he becomes aware of his life. He accepts situating himself in the past and within a set period, as part of the flow and continuity of time. In remembering former pleasures, he revives them and enjoys them a second time; as for the pains, they make him laugh, since he no longer feels them. But now he knows that the passage of time is inescapable. Whether worthy or unworthy, his life is his material and his material is his life. He has no other and he cherishes it. He has always seen himself as fit to be his own pupil and as having the duty to love his tutor. His great strength, his great secret, is this: he takes pleasure without shame or guilt. He has a taste for happiness, Giacomo Casanova.

THE VOLUPTUOUSNESS OF LIVING, THE VOLUPTUOUSNESS OF WRITING

Isolated from society and women, a toothless old man mocked by the castle flunkies, Casanova makes love with the French language, the language of love and the Enlightenment. His final conquest, his most beautiful courtesan, is writing. His childhood was mute and his family ignored him, but now he gorges himself on words, never setting down his pen. Things and words merge. Words capture the scents, flavors, curves, textures, sounds, and colors of memories. Words encapsulate living things and heighten them—the shiny and the downy, the rotten and the sweet, the velvety and the rough, the smooth and the bitter, the husky and the sticky, the pallid and the spicy—a display that runs the entire gamut of the senses, warming the soul of an exile who dreads boredom.

Courtyards, gardens, boudoirs, prison garrets, convent parlors, literary conversations and theological arguments, women, books and faro banks, ecclesiastical robes and military uniforms, Pierrot masks and dominoes, gondolas and berlins, the cabala and philosophy, parties, pox, duels, tactlessness, flight and glory—all the events and curiosities of his life file by again before the creased eyes of the triumphant old man.

He describes dishes that are the "height of taste": cheeses whose perfection is reached when the little creatures that inhabit them become visible; sticky Newfoundland cod and high game "on the very edge"; above all else, champagne, oysters, and the foamy, thick morning chocolate he insists on preparing himself. As for women, he has never made a secret of it: he has always found that the one he loved smelled good, and the stronger the smell of her perspiration the sweeter he found it.

The Venetian laughs at the thought of those who are bound to exclaim: "What depraved taste! How shameful to acknowledge this without blushing!" Yet defiantly he believes that he is happier than the next man precisely because his appetites afford him greater pleasure. He had never had qualms about betraying scatterbrains, rogues, and fools when the need arose. He himself reports the opinions of people who mince no words in describing him as a sorcerer, forger, thief, spy, slanderer, petty robber, traitor, gambler, rascal, counterfeiter of bills of exchange and of handwriting, impious liar, atheist. He does not hide his misdeeds but converts them into stories—just as he took the title Chevalier de Seingalt, thanks to the alphabet which belongs to all and which anyone is entitled to use in order to create his own name.

THE WRITER AND HIS DOUBLE

He is seated at his table, next to his window, looking out into the park that extends all the way to the foot of the mountain. It is full of rare species. The castle where he is living the last days of his nomadic life, like the Château of Chantilly, in France, is built on a large square, at the end of a courtyard, flanked by a Jesuit church and a pavilion. A double stairway leads to the terrace and the main entrance. Lattice windows with white lintels adorn the façade. The bedrooms and the enfilade of drawing rooms are beautifully furnished. Paintings and suits of armor recall the glorious past of his host's family. At the place of honor is the portrait of the Duke of Wallenstein, who is soon to become Schiller's tragic hero. The aroma of glory and valuable old books permeates the atmosphere.

Yet Casanova is languishing in this golden retreat. He tries to get away for a few escapades in Dresden or Prague. When the master of the castle is away, as he often is, the steward, Georg Feldkirchner, persecutes and humiliates the old Venetian, who then takes revenge with his pen, writing letters to the steward that stay undelivered.

Casanova demands the respect which "a polite man owes to a man who, though not a gentleman by birth, became one through the study of the sciences and of literature."

Since childhood, he has understood that writing alone gives power to people who do not have it by birth as a privilege of caste. Writing is a way of wearing a mask, of scrambling genders and social identities, of inventing one's own rules, of benefiting from an artist's impunity and an ambassador's extraterritoriality. Writing is essential to his health, since anger kills, he believes, unless one can find a way to purge oneself of it. Writing changes the course of events. He has often had the opportunity to confirm this truth during his lifetime. At eighteen, as a poor but literate young friar incarcerated at the Sant'Andrea fortress for a peccadillo, he helps a lieutenant colonel who dreams of being promoted but does not know how to write. Casanova laughs as he remembers the scene: *I wrote a short petition for him, but so forceful that the Savio [the Minister of War], after asking who had written it, promised to fulfill his request.* Well rewarded for interceding, Giacomo ends up a public scribe, in a position to determine promotions for the entire regiment. *The effect of my petition made all the other officers believe they would never get anything without the help of my pen; and I refused it to no one.*

Casanova remembers that, being inexperienced, he offered his services indiscriminately to everyone and that the rivalries between his clients earned him a few quarrels. As well as his first love disease. When a beautiful Greek woman solicited the nimbleness of his pen, he asked to be repaid with favors. *But two days after the exploit, instead of finding myself rewarded, I found that I was punished,* he had to admit.

Twenty-five years later, seeking release from a Madrid prison, he dispatched four strong letters to the authorities. After obtaining his freedom, he questioned the alcalde:

—*Admit that if I had not known how to write, you would have sent me to serve in the galleys.*

—*Alas! It is possible,* the Spanish judge answered laconically.

He experienced his first literary triumph as a child in Venice. As a little boy of eleven, he had been exiled in Padua for two years, brought there by his mother to recover his health and receive the rudiments of an education; she had thought he was stupid and had abandoned him in a sordid boardinghouse. But soon grammar, Greek and Latin, as well as the basics of philosophy, astronomy, and music, held no secrets for him. He had become a brilliant student. Summoned back to Venice to wish his mother farewell, for once again she was setting off on a journey, little Giacomo made her eyes shine with admiration by improvising Latin verses full of wit and intelligence. The neglected child saw himself accepted for the first time.

It was my first literary exploit, and I can say that it was at this moment that a love for the glory which comes from literature was planted in my soul, for the applause brought me to the pinnacle of happiness.

In his Bohemian retreat, Casanova recalls his mother's look of surprise and pride. As beautiful as daylight, is the way she seemed to his childish eyes. Beautiful and distant. For a fleeting moment he had succeeded in capturing the attention of this inaccessible mother who had turned away from him right after his birth. For a fleeting moment he had felt happy under her gaze. He never admitted to the least sadness, or hint of regret or anger toward her. She was the unchallenged queen, the magnificent lady who appeared in his dreams at night, but she did not trouble his childish soul. She had not loved him, perhaps, because he was frail and sickly and she was afraid of losing him. She had left him in the care of her mother and run off to London with her husband. Little Giacomo had no strength, no resilience, and hovered between life and death. He kept losing all his blood, which flowed constantly from his nose. Had he thought this bleeding might retain her? Another woman had turned her attention to him, a gentle grandmother, determined to look after him, who loved him with constancy to the day of her death. She took him to see a witch, who exorcised the blood that was emptying him of substance. Then, belatedly, he acquired the desire to live, but with intensified force. His kind-hearted grandmother had instilled in him both a taste for life and absolute self-confidence. He never lost either, except on a day of despair in London when he considered throwing himself into the Thames because he had been deceived by La Charpillon, a young prostitute.

It was on that fatal day at the beginning of September 1763 that I began to die and ceased living, he admits. *I was thirty-eight years old. If the perpendicular ascending line is equal in length to the descending one, as it should be, today, on the first day of November 1797, it would seem I can count on almost four more years of life, which given the axiom "Motus in fine velocior" [Motion is increased in speed toward the end] will go by very fast.*

This is what Love did to me in London "nel mezzo del cammin di nostra vita" [midway on the journey of this life], at the age of thirty-eight. It was the end of the first act of my life. The end of the second was when I left Venice in the year 1783. The end of the third will apparently take place here [in Dux], where I amuse myself by writing these memoirs.

For Casanova, the urgency of writing is also, at death's door, a last revenge on life. Fleetingly conjuring up a shine in his mother's eyes. Wagering on immortality. Casanova is a gambler who has participated in every kind of game of chance—basset, piquet, prime, whist, quinze, and faro—in the *ridotto* in Venice, at the Marchese Grimaldi's table or Lady Harrington's, at tables of rogues and cowards. For his twenty-first birthday, his Venetian protector, Senator Bragadin, almost like a father to him, gave him advice that he always followed, never to lay a stake against the one who holds the bank: *Since you like games of chance, I advise you never to punt. Deal. You will have the advantage.*

What compelled me to play was a feeling of avarice; I loved spending money and I was sorry when it was not gambling that provided me with the money to do so. I felt that money earned gambling had cost me nothing.

Now Giacomo Casanova is playing his last card. He has no other life but his narrative. His pen gives him the only way to seal his destiny permanently: writing in order to transform his life into a work of art, to make himself into a literary character.

LIFE IS THEATER

Having taken refuge in his room, as he writes he turns his back on the nasty people who harass him in his host's absence. His memories are a revenge against their insults. He spoke in German; they did not listen. He became angry; they laughed. When he dances the minuet at the balls, bowing as he was taught to by Marcel, the famous Paris ballet master, they make fun of him. He wears his white plume, his gold silk drugget, his black velvet jacket, and has garters with brass buckles over rolled-up silk stockings. They laugh again. *Cospetto!* he yells, *you riffraff, you are all Jacobins, you wrong the Count, and the Count wrongs me by not punishing you.*

He has always been particular about his appearance. He readily acknowledges as much. *We men, though devoid of a uterus, were extraordinarily fond of dressing up in our youth*, he likes to remind us. He remembers unusual costumes he thought up for some friends during carnival in Milan. He recalls the scene.

Having gone to the best secondhand-clothes dealer in town, he acquired two velvet suits, one blue, the other sulfur yellow, and satin dresses, one flame-colored, the other lilac, the third in multicolored striped floss silk. He also bought batiste shirts and several yards of velvet, satin, and striped fabrics in various colors. At home, where a tailor waited for him, he slashed each garment haphazardly with a stiletto in about sixty places, then instructed the frightened artisan to create the most attractive effect by patching up the holes with pieces of contrasting cloth. He asked the tailor's wife, the beautiful Zenobia—whom he couldn't help fondling a bit—to ill-treat the dresses. She ripped the fabric at the bosom, shoulders, and sleeves, just enough as to arouse desire without excessively offending decency. Several days were needed to prepare these costumes of *pitocchi*, which transformed

noble marchesi and marchese into luxury beggars. Casanova
wanted to keep the disguises secret. His friends would know
nothing until it was time to dress. *Do not ask me how*, he said to
them, *for I want to enjoy your complete surprise. Coups de théâtre are
my passion.*

Dressed as Pierrot, Casanova was amused by the spectacle his
friends offered at the ball. Shoes deliberately slashed, fine lace
cuffs all torn up, hair disheveled, masks with despairing expressions—like beautiful but chipped porcelain plates used for begging: it was a masquerade of sumptuous poverty. Everyone
applauded this unusual and extravagant invention, an inverted
world portrayed with the insolence that carnivals permit. Incognito in his white mask, Casanova took great pleasure in his creation and broke the bank. Several days later, a new costuming
was required for an intimate gathering. This time, genders, not
the social classes, were overturned. Men and women exchanged
clothes. The men were told to imitate the fair sex's modesty and
chaste reserve, while the women, under the protection of their
disguise, became bolder and indulged in ribald caresses. The
night ended just as the director had predicted—everything was
meticulously planned—to the delight of all.

Life is theater, the only condition under which it is worth
living. Casanova likes to challenge convictions. With the joyful
impertinence of a commedia dell'arte character, he reverses the
established order, pokes fun at identities, and blurs the boundaries of certainty. He amuses himself redesigning reality and re-
arranging it for his own little pleasure. A pleasure that includes
the pleasure of others. Casanova is generous, even to excess. He
loves spending and squandering. He needs a public to applaud
and marvel at his magical tricks. He withholds nothing and
hoards nothing. This he sees as the best proof of his disinter-
estedness and deep-seated honesty. He shares the joys of the

artist or magician who pulls wondrous illusions out of a hat. Nothing remains afterward except a bow, some applause, and pleasure, nothing but pleasure.

The reason why he accepted Count Waldstein's hospitality and pension is because he no longer has any hopes of seeing his purse filled—or his bed and barouche. Irresistible youth has vanished. He lacks the resiliency to jump into new journeys and new conquests. He can no longer say to himself, as he used to, *In the morning, on waking, I take a look at my physical and moral state, and I find I am happy*. From present moment to present moment, old age has caught up with him. Plunged in melancholy thoughts, he notes down the first effects of time.

I felt I had aged. Forty-six seemed to me an advanced age. Sometimes I found the pleasure of lovemaking less intense, less seductive than I had imagined . . . For eight years already my potency had been diminishing little by little . . . Try as I might, women no longer tended to fall in love with me . . . I felt I was a completely different person . . .

What he can pass down of his life is neither a title nor property nor wealth, nor even a name—for if he has children, he recognizes them solely on the basis of physical resemblance and their mother's word. Casanova's legacy lies in the pages he is busy writing, as hastily as possible in order to go over his entire life's journey. He is unsure of succeeding. At times he is overcome by fatigue and melancholy. When his glamour as an adventurer declines with age, he finds the narrative less pleasant. But before death catches up with him, he still wants to give a firsthand account of a century and style of life that are drawing to a close. He wants to tell of his extraordinary aptitude for happiness, a trait he wishes everyone to have.

His pen glides along the page with the eagerness he applied

to living his life. He recalls the sumptuous luncheon he gave at the wish of the Burgomaster of Cologne's wife, whom he hoped to seduce. She urged him to go and see Count Verità in order to organize a meal that would be identical to one that had been given by the Duke of Zweibrücken.

—*Just tell me how much you wish to spend*, the Count asks him.

—*As much as I can*, Casanova replies.

—*In other words, as little*, the Count corrects him.

—*No. As much, because I want to be magnificent.*

—*You must say how much, because I know the man.*

—*Tell him two hundred ducats.*

—*That's enough. The Duke of Zweibrücken gave no more.*

The table is set for twenty-four people, spread with damask linen, and covered with vermeil and porcelain. The menu includes twenty-four oysters per person, an enormous ragout of truffles, followed by a dessert buffet representing portraits of all the sovereigns of Europe. Casanova plays the gallant escort, stands and serves the ladies, ministering to one after the other (without favoring his lady love, who is dazzled by such lavish treatment). He notes with pleasure that not a single drop of water is consumed in the course of the luncheon: champagne, Tokay, maraschino, wines from the Rhine, from Madera, Málaga, Cyprus, Alicante, and the Cape are not meant to be mixed with water and were served pure. The Venetian enjoys feeling he is the equal of a prince of the Empire. The Elector of Cologne, as a reward for having been amused with the tale of Casanova's escape from the prison in Venice, gives him a lovely gold snuffbox with a portrait of the Elector as Grand Master of the Teutonic Order, encircled with brilliants. Casanova has the snuffbox passed around among his guests. No one doubts the nobility of the host anymore. And the Burgomaster's wife gives him discreet instructions on how to meet her on a forthcoming night: he must hide in the church adjoining her house and stay locked inside until she comes to set him free. The wait was as exquisite as the embrace given in reward.

Casanova likes to remember, as though memory alone could accord love its full significance. He mentally summons faces, conversations, and events. He ceases to be the old man harassed by the castle steward and his nasty stooge, Vidarol, who has just defiled his effigy in the lavatory with a nauseating and degrading substance. No, he is the Venetian rushing happily from place to place, always generous with his speech, his seed, his imagination.

CATALOGUE

Casanova is a man who undertakes things. Success or failure, nothing stops or demoralizes him. He forges ahead with the same enthusiasm, never short of ideas or energy. If he encounters obstacles along the way, a good night's sleep and a strict diet for several days get him back on his feet. He admits to having wasted only one day of his life: a day spent in oblivion sleeping uninterruptedly for twenty-seven hours after a masked ball in St. Petersburg, one Sunday in December 1764.

For pleasure, he enjoys leafing through his amusing, surprising catalogue of his countless projects, employments, and initiatives throughout Europe—full of inventiveness and unexpected developments. In Paris, he learns French with Crébillon the elder, takes part in the founding of the national lottery, sets up a silk-printing workshop, devotes himself to the study of the cabala, keeps company with Silvia, a performer of Marivaux plays, takes minuet lessons from the renowned ballet master Marcel, applauds two of the most famous dancers of his time, Louis Dupré and La Camargo, is employed to do some espionage work by Louis XV, and has ingenuous conversations with Madame de Pompadour and the Duke de Richelieu.

In Spain, he discourses on the colonization of the Sierra Morena and the cultivation of tobacco. With Catherine the Great of Russia, he discusses the Gregorian calendar and suggests introducing the cultivation of blackberry bushes. For the Duke de Courlande, he acts as a mining inspector, delving into the topic as though he knew it perfectly, in both theory and practice; he surprises himself with his ability to talk so easily about a subject he knew nothing about a minute ago. From London, he wants to sell the secret of a cotton red dye to his own country. In Prague, he invents a "grammatical" lottery that teaches players the French language and "more imperfectly all the languages of the universe"!

With gamblers, he is Greek; with actors, he becomes a theater entrepreneur or playwright. With fools, he admits he is a cheat; with gentlemen, he is a man of honor. For Madame d'Urfé, he is a cabalist by the name of Paralis; at the Roman Academy of Poetry, his alias as an Arcadian shepherd is Eupolemo Pantaxeno. At eighteen, he asks Pope Benedict XIV to give him the license to eat meat on fish days and read banned books. At thirty-five, with Voltaire, he recites Ariosto and discusses Homer, Dante, Petrarch, and Goldoni. He has been in turn a priest, a doctor of law, a soldier, a public scribe, a violinist, a physician and magician, the adopted son of a Venetian patrician, a libertine, a gambler, a financier, a Pierrot, a dancer of the furlana— and a lover and friend of women.

THE TIME OF HAPPINESS

Casanova falls in love with one woman and then another but never keeps a tally of them. He loves the woman whom he desires and remains attached to her. He enjoys the attractions of her body but only if they are associated with the refinements of intellect and conversation. He gives joy as much as he takes it. When love is at stake between a man and a woman, deception is inevitably reciprocal. Everyone is both a loser and a winner. Pleasure in the present is always innocent. What could be the price of joy except paying with one's own person?

Fickle and enamored of freedom, when he parts with a mistress he has the decency to arrange a happy sequel—marriage, dowry, theater engagement. Though he derives happiness from the momentary and the ephemeral, they also exhaust him. He escapes duration but cannot always avoid tears and distress. He knows the suffering caused by certain separations. Bettina, his first love; Teresa, or Bellino, of whom at first he did not know whether she was a woman or a castrato; Henriette, his greatest love; M.M., the Murano nun; and Pauline, the Portuguese noblewoman he met in London—all these women plunged him into a state of despair which his desire for voluptuousness would have liked to avoid. The time of happiness—always outside time, no matter how long—consists of a progression of uninterrupted sensual pleasures, the end of which, if it is not immediately negated and superseded by a new liaison, plunges him into a state of great pain and bereavement.

Nothing is more bitter than separation when love is undiminished in strength, he writes, admitting to himself that he is more sentimental than libertine. *The pain seems infinitely greater than the pleasure previously experienced. The pleasure no longer exists, we are aware*

21

only of the pain. We feel so unhappy that, to be relieved, we wish we had never been happy.

He sinks into a deep and prolonged sleep, a state similar to prostration. He stops eating, and succumbs to a languor that consoles him by preventing him from thinking. Sometimes he punishes himself for an unbearable attachment by taking up with venal women who, with perfect timing, give him a love disease. To avoid the feeling of loss, perhaps even of abandonment, he seeks to keep the ties alive which bind him to the women whom he has known through chance and love. Every now and again, as the years go by, all through his life, in any number of places—barouches, gambling tables, theater boxes, princes' palaces, anywhere from Paris to St. Petersburg, or Rome to Spa—in this Europe where the same people are always traveling about, separating and meeting, he resumes a conversation that was interrupted some time before. How sweet to see familiar faces again and catch up on the years gone by! Is this not the most deliberate way of cultivating constancy? Love may simply be meeting and rediscovering each other again.

You will forget Henriette, too, are words she had engraved with the point of a diamond on a windowpane in their hotel room in Geneva. No, he does not forget her. He wept over this Provençale noblewoman, beautiful, witty, and cultured, in whom the loftiest feeling coexisted with the appearance of great libertinism; she reasoned like a geometer but merrily maintained an air of frivolity. She played the cello so magnificently that he shed tears over it, hiding in a shady garden in Parma. She was really Marie-Anne d'Albertas, and later married François Bougerel de Fontienne; she had to leave him after three months of complete happiness—that was in 1749—and avoided being seen by him when, fourteen years later, fate led him to seek hospitality at her castle just outside Aix. In 1769, gravely ill, he spent four months in Aix, nursed by a discreet governess who refused to reveal the name of her employer; this kindly good fairy who looked after his health so self-effacingly was called Henriette. She had not forgotten the man she called the "most honorable I have known" any more than he had forgotten her. She sent him a short letter just as he left Aix for Marseilles:

Nothing, my old friend, is more like a romance than the story of our meeting in my country house six years ago and our present meeting, twenty-two years after we parted in Geneva. We have both aged. Will you believe that, though I still love you, I am happy that you did not recognize me? It is not that I have become ugly, but being stout, I have a different appearance. I am a widow, happy, and comfortably off enough to tell you that if you ever lacked money at the bank, you could find some in Henriette's purse. Do not come back to Aix to search me out, for your return might lead to conjectures . . .

Twenty years after this letter, they are still writing to each other. Neither has forgotten the period of complete happiness they once shared: never a moment's quarrel, never a yawn, never a rose leaf folded in half, as Casanova puts it, ever troubled their bliss.

Now that Casanova has nearly arrived at the end of the third act of his life and the curtain is slowly coming down, he tastes the appeasing happiness of memory.

His last lady friend, Cecilie von Roggendorf, a twenty-two-year-old canoness, arouses a final passion, Platonic and epistolary. In a letter dated June 25, 1797, this is what she says: *Oh, dearest friend, you are the only person among all that I can still love easily, if you knew how much I esteem you, the confidence I feel when I reread your lines, where I discover such purity of morals, such sound principles, and a subtlety of mind and tact that enchant me.*

For her, the exiled old man writes a "précis" of his life. And he makes an assertion to her that he would never have thought possible: he, the voluptuous and carnal man, the libertine, dares to write that true love is unrelated to sensual pleasure. *Real love is the love that sometimes arises after sensual pleasure: if it does, it is immortal; the other kind inevitably goes stale, for it lies in mere fantasy.*

The Child from Venice

Giacomo's childhood was silent. His parents believed he would not live long. No one thought of speaking to him. Words formed a faraway, indistinct jumble of sounds. He discovered the power and pleasure of language only very belatedly. His earliest memory dates back to his ninth year. Until the awakening of his mind—and with it, memory, sense impressions, and the imagination—life seemed to seep out of him laboriously, like a shallow trickle of subterranean water, oozing involuntarily, a light mildew deposited by time.

He lived his first years under the sign of blood—blood in mysterious overabundance pouring from the nose. It seeped out continuously. As the little boy grew, he was slowly dying. His blood poured out unremittingly, announcing to his indifferent family that his death would not be long in coming. The physicians argued over the cause of his illness: how could he be losing more blood than his little body could contain? They said that out of a maximum of sixteen to eighteen he was losing two pounds of blood a week. What could cause such copious bleeding? One medical scientist claimed that all his chyle was converted to blood, another that with each breath the air increased the amount of blood in his lungs, which was why the child always kept his mouth open. Alexander Knipps-Macoppe, a famous physician and professor of medicine at the University of Padua, declared that since blood was an elastic fluid whose viscosity could diminish or increase but never its quantity, Giacomo's hemorrhages could only be caused by the thickness of the blood, which was relieving itself naturally in these discharges and hence facilitating its circulation. He added that the child would already be dead if Nature, which seeks life, had not come to her own assistance.

His parents thought he was doomed to a premature death; they did not talk to him. The child remained silent, motionless, a dull look in his eyes, glum, dazed. Everyone pitied him and left him alone. No one played with him or was interested in him, certainly not his mother. Little Giacomo showed no curiosity about the world. He lived in Venice, in the Calle della Commedia.

When he was a year old, his mother, Zanetta, left him in the care of her mother and went off to London with her husband to make her debut in the theater. His widowed grandmother Marzia kept a household of cleanliness and honest abundance. His maternal grandfather, Girolamo Farussi, had died of grief and disappointment twenty-two days before his only daughter's marriage to the actor Gaetano Casanova. Farussi was an artisan—a shoemaker originally from Burano, the lagoon island known for its fishermen and skilled lacemakers—who lived with his family in the San Samuele quarter of Venice. A young actor from the Grimani theater troupe came to live across the way and fell in love with Zanetta when she was barely fifteen years old.

Gaetano Casanova, born in Parma in 1697, the son of Giacomo Casanova and Anna Roli, had left his family and hometown at the age of nineteen to follow an actress nicknamed La Fragoletta who had a talent for soubrette roles. Having no profession or money, he became a dancer and then an actor. Eight years later, whether through fickleness or jealousy, he left his mistress, came to live in Venice, and joined the troupe that performed at the Teatro San Samuele.

The shoemaker Farussi considered it a disgrace to make a show of oneself onstage; it was out of the question for him to grant his daughter's hand to an actor. So when Gaetano succeeded in winning the beautiful Zanetta's love, he abducted her from her father. With witnesses and the necessary papers in hand, the two lovers presented themselves before the Patriarch of Venice, who joined them in holy matrimony on February 27, 1724, at the Church of San Samuele. From this union, thirteen months later, on April 2—Easter Day of the year 1725—Giacomo Girolamo Casanova was born. The day before, Zanetta had had a strong craving for crayfish.

Casanova's mother, Giovanna Maria Farussi, known as Zanetta, was a perfect beauty. She kept her looks for a long time; then suddenly her beauty faded. She was born in August 1708, probably in Burano, her father's island, and as a reminder of this origin, she was nicknamed La Buranella. We know nothing about her youth, except her beauty and her willingness to be abducted by the actor living in the house across the way, which brought on her father's death. Her mother forgave her misalliance, after she pledged never to go on the stage, a promise she did not keep. Her husband, on the other hand, soon quit the theater for optics. Zanetta left the task of bringing up her children to her mother, so she could devote herself to the commedia dell'arte. She began by putting the firstborn in her mother's care so she could leave for London, where, two years later, she gave birth to a second son. (Rumor had it that this child's real father was the Prince of Wales, the future King George II. Francesco Casanova became a painter of battle pictures, a member of the Royal Academy of Painting and Sculpture in Paris, then a protégé of Prince Kaunitz in Vienna.) At the end of 1728, Zanetta and Gaetano returned to Venice and performed at the Teatro San Samuele. Giacomo was three years old. In 1730, a third son was born, Giovanni Battista; he also became a painter and draftsman, a pensioner of the Elector of Saxony in Venice, a student of Mengs in Rome, and subsequently director of the Dresden Academy of Fine Arts. A year later, Faustina Maddalena arrived; she fell ill and died at the age of five. In 1732, Zanetta gave birth to Maria Maddalena Antonia Stella, who became a dancer and accompanied her mother to the court of Saxony. It is to his sister's family, indeed to his sister's son-in-law, Carlo Angiolini, that on his deathbed Casanova handed the manuscript of his *History of My Life.*

A sixth "posthumous" child, Gaetano Alvise, was born in 1734. (He became a priest.) A widow at twenty-five, Zanetta turned down all her suitors and decided to support her children on her own—but from a distance. Very soon she left Venice for Verona, St. Petersburg, and finally Dresden, where she remained for the rest of her life as a member of the Comici Italiani ensemble recruited in 1738 by Andrea Bertoldi for Count Heinrich von Brühl, Cabinet Minister in the court of Saxony and Poland. Onstage, throughout her life, at whatever age, Zanetta Casanova played with grace and talent the parts of the *prima amorosa.*

THE FAIRY AND THE WITCH

Giacomo's first childhood memory is set in Venice at the beginning of August 1733, in a house on the Calle della Commedia, in the shade of the church and theater of San Samuele.

Giacomo is standing in the summer heat, leaning against the wall. He is holding his head and staring down at the blood streaming to the floor. His beloved *nonna* washes his face with cool water and without anyone in the house knowing makes him board a gondola which brings him to Murano.

After disembarking, the grandmother leads her grandson away from the beautiful gardens and country houses and into a dark hovel. There they find an old woman sitting on a pallet, surrounded by five or six cats, and holding a black cat in her arms. The two women confer in a low voice for a time that seems endless to the child. After a silver ducat is slipped into her hand, the witch opens a chest, picks Giacomo up, and puts him inside. She closes the chest and tells him not to be afraid—this in itself would have been enough to scare him if he had had any brains, but he has none. He remains dazed, sitting in a corner, holding his handkerchief to his nose, unruffled by the racket outside. He hears, in turn, laughter, weeping, singing, shouts, and thumps on the chest, and is indifferent to it all. Finally he is taken out of the chest. The witch then lavishes caresses on him, undresses him, wraps him up, puts him to bed, burns some medicinal herbs, performs some incantations, unwraps him, makes him eat some pleasant-tasting dragées, and rubs his temples and the nape of his neck with a sweet-smelling ointment. After all this, the witch promises the child that the blood will gradually stop flowing as long as he tells no one about her, but threatens him with death if he divulges her secret mysteries. She also tells him that a beautiful lady will pay him a visit the following night. As soon as the child returns home, he falls asleep.

A dazzling woman, wearing a dress of magnificent fabric with a huge puffy pannier, crosses the darkness. She comes down the chimney in the bedroom where the little boy is resting. He wakes up and sees—or thinks he sees—a luminous woman wearing a crown of sparkling precious stones. With slow steps and a majestic, gentle air, she comes and sits on his bed. She takes several small boxes out of her pocket and, murmuring some words, empties them over his face. Unknown words, strangely tender, envelop him. She speaks for a long time, a very long time. The child listens to her, paralyzed and dazzled. He sees the little boxes, hears the music of her words, and watches the queen shining so brightly in the night. He is unable to understand what is happening to him. He is at the theater but in his own bed. The fairy bends over him, kisses him, and disappears just as she had appeared. The little boy immediately dozes off.

In the morning his grandmother comes to his bedside. She talks to him about the nocturnal visit and imposes silence under penalty of death. This threat, made by the only woman whose influence over the little boy is absolute and who has accustomed him to give blind obedience to her every command, remains anchored in his memory. And the injunction is not hard to comply with. For to whom could he describe the magical vision, he who speaks to no one and to whom no one thinks of speaking?

After the expedition to Murano and the night that followed, the nosebleeds gradually subside from day to day. Giacomo's mind opens. He learns to read in less than a month. He acquires a taste for knowledge and for life. He is eight years and four months old.

THE STOLEN CRYSTAL

The second scene Giacomo remembers goes back to mid-November 1733, three months after the trip to Murano, six weeks before his father's death. He and his brother Francesco, two years younger, are in their father's room. Giacomo is watching his father work with optical equipment. A large, round piece of multifaceted cut crystal attracts his attention. He takes it in his hand, holds it up to his eyes, and marvels at seeing objects multiply. He suddenly has an urge to steal it; since no one is watching, he drops it into his pocket. A few minutes later, his father stands up and, unable to find the crystal, turns to his sons and says that one of them must have taken it. Francesco denies having done so, and Giacomo, though he is guilty, denies having done so as well. The father threatens to search them and swears to give whichever one is lying a whipping. The older son, while pretending to be looking for the crystal in every corner of the room, deftly slips it into his brother's pocket. Their father, irritated by the futile hunt, searches the children, finds the lost object in the innocent son's pocket, and inflicts the promised punishment.

Six weeks after this incident, Giacomo's father suffers a cerebral abscess that sends him to the grave in a week. The physician, after having given him "opiate" remedies, tries to correct the blunder by administering "castoreum," an anti-spasmodic substance that makes his patient die in convulsions. The tumor bursts through the ear a minute after his death: having killed him, Doctor Zambelli leaves as though there was nothing more he could do at his patient's house.

Gaetano Casanova had been only thirty-six years old when he died. His death is mourned by the public, especially by the nobility, who realized he was superior to his station, not just in his behavior but also in his knowledge of mechanics. Two days before his death, in December 1733, sensing that the end was near, he had summoned his wife and five children to his bedside, as well as the Grimani brothers—Michele, Alvise, and Zuane, the three patrician owners of the San Samuele theater, whom Gaetano urged to become his family's protectors. He makes his weeping wife swear that she will let none of their children go on the stage. Zanetta takes the oath and the three Venetian noblemen promise to see to it that it will not be broken.

"THE TREES ARE WALKING!"

Pregnant and a widow, Zanetta is excused from performing until Easter. She refuses her hand to all the suitors who come forward. She believes that she can support her children on her own. For the first time, perhaps, Giacomo's mother takes an interest in her oldest son, not so much out of affection as because of his illness. Marzia, her mother, draws her attention to the child, who is always weak and has no appetite. On the day of his ninth birthday, April 2, 1734, Giacomo is taken to Padua by Zanetta, the abbot Alvise Grimani, who is his tutor, and Signor Baffo, a libertine poet and friend of his late father.

All four board a *burchiello* at ten o'clock at night. The boat is like a small floating house, with a sitting room and cabins and glass windows along the sides. Zanetta rises at daybreak and opens a window; the rays of the rising sun shine on the child's face and wake him. The bed is too low for him to see at ground level; he can see only the tops of the trees lining the riverbanks. The craft is sailing along calmly and smoothly, so that the trees slip past one by one and move rapidly out of his sight. Giacomo is astonished and cries out to his mother: *What is happening? The trees are walking!*

When the two patricians join them, the child asks the question again. They all laugh. The mother sighs and answers, exasperated: *It is the boat that is walking, not the trees. Get dressed!*

The child, with nascent good sense, thinks he understands the meaning of the phenomenon and says: *Then it is possible that the sun does not walk either but that it is we who move from west to east.*

His mother makes fun of him, Abbot Grimani calls him an imbecile. Dismayed, Giacomo is on the verge of tears when Signor Baffo rushes up to him and kisses him tenderly, saying: *You are right, my child, the sun does not move. Have courage, always reason accordingly, and let people laugh.*

Giacomo never forgets this lesson, for which he is grateful to his teacher. From then on, thinking is living—thinking independently without fear of those who laugh. He discovers the taste for transgression which goes with the taste for knowledge. From then on, his curiosity is limitless: grammar, law, theology, mathematics, ancient and modern languages, the writings of Virgil, Seneca, Ariosto, and Aretino, the arts of prose and verse— the most sophisticated erudition absorbs him. From then on, Giacomo's thinking is this:

The stupidity of the two others (my mother and Abbot Grimani) would certainly have blunted the sharp edge of a faculty that perhaps did not take me very far, I don't know; but I do know that to it alone I owe all the happiness I enjoy when I am alone with myself.

Arriving in Padua early on that April morning, Zanetta and the two noblemen leave the little boy and his little suitcase in a squalid boardinghouse. They do not see the rats and vermin scurrying around the children's room, nor do they inquire about the meager, coarse meals that the children are served. They count six zecchini to pay six months in advance. Signora Mida protests that this is not enough to feed the boy, keep him clean, and see to his education. Her objections are ignored. His mother, Abbot Grimani, and Signor Baffo kiss little Giacomo, instruct him to be obedient, and abandon him.

This is how they got rid of me.

THE SILVER SPOON

When he is seated at the table for his first meal, the child asks for his set of silver cutlery, a personal article which he cherishes because it was given to him by his kind grandmother, Marzia. His request is denied; he must use a wooden spoon like everyone else. A bad soup, a small portion of dried cod, an apple, and as a beverage (drunk directly from the earthenware jug, there being no glasses or cups) water boiled with grape pomace—this was the menu. Giacomo is surprised, but he does not know whether he is allowed to consider it bad and complain.

Hunger gives him rosy dreams of sitting at a big table, busily satisfying his cruel appetite, and it drives him to steal and gobble up anything he can find. In a few days, he devours fifty smoked herrings he finds in a cupboard in the kitchen, to which he steals down in the dark of night; a string of uncooked sausages fastened to the chimneypiece, normally indigestible; and as many eggs as he can lay his hands on in the poultry yard, just laid and still warm. At school, he makes such rapid progress that his schoolmaster, Doctor Gozzi, puts him in charge of his thirty classmates. He shows great forbearance for their misdeeds, in exchange for a few roast cutlets or pieces of chicken. Soon his trial comes to an end, thanks to Doctor Gozzi, who suggests that he write Abbot Grimani, Signor Baffo, and his grandmother—his mother was absent from Venice, for she had started performing again—for permission to come board with him. Grimani answers with a reprimand.

But in a week his *nonna* comes and rescues him from the boardinghouse where his mother had brought him six months earlier. Giacomo flings himself on her and breaks into tears. His grandmother, too, becomes tearful, takes him on her lap, asks him to tell her about his unhappy stay. He does not omit a single detail. She then packs his few old clothes in the trunk, retrieves the silver cutlery, and takes her grandson to the inn. Giacomo is brimming with inexpressible joy; his heart is ready to forgive and his mind to forget the torments he has endured. She settles him into Doctor Gozzi's house, outfits him as a friar, and has a wig made for him, his hair being so filthy it has had to be cut off. Marzia returns to Venice by *burchiello*, relieved to have been able to rectify, once again, her daughter's casual negligence.

ZANETTA, A GOLDONI ACTRESS

After placing him in the boardinghouse in Padua, Giacomo's mother had gone to Verona with the troupe affiliated with the Grimani theater. The company performed in Venice over the fall and winter, and spent the summer months on "firm ground." Giuseppe Imer, the director of the troupe, was a very eloquent but physically unattractive Genoese—short, fat, with no neck, tiny eyes, and a small, flat nose—who lacked neither intellect nor knowledge nor talent. Since he had a good singing voice, he thought of introducing musical interludes into comedy, a novelty that become a great success. He invited Carlo Goldoni to write for his actors.

In his *Memoirs Forming a Complete History of His Life and Writings*, Goldoni notes that the troupe had two actresses for the interludes: one was "a very pretty and very able widow by the name of Zanetta Casanova, who played the part of young lovers in comedy." Though the two actresses and the director could not read music, Goldoni finds that all three have taste, perfect pitch, and a perfect execution. The delighted public applauds.

Goldoni accepts a commission to compose an interlude in three acts with music, which he entitles *La Pupilla*. He takes his plot from the director's private life, since he has perceived that the Genoese has a decided inclination for the pretty widow and is jealous of her. Goldoni plays the part himself, and Imer is quick to discover the trick; but he finds the interlude so well written and the criticism so respectful and delicate that he pardons him this piece of pleasantry.

In the spring of 1735, Goldoni joins the troupe again, but finds it much changed. "The greatest loss experienced by the company," says he, "was that of the widow Casanova, who, not withstanding her connection with the director, had accepted an engagement in the service of the King of Poland." Zanetta had left, but was not yet working for the King. She had gone to Russia, with a troupe of Italian actors assembled by Pietro Mira, known as Pedrillo, a Venetian violinist who was Empress Anna's favorite jester and whom the Empress had sent to Italy to hire actors and musicians. Among those hired were the actors Vulcani, Giuseppe dall'Oglio, and Zanetta Casanova.

A BLOND WIG AND LITERARY SUCCESS

Before departing for the far north, the mother summons her oldest son and his tutor, Doctor Gozzi, to Venice. She receives them with aristocratic grace. Giacomo and his teacher are very impressed. The child finds his mother incredibly beautiful. Gozzi, intimidated and unaccustomed to society and fine manners, blushes and lowers his eyes; he is too shy to look her in the face when she speaks to him, and even more so when she offers her cheeks to receive his chaste kisses. This seems to amuse Zanetta.

The first thing she notices about her son, which appalls her, is the blond wig, which jars with his dark complexion, an incongruous mismatch with his eyebrows and black eyes.

—*Why not let him wear his own hair, my dear doctor?* the actress asks.

—*Because, madam, my sister, Bettina, keeps him clean more easily with a wig.*

This naïve remark draws laughter from those present, who then ask the doctor whether his sister is married. It is Giacomo who replies at once: *Bettina is the prettiest girl on our street and fourteen years old!*

This provokes even more laughter and Zanetta promises to make Bettina a fine gift if she cares for her son's hair. She sends for a wigmaker to bring the right color wig. Then everyone starts playing cards.

At supper, an Englishman, a man of letters and an expert Latinist, notes down an ancient distich which he gives to Giacomo to read:

Discite grammatici cur mascula nomina cunnus
Et cur femineum mentula nomen habet
(Teach us, grammarians, why *cunnus* [vagina] is masculine
And *mentula* [penis] feminine)

The young scholar, after a moment's reflection, writes out the following pentameter:

Dice quod a domino nomina servus habet
(Because the slave always takes the name of his master)

Everyone at the table bursts out laughing. They are surprised at such precocity and noisily cheer the young hero whom they had once known as a quasi-imbecile and who, in two years, has blossomed into such a clever child. Zanetta gives the master a gold watch, and Doctor Grimani gives Giacomo four zecchini to buy books.

THE PRIMA AMOROSA

Back in Padua, the tutor now talks of nothing else than his pupil's mother; and Bettina develops a fondness for Giacomo when she opens a package and discovers many yards of satiny light silk fabric and twelve pairs of gloves. The young girl takes good care of the little Venetian; she comes to comb his hair every day, sometimes when he is still in bed. She washes his face, neck, and chest, dispensing some childish caresses, which trouble him greatly. The pretty adolescent girl, cheerful, mischievous, and a great reader of novels, arouses him with ever more brazen gestures. He can hardly control himself but, much to his own regret, remains locked in his timidity.

One morning, Bettina, seated on his bed, carries her zeal for cleanliness too far, and her curiosity gives Giacomo such voluptuous pleasure that "it ceased only when it could not become greater." The young man is now initiated, not to love as yet, but to badinage and to women's desires—sometimes so difficult to interpret. Giacomo Casanova has just met with his first love intrigue.

Bettina spends the early hours of the morning igniting his sensuality, but she spends her nights locked up with another boarder in the house. Young Giacomo is terribly jealous. He feels superior to his rival in education, intellect, and manners, but, alas, his rival has the advantage of being pubescent. Giacomo demands explanations. Bettina then extends him a very strange invitation: she asks whether he would like her to dress him up as a girl and go with her to a ball in five or six days. There they could talk things over. Eager to prove he is a boy and not a girl, as she bids him to become, he informs her that he will expect her in his room that night.

He waits all night. Outside, snow is falling in great flakes. Early in the morning, numb more with rage than with cold, he approaches Bettina's room, hears noises, and sees his rival walking out in triumph. The young man kicks Giacomo in the belly with such force that he lands some distance away, buried in snow.

Giacomo is concocting dark schemes of revenge when he finds Bettina stretched out on the bed in the throes of dreadful convulsions. Half undressed, her body arched, writhing from side to side, kicking and punching the air at random, and avoiding with violent tugs all attempts to restrain her. A midwife says the convulsions are hysterical; a physician orders cold baths. As for Giacomo, he knows or thinks he knows that Bettina's sudden illness stems from her nocturnal exercises and the fear of being denounced by her rejected young lover. Still, he does believe in the genuineness of the convulsions, which often recur over the next few days.

The family rallies around her. A servant is accused of being a witch; Doctor Gozzi tries to ward off the demons. All to no avail. Giacomo whispers into her ear: *Take courage, get well, you can rely on my discretion.* Bettina does not have convulsions that day. Giacomo thinks he has cured her, but then the convulsions recur. A Capuchin is called in to exorcise the possessed girl. In his room the young boarder finds the following note: *Either come to the ball with me dressed as a girl or I will show you a sight that will make you cry.* Giacomo refuses, he says he loves her as if she were his sister. He sees her as a creature bewitched by her own temperament.

I felt a kind of pleasure in accepting at face value all the counterfeit currency she had passed off on me.

Smallpox has ended the story. Desire gives way to tenderness and leniency. He no longer bears her a grudge; he understands her suffering. From then on, and for the rest of his life, Giacomo accepts being the dupe of women. He shares their secret: woman loves man, but she must sometimes disguise her desire.

A short time thereafter, Giacomo's mother returns from St. Petersburg, where Empress Anna Ivanovna had not found Italian comedy sufficiently amusing. Zanetta had traveled with Carlino Bertinazzi, the famous Harlequin, who then left for Paris. Six months later, she says goodbye to Giacomo and goes to the court of Dresden, where she has just been offered a lifetime engagement in the service of August III, Elector of Saxony and King of Poland. The year is 1738; young Casanova is thirteen years old. He makes believe that his mother's departure does not sadden him. He will be like her, carefree and dissolute, absolutely sincere and completely inconstant. Love is a game, a festive celebration. Life is theater, a comedy—performing it well is all that matters.

The Curtain Rises

THE OMNIPOTENCE OF WOMEN

As the first act of his life begins, here are the characters whom Giacomo Casanova summons onstage in their order of appearance: an absent mother, a father who dies too soon, a kindly grandmother, a Murano witch, a nocturnal fairy, several quack physicians, a lecherous poet, several Venetian noblemen, a sordid Slavonian woman, a schoolmaster in Padua, a young hysteric, a handsome exorcist, debauched schoolboys, the San Samuele parish priest, the old Senator Malipiero, the daughter of the actor-director Imer, a peasant woman, two sisters, a skilled hairdresser, seminarians, a Minister of War, a man beaten with a stick at midnight, a Greek woman who gives him his first love disease, and Bernardo da Bernardis, bishop by the grace of God, the Holy See, and Giacomo's mother.

The curtain rises on a scene of witchcraft.

Giacomo bleeds as other children cry. He cries blood. His life is seeping out of his nose, it is being snuffed out drop by drop. What makes him summon death like this? Is it a way to hold the attention of a mother who turns from him and moves farther and farther away? A mother who plays the lover in comedies in London, Verona, St. Petersburg, Prague, and Warsaw? How can he make her like him, attract her to him for a moment, experience the warmth of her arms, the softness and fragrance of her skin, the melodious sound of her voice?

The small child from the "back street of comedy" is born under the sign of loss. His childhood is threatened. The incantatory and mysterious gestures of an old witch succeed in belatedly waking him to life, memory, and the intelligence of the senses. In his parents' absence, three female characters show concern for him: a magician, a queen of the night, and a supportive grandmother surround him with solicitude and kindness; they have faith in him. To strip the mask of death from his sad face, the three women plunge him into a ritual of gestation and rebirth. The primal scene is replayed; pregnancy and childbirth are relived. Through the symbolic power of their words and gestures, life is transmitted to him anew and the feeling of being loved instilled in him.

When he is locked in a chest, all his senses are stimulated: hearing, smell, taste, touch, sight. He is made to hear the sound of laughter and cries, prayer and song. He is enveloped in the acrid odor of smoke, followed by the sweet smell of ointments. He is given five deliciously flavored dragées to taste. Every inch of his skin is touched—covered with caresses, wrapped and unwrapped, rubbed, massaged. The witch accompanies her gestures with words in the Friulian dialect. This immersion in sounds so foreign to young Giacomo are soothing to the child whose mother and father had never talked to him. Blood—blood of women, of death, of castration, blood flowing and spreading outside the body, the vegetative, uncertain, ignored life—comes to an end. The chest retains, contains, envelops, protects, sets free. Then, after complete darkness, in the half light of night, the most luminous, most majestic of women appears before him, a dream mother who bends over him and lavishes kisses, sweet words, and myriad little boxes on him. Giacomo is restored to life.

After the trip to Murano and the gentle nocturnal visit, the metamorphosis takes effect; the dangerously flowing blood is exorcised and death backs off. Having sworn a vow of secrecy, the child has been initiated into magic; later, he will become a magician himself, sometimes in play, often from inward necessity. All his life, Casanova strives to recapture this moment of wondrous fusion, this magical regression with the fairy mother and sorceress grandmother. He regularly thinks up stratagems to maintain this illusion of blessed euphoria, this providential union prior to any kind of differentiation, severance, or law. At the genesis of memory, little Giacomo experiences the magical omnipotence of women.

When he is writing his memoirs, Casanova finds it ridiculous to attribute the healing of his hemorrhaging to a sorceress, to a fairy's eccentricities, but he believes it would be inaccurate to say they did not contribute to it. As for the apparition of the beautiful queen, he always believed she had been a dream, unless a masquerade had been staged for him. The old man in Dux does not believe in sorcerers, but he is convinced their spells have true power over those who believe in them. Remedies for some of the greatest afflictions are not always found in pharmacies; such is his conviction.

Some things, he writes in his Bohemian retreat, *become real that previously existed only in the imagination, and therefore some effects attributed to faith may not always be miraculous. They are miraculous for people who attribute limitless power to faith.*

CASANOVA'S MOTHER

Casanova's mother was marvelously beautiful and inaccessible, distant and enchanting. The only thoughts the son associates with the woman who gave birth to him are beauty and absence. He is unemotional in describing her abandoning him; he denies suffering and loss. To avoid the pain of sadness, Giacomo idealizes his mother. He looks upon her in the wonder of unconditional admiration. He sees her as a fairy, a queen, a magician.

Glistening with supernatural light, covered with jewelry, radiating luxury and glory, she glides through the night as in a dream and guides him to success from afar. She towers over everyone, high above, under the bright glow of the footlights. She is the magnified image of love. He avoids all conflict with her and has no resentment or ill feeling toward her. As a way of protecting himself against the void and separation, he tries to erase all trace of confrontation, all forms of otherness, all difference—of sex, location, generation, and social condition. All his affairs present a similar pattern: staying on the safe side of a disquieting otherness, meeting the other while avoiding the threat of her rejection. The child from Venice wants to keep the illusion of motherly perfection intact. Thus does he maintain the conviction of being enveloped in her omnipotence and magic. She is the blind goddess—Providence, Destiny, Lady Luck—and he is under her protection.

In order to reach this inaccessible mother, he must identify with her and live an exceptional life. He will stand above, apart, or beyond the common laws of men. He strides across frontiers, flouts the rules, braves the lightning, escapes from prisons, conquers every woman he falls in love with, and considers no enterprise impossible. Casanova has extravagant ambitions and the nerve, guts, and inexhaustible energy to match. He always has the overpowering feeling of being protected by an invisible intelligence, a benevolent genie goading him to seek happiness.

Because he has been on close terms with death since childhood, life belongs to him. From the beginning, he knows that he is owed nothing; thus anything is allowed or, at least, possible. The past is gone, the future is yet to come, and both are nonexistent: all that counts is the present moment. He jumps into things with ever greater resiliency. He springs up out of nowhere to save the virgin, widow, peasant woman, countess, or a gentleman he happens to meet. He offers to them all his arm, his sword, his honor, his expertise in the cabala, his purse, his connections, his conversation, his knowledge of love, his imagination. Thanks to his daring, his cleverness, his know-how, he inverts bad luck for those he meets. In exchange, he gains something for himself: adventure, pleasure, novelty, rewards, and amusing stories to tell.

Like the three sorceresses of his childhood, he seeks to play the part of deus ex machina who has the power to save, repair, change, erase, or provide whatever the circumstances and needs require. He enjoys playing with taboos and impossibilities, but with a light touch. Tragedy is not his element, and he flees from it more than from anything. He is the providential, beneficent hero whom everyone, man or woman, is pleased to have met. He wants to be attractive and convincing, to prevail through charm, persuasion, eloquence, and talent—sometimes with gifts or even money, but never through violence or coercion. He prides himself on conquests, never on victims. Laughter, thankful appreciation, satisfied sighs, applause intoxicate him. They are like an enchanting echo of his mother's acclaim on the occasion of his first poetic exploit, an evening in Venice, during Lent in 1736.

Giacomo is bleeding, Zanetta turns away. He dares to ask a question; she proclaims him an idiot. Nothing will ever come of the boy. She abandons him in Padua with no compunctions, alleging he needs a change of air, and returns to the stage, a pretty widow surrounded by attentive men. Two years go by. She is about to make a long journey; she remembers her first-born and summons him to Venice to say her farewells. A blond wig mars his appearance; she is suddenly interested in his hair and his looks. She wants her son to cut a handsome figure, if nothing else so that he not detract from the elegance of her dinner table, and for his manners to blend with the aristocratic society she is surrounded by. Suddenly the little fellow speaks and produces some Latin verses. Her guests begin to laugh, charmed by such vivacity and precocity. His mother is now delighted, joyful, even proud. He is not so bad, this little Giacomo. What does he say? That each sex depends on the other for its pleasure? That the slave is always named after his master? How does he know these things at his age? He is only eleven, but already erudite, self-assured, and capable of repartee. Zanetta applauds. His mother's applause sends him to the pinnacle of bliss.

She looks at his wig; she laughs when he speaks. Is this what it takes to make oneself attractive to women—appearance and speech? She would have nothing to do with him before, with his bleeding, with his weak body and dull mind. She wants him to be lively, brilliant, a fine talker, well dressed and perfumed. That is how he will be.

Casanova responds, mirror-like, to his mother's narcissistic interest in him with increased brio, travels, festivities, ecstasies, feasts of the mind and the senses. Any excuse will do for sensual enjoyment. The joyful excess of all these pleasures takes him beyond despair and the sense of void and death. The neglected child, silently languishing, now believes in happiness. And since his movements are unhindered by fear, including the fear of displeasure, he is capable of all acts of daring and generosity.

His mother is an actress onstage; Casanova is an actor in life. His theater includes all Europe. Forever performing, he is quick to pick up signs of contentment from his audience, and he is unsparing in his efforts and use of effects. His pleasure lies in the pleasure of others. In drawing rooms and boudoirs, or in the course of travel, he tries to fulfill the expectations of his partners of the moment. He has an irrepressible need to know he is loved, appreciated, esteemed, admired, respected. In social settings, he cannot bear silence or the slightest hint of disapproval. *In the most brilliant company*, he admits, *a single person present giving me the eye ruffles me; I become ill-humored and stupid. It is a failing.*

His desire is to arouse the desire of the other. He would like love, esteem, interest, or friendship to be unfailing and unconditional, like his grandmother's, which confirms the omnipotence he had as a child. A love suspended in time with no beginning or end. He watches for signs—even furtive ones—of alliance and complicity. He always feels compelled to test his luck—at cards, with women, in all his undertakings—to see his illusion of impunity, the fortunate hallmark of his destiny, confirmed by chance.

"FAREWELL, VENICE!"

Since he proves to be gifted beyond her hopes, Zanetta dreams of success for her son. In spite of his inclination toward medicine, she encourages him to prepare for an ecclesiastical career, the only possible calling for talented persons of humble birth. Let him study ecclesiastical law and he is certain to go far!

At the court in Dresden, she appeals to the Queen of Poland to persuade her daughter, the Queen of Naples, to obtain a bishopric for her protégé, Bernardo da Bernardis, a monk in Warsaw, in his native Calabria; in exchange, this monk has promised to take Giacomo into his service. *He will set you on the road to the Church's highest dignities*, she writes to her eighteen-year-old son. *Imagine the comfort for me, when, twenty or thirty years from now, I see that you have become at least a bishop.*

This sudden interest on the part of his mother goes to his head. *Farewell, Venice!* She sends him south to Naples on foot, by way of the Eternal City. He takes to the road with a light step. In spite of the trials he has along the way, he is deeply convinced that brilliant Fortune awaits him, since she shares the features of his distant and powerful mother. Nothing can harm him anymore. He is protected!

On the road, as he approaches Rome for the first time, he sees a huge pyramidal flame which accompanies him to the entrance of the city. The sight of this little meteor gives him singular ideas. He begins to dream about some uncommon destiny. The thought never leaves him. He will become a Pope or a great philosopher. He knows he is at an age when a young man can count on Fortune, if he has a bit of courage and a physical appearance that favorably predisposes the persons he approaches. He does not see himself as handsome but as having some ineffable quality of greater worth. He feels he can do anything. He is convinced that an open, "rose-colored" expanse lies permanently before him. He is not yet ready to hear of old age, disillusionment, and death.

Surrendering to fate, I believed that thinking about the future was a wasted effort.

When he arrives at the Bishop's in Calabria, Casanova is distressed to find him poorly lodged and fed, with no interesting company. When he asks him if there are any good books, a literary circle, or an aristocratic set with which to spend a pleasant hour or two, Bernardo da Bernardis smiles sadly. Thoughtful and demoralized, the adolescent wonders:

Without a good library, or group, or rivalry, or literary correspondence, was this a country where I could see myself settled at the age of eighteen?

The Bishop decides to send the well-read, ambitious young man on to Naples, supplied with good letters of recommendation. He is very soon received into the best homes there, each aristocratic father wishing to keep him as a tutor for his children. A Neapolitan by the name of Antonio Casanova is curious to meet him.

—*Your family is Venetian, my young friar?* he asks him.

—*Signore,* the adolescent answers modestly, *I am a great-grandson of the grandson of the unfortunate Marcantonio Casanova who was secretary to Cardinal Pompeo Colonna and who died of the plague in Rome in the year 1528, during the pontificate of Clement VII.*

Giacomo, who knows his family tree by heart, reels off his ancestral line starting with Don Juan of Saragossa, son of Don Francisco of Aragon, born at the end of the fourteenth century. When he hears all this, the Neapolitan kisses him, calls him cousin, and orders a blue redingote made for him of the finest wool and with gold buttons; then he introduces him, nobly attired, into the best society of Naples and the surrounding area.

Giacomo soon has countless magnificent gifts and agreeable invitations heaped upon him. It is even suggested that he be given the honor of kissing the Queen's hand. At this prospect, the young Venetian is overcome with shame. He has boasted that his ancestors included a poet, a theologian, a king's secretary, one of Christopher Columbus's companions, and a colonel, but he has left out that he is the son of mere actors. The Queen knows of Zanetta's employment at the court of Saxony and might well divulge the fact, a disclosure that would cause a scandal; his pedigree would be cast in a ridiculous light, and the power of prejudice would erase the good impression he has made. In spite of his brilliant conversation, his good manners and talents, and the friendship with which he is honored by dukes and duchesses, he does not belong to their world; he is an intruder—almost an impostor. For fear of being unmasked, he quickly decides to leave Naples. He proudly announces his intention to seek his fortune in Rome. His new friends do not let him leave empty-handed: he now has in his possession a snuffbox, a tortoiseshell watch with gold inlays, a valuable walking stick, silver ducats, traveling clothes, and letters of recommendation to the powerful Cardinal Acquaviva. Already a master in the art of the evasive pirouette, the young friar exits the stage, head held high.

In his heart of hearts, he is wounded. The social insult, the shame of having no social standing drives him from then on. Sometimes his aim is to force the nobility to recognize that he has a nobility different from theirs, a personal nobility independent of birth or fortune; sometimes he gives himself the appearance of belonging to the cream of society by taking the title Chevalier de Seingalt or by borrowing his mother's maiden name—in Russia, for example—and calling himself Count Farussi. Great is the young Friar Casanova's temptation to disregard his genealogy, erase all trace of ancestry or belonging, and roam the world with no family ties, basking in the euphoric illusion of being his own father and his own mother.

WHAT IS A FATHER?

In recalling his childhood, Casanova the writer summons three consecutive scenes: the healing of his hemorrhaging through witchcraft, the theft of the crystal, and his father's premature death.

As soon as his curiosity awakens, the young Giacomo turns to his father. In his father's mechanics and optics workshop, he marvels to discover the infinite mirror in a piece of cut crystal. His urge is to take possession of this paternal magic—more concrete, less mysterious, and more accessible than women's magic. When his father asks for his work tool, the child dares not admit that he would like to keep it and that he would like to hold the glass up again to his enchanted eye. Adding cowardice to theft, he slips the object into his younger brother's pocket. Gaetano punishes his younger son instead of his oldest.

The culprit goes unpunished while, unjustly, the innocent brother pays for a misdeed he never committed. How is it possible for a father to be so easily fooled, deceived, deluded? How could he not have distinguished truth from falsehood and restored justice? This double mistake renders the paternal law derisory, powerless, and unfounded. The father's authority is not denied—the threat of punishment was carried out, after all—but ridiculed, deflected, and mocked. This incident, in itself rather banal, is immediately followed by the father's grievous, premature death.

The old man in Dux links the two events yet feels no guilt for the "murder" and forcefully asserts Doctor Zambelli's responsibility. The doctor's incompetence contrasts sharply with the skill of the Murano witch. These two protagonists implicitly duplicate the parental couple: female omnipotence and male impotence, a motif Casanova embroiders endlessly. Throughout the narrative of his adventures, as he tries to solve the equation of his origins, he repeats the same pattern: duping authority, being the dupe of women, demonstrating his inexhaustible energy.

The little boy's attempt to identify with his father goes wrong and is converted into deception; the failure of authority is exposed; the victory over the father is bitter-tasting, and, dodging the law, Giacomo deflects its burden onto someone else. Secretly he wins, but he loses his father. Defiance and triumph are followed by loss and emptiness. With his father dead, a punishment is left unsettled and the question of blame remains. Casanova refuses to feel guilty—he will not hear of it. And yet, from time to time in the course of his life, he attracts failure—he is imprisoned, hunted, exiled, dispossessed, and treated as undesirable.

Too easily fooled and then dead so soon, having failed to protect his son from maternal excess (excessive absence, excessive fascination, excessive magic), Casanova's father fails to perform his part on the family stage. He leaves the role free for others. An orphan, Giacomo tries to find adoptive fathers— teachers capable of guiding him and shaping his impetuousness. At eighteen, as he is about to enter Rome, this is how he sees himself:

I was an interesting scatterbrain, a rather attractive thoroughbred horse, unbroken, or, which is even worse, badly broken.

Throughout his formative years—wherever Fortune leads him, in Padua, Venice, Rome, or Constantinople—he encounters learned individuals whose reliability he questions and whose breadth and wisdom he puts to the test. With an always slightly mocking critical acuity, he measures their limits, their weaknesses, and, worst of all, their inconsistencies. Casanova—as a child, a schoolboy, a student, a friar, or a young soldier in the service of his country—constantly wavers between his tendency to call into question the authority of princes and teachers and his need to have dependable, clear, stable, just laws to rely on. He needs to seek out respectable adoptive fathers who cannot be deceived or exposed.

To Giorgio Baffo, a great friend of his father's, he is ever grateful for stimulating his curiosity and for encouraging him to think for himself and ignore the laughter of others—a gratitude that is probably even less ambivalent since this patrician was a poet in "the most lascivious of all genres." Casanova, when exiled from his country by the Inquisition, notes with irony:

The State Inquisitors of Venice, with their piety, will have contributed to his fame. By condemning his manuscripts, they made them available.

His first schoolmaster, Doctor Gozzi, is submissive to law and the Church, and mistrusts thought because it gives rise to doubt. He imparts to Casanova everything he knows, which according to his pupil is very little but enough to introduce him to all the sciences and teach him to play the violin. For Doctor Gozzi, who shares his bed with young Giacomo, the sin of the flesh is the greatest sin of all, and he becomes angry when the impertinent Giacomo claims it can only be the least. His morals, consistent with his religious convictions, are irreproachable. As an adult,

Casanova stays with him whenever he returns to Padua. He has an enduring affection for him even if he is quick to rid himself of the religious relic his teacher gives him as a gift.

Which I might still have had in my possession, he admits, *if it had not been set in gold. The miracle it performed was that it was of use to me in a moment of emergency.*

On January 22, 1741, in Venice, Giacomo is received into the ranks of the four minor orders, to his grandmother's great satisfaction. The parish priest of San Samuele introduces him to Senator Malipiero, an old gentleman of seventy who entertains the best Venetian society in his nearby palace. Subject to attacks of gout that leave him crippled in one limb, then in another, and toothless, he is obliged to eat alone because he takes twice as long as everyone else to finish his meal and is unwilling to rush or make his guests wait. When Casanova is introduced to this witty man, our young monk persuades him to invite to dinner guests who eat twice as much as other people.

—*Where can they be found?*

—*It is a delicate matter. Your Excellency must test dinner guests and when you find them to be as you want, you must know how to keep them without telling them why: for there is no well-bred person in the world who would want people to say that he has the honor of eating with Your Excellency only because he eats twice as much as another.*

The logic appeals to Senator Malipiero, who makes the young friar his daily table companion. He instructs his new favorite to read Gassendi, and he includes him in the evening gatherings, among men of wit who are well informed about all the latest happenings in Venice, and among respectable women who his protector asserts are models of correct behavior, adding that everyone would consider him a scoundrel if he said anything about them that reflected poorly on the good reputation they enjoyed in society. First lesson in the social graces.

In a matter of days, all the lady guests of the Palazzo Malipiero adopt Giacomo as the fair-haired boy in their households.

In my capacity as young friar of no importance, they wanted me to accompany them when they went to see their daughters or nieces in the visiting rooms of the convents where they were being educated; I went to their houses at all hours and was admitted unannounced; I was scolded when I allowed a week to go by without going to see them; and when I entered the ladies' apartments, I could hear them running away, but they said they were foolish as soon as they saw it was only me. I found their trust charming.

He sees all doors open to him, he is let into boudoirs, gondolas, and secrets; he is fifteen, barely sixteen, an age of androgynous charm and dawning sensuality. No longer a child but still a child. In this hazy borderland, he still benefits from the privileges of childhood but is already entitled to a few liberties. Without batting an eye, he receives the caresses of "old women," some of whom wish to pass for old though they are not, just so they can kiss him with a semblance of propriety.

A "friar of no importance," such is his position in society; the phrase reveals his lowly social stature but also his ideal of casual seduction with impunity, with no consequences or commitments. As a young man of no importance, answerable to no one, he avoids rivalry. Giacomo remains out of the running.

His admission into Venetian palaces, the company of society women, the delightful rustle of their gowns and their ambergris-scented powder, their witty conversation, their glances—all this flatters the adolescent and motivates him to be attractive and elegant. Tosello, the priest of San Samuele, does not look upon this approvingly; seconded by Casanova's grandmother Marzia, he condemns Giacomo's excessively studied curls and the delicate odor of his jasmine pomade. Our young clergyman retorts that if he had wanted to stink he would have become a Capuchin. Very early one morning, the priest slips into his room and, armed with a good pair of scissors, ruthlessly cuts off the sleeping friar's pretty curls. What anger! What indignation when he wakes! His brother Francesco laughs, his *nonna* tries to calm him by conceding that Tosello overstepped the bounds of acceptable punishment. Giacomo is enraged, determined to take revenge "in blood without fear of the law." He consults a lawyer to seek compensation, when a skillful hairdresser, sent by Senator Malipiero, comes on the scene and redresses the wrong. After assessing the damage, the hair stylist laughingly announces that he will fix his hair *"en vergette"* and that it will look even more elegant than before. Giacomo is pleased and avenged. Once again he triumphs over authority by greeting it with derision.

The incident amuses the elderly Senator Malipiero, and he insists that his protégé be the preacher for the day after Christmas. The victory is complete; it includes fifty zecchini in alms and several love letters written by beautiful ladies in the pews below—scandalizing the bigots. Giacomo dreams of becoming the century's leading preacher, while his grandmother dreams he will become an apostle. But the second time he steps up into the pulpit, because his conceit is such that he had not taken the trouble to learn his sermon by heart, and his love of food so great that he had lingered at the dinner table, he wanders aimlessly from his subject. The congregation becomes uneasy. He sees several people leave the church and thinks he hears laughter. Alarmed, he falls into a swoon, half sham, half real—an escape that certainly lacks panache. This time he has lost his audience. Shame drives Giacomo to leave Venice immediately for the University of Padua, where he takes his third-year law exams and studies for his doctorate. A scatterbrain of no importance can succeed only so far.

LAUGHTER AND GUILT

Some time later, as Giacomo prepares to go south, Malipiero, delighted to see his pupil eagerly following the calling his mother wished for him, teaches him a lesson he never forgets. The well-known precept of the Stoics, *Sequere Deum*, has no other meaning, he explains, than "Abandon yourself to what fate has to offer." A month later, an incident occurs that causes Giacomo's disgrace. He becomes too intimate with Teresa Imer, the old man's pretty favorite.

Sitting side by side in front of a small table, with our backs to the door of the room where we assumed our employer was sleeping, at a certain point in our conversation—in our innocent gaiety—we suddenly wanted to explore the differences between our two shapes. We were at the most interesting point of our examination, when I was violently struck on the neck with a cane, and struck by another blow, which would have been followed by others, if I had not escaped from the hailstorm by making a quick dash for the door.

A quarter of an hour later, Giacomo is given his coat and hat with a note warning him never to set foot in the palace again. He immediately pens a vengeful response:

You struck me in anger, therefore you cannot boast that you taught me a lesson. Indeed, I choose not to have learned anything. I can forgive you only by forgetting that you are wise; and that I will never forget.

The adolescent has exposed his teacher, who was unable to master his anger and jealousy. And what is the value of a teacher who cannot abide by his own wisdom? The servants guess the cause of Giacomo's sudden exile, and soon the story makes the rounds of Venice.

A strained relation with authority ends thus—with roars of laughter. It is a strained relation, not a real confrontation. Giacomo mocks the wise old man, greets his lesson with derision, and declares he has learned nothing. He laughs at authority without directly confronting it, underscores the father figure's inadequacy, and avoids conflict. Several pirouettes accomplish the trick. Harlequin, servant of two masters—in other words, a servant to no one, or only to himself, which comes to the same thing—leaves the stage thumbing his nose. And the public applauds.

Yet guilt is not unknown to Casanova, who periodically throws himself head-first into failure, traps, love diseases, gambling losses, and state prisons. Relying on the magical omnipotence of women, he seems to belittle the paternal function, and yet, when moved by a feeling of being in the wrong he gets himself punished:

I have never done anything in my life but work on making myself sick when I was enjoying health, and work on regaining my health when I had lost it.

There is certainly an irony to this pattern, for punishment often becomes the occasion for a new exploit, as though he were only seeming to submit to the law. He always triumphs over it in the end, holding it up to ridicule, laughing at it and making others laugh. Come, now! he seems to be saying, From disease, I can be cured; from prison, escape; from gambling, recoup my losses; from disappointments, be consoled by several good nights' sleep!

Casanova's arrogant desire to be above the law coexists with a secret need to pay for his escapades. He jumps back and forth with great speed, from health to sickness, from beauty to squalor, from wealth to poverty, from princes to swindlers, from palaces to prisons. Thus does this friar of no importance crisscross Europe from north to south and east to west, going from the prettiest marquises to infected courtesans, from the greatest nonbelievers to the Holy Pontiff. From Pope Benedict XIV, he requests permission to eat meat on fish days and to read banned books; it is as though he had the irrepressible urge to try to change any authority into an obliging mother figure who encourages his fantasies of immunity. He remains the outlaw son of a magical mother and eliminates, through laughter or trickery, any paternal prohibition.

THE RED SUIT OF FORTUNE

Giacomo gives up his ecclesiastical robe for a military uniform, but since he is neither patient nor hypocritical enough, he is no more successful in this career than in the other, and after these years of apprenticeship, he returns to his native city in 1746. He is twenty years old and penniless. He decides to become a violinist in the orchestra of the San Samuele theater. He is back at square one.

In the spring of that year, he is working in one of the orchestras hired to play for a big wedding at the Palazzo Soranzo. Toward the end of the festivities, our musician leaves the palace to go home. On his way down the stairs, he notices a red-robed senator getting into his gondola. A letter falls out of his pocket. Casanova picks it up and hands it to the patrician, who insists upon seeing him home. Three minutes later, the senator asks the violinist to shake his left arm, then, with a few poorly articulated words, mumbles that he can no longer feel his leg; his mouth contorts and his eyes take on a deathly blank look. Giacomo yells to the boatmen to stop; he runs to get a surgeon, who bleeds the dying man, and he tears his shirt to make him a bandage. The dying senator is brought home to bed. Giacomo insists on watching over him. Signor Dandolo and Signor Barbaro, two of the patrician's friends, come in and question the young stranger whom they find at his bedside. After describing the circumstances of the stroke, Giacomo announces his intention of spending the night in an armchair, not leaving the senator for a moment. He adds that he must spend the night at the patient's bedside to prevent his dying. The two friends are impressed; though the young man is unknown to them, they dare not question him, and our violinist volunteers no further information.

A physician, Doctor Ferro, is summoned to the patient's bedside and begins to administer a mercury treatment. During the night, the senator is on fire, in a state of great agitation, and hardly able to breathe. Without delay, the young Casanova takes the liberty of uncovering his chest, removing the plaster, and washing him with warm water. The dying man comes back to life and falls peacefully asleep. The following day, Doctor Ferro prides himself on the nobleman's recovery, but the three patricians point to the young man and declare him the more knowledgeable physician.

I kept a modest silence, controlling a desire to laugh, while the physician looked at me, rightly regarding me as a brazen charlatan who had dared to supplant him . . . He leaves, and now I had become physician to one of the most illustrious members of the Venetian senate.

Having recovered from his stroke, Senator Matteo Giovanni Bragadin, who is attracted to the occult sciences, finds the young man too knowledgeable and believes him to be endowed with supernatural abilities. The child from Venice who had been saved by witchcraft immediately slips into the assigned role: he makes the mad claim that he is in possession of a magical numerical calculus. Bragadin replies that it is the key of Solomon, also called cabala. Giacomo knowingly deceives him and then sees no reason to set him right, since his deception is to their mutual advantage. He has read the ancients and knows that next to reason is cunning intelligence, or *metis*.

Deceit is a vice, but honest cunning is merely prudence of mind. It is a virtue. True, it resembles mischievousness, but that is inevitable. He who does not know how to exercise prudence is a fool.

Giacomo decides to secure the three patricians' friendship. He discovers he has found a father.

Whoever you are, says the senator, *I owe you my life. Your protectors, who wanted to make you a priest, a doctor, a lawyer, a soldier, and finally a violinist, were fools who did not know you. God instructed your angel to bring you to me. Now that I know you, if you wish to be my son, you have only to accept me as your father, and from then on I will treat you as such in my house until I die. Your apartment is ready; have your clothes sent for; you will have a servant and a paid gondola; you will share our table and receive ten zecchini a month.*

Giacomo throws himself at his feet in gratitude. Within a matter of days, he makes the jump from lowly professional fiddler to nobleman's son. He has just avenged his father's death by saving the life of an adoptive father. He fools one just as he fooled the other, but the second one survives and is amused. The senator proves to be a permissive, lenient father who identifies with Giacomo's mad youth, for he remembers his own, which was hardly more sensible. He gives him a few lessons on not overstepping authority beyond certain limits, but above all he instructs him to enjoy life in the present: *Think of having fun!* he commands him and gives him the means to follow his commandment.

Giacomo is twenty-one; he thinks he has risen above all prejudice. He is convinced he can live in complete freedom, and he refuses to believe that true freedom does not—and cannot—exist anywhere, not even in the aristocratic city. But his casual ways will land him in prison. He is the adoptive son of a Venetian nobleman, not his legitimate son. Nothing can erase the blemish of his birth. He feigns not to know this, intoxicated with the feeling of impunity.

Sufficiently wealthy, endowed by nature with a striking appearance, a confirmed gambler, a spendthrift, a great talker, always forthright and not modest, intrepid, running after pretty women, supplanting rivals, accepting as good company only those whom I found amusing—people could only hate me. As I was always prepared to pay with my life, I thought I could do whatever I pleased, for any authority that was in my way seemed to me an obstacle to be challenged.

Inexorably, the wheel of Fortune brings Casanova back down. The Inquisition is on the prowl. Who is this actor's son who behaves like a patrician nobleman, owns banned books, keeps company with foreign ambassadors, courts women with utter disregard for their lovers, and professes impious ideas?

Bragadin, who had been State Inquisitor for eight months, urges him to seek refuge in a safe place.

—*Prudence requires you leave. Believe me, my dear son, go, take a day and night post to Florence and stay there until I write that you can return. Have four oars put on my gondola and go!*

—*I do no not feel guilty of anything, and therefore I cannot fear the Inquisitors' tribunal.*

—*The tribunal can find you guilty of crimes you are not even aware of.*

—*By leaving I would be showing a fear which would proclaim my guilt.*

—*Stay and sleep at least for tonight in your apartment at the palace; the police agents cannot come to arrest you in the house of a patrician.*

—*They will find me during the day; I must not be afraid.*

—*We may not see each other again, my dear son.*

IN WEDDING ATTIRE

At daybreak on July 25, 1755, they come to arrest him. His manuscripts, letters, and books are seized: Ariosto, Horace, Petrarch,
as well as works on magic, *Le Portier des Chartreux*, and Aretino's
little book on sexual positions. Meanwhile, Giacomo performs
his toilet carefully, shaves, has his hair combed, and dresses in
silk and lace as though he were going to a wedding. Is this derision, provocation, a way of asserting that he does not feel in
the wrong and that a mistake has been made? Such a nobly
attired man cannot possibly be locked up under the lead roofs
of the Ducal Palace by Venice's wise Inquisitors; he cannot possibly be guilty of anything. Several hours later, the secretary of
the tribunal having called for his imprisonment, Giacomo crosses
the Bridge of Sighs and, dazed and overcome, ends up in a dark
dungeon with ceilings so low that he cannot stand upright. It is
extremely hot, he hears the rats scurrying about, he is alone with
his rage, indignation, and despair. *Never in my life had I had such
a bitter taste in my mouth*, he later wrote.

On October 31, 1756, at midnight, Casanova escapes. From
the roof he enters the attic of the Ducal Palace, finds a narrow
little stone stairway leading to the chancellery office, breaks
down some doors, and is in the study of the *Savio alla scrittura*,
the Minister of War, faced with an impregnable door. His vest,
shirt, and trousers torn, his hips and thighs drenched in blood,
he sits down and tells the monk who is escaping with him that
he has done all he could. Things are now in the hands of God
and Fortune.

*I ripped up some handkerchiefs and made bandages for myself as best
I could ... I put on my fine coat which seemed comical on this cold day
... I looked like a man who had gone to a den of vice after going to a*

ball, and had come out disheveled. The bandages that were visible on my knees were what marred the elegance of this persona.

In this dramatic moment, when everything hangs in the balance, Casanova is worried about his appearance. Or at least the old man in Dux makes a point of stressing his hero's vanity for the reader. As though he were trying to show that nothing had happened between his arrest and his escape, that neither his sentencing for atheism nor the strain of living in a dungeon had gotten the better of him, that none of this had had any effect. The libertine—forever bold, rebellious, carefree, and elegant— leaves his prison just as he had entered it, in wedding attire! The Inquisition has had no power over him. Casanova proclaims, once and for all, that he is a young man of no importance, and that a man can owe his life to a formal coat.

Providence takes the shape of a guard in the palace courtyard who notices, next to an open window, Casanova's face and his fine hat trimmed with gold Spanish point lace and a white plume. The man thinks he might have inadvertently locked up a patrician nobleman the night before, and he comes up to set him free. Once the door is opened, the two escapees take flight with great speed, down the royal stairs—the stairway of the Giants, *la scala dei Giganti*—leaving the guard, Andreoli, transfixed. Casanova and his companion, Father Balbi, cross the piazzetta, and with hardly a glance right or left make their way to the shore and set off in the first gondola they find moored at the embankment.

I then turned and looked at the entire length of the beautiful canal, and, seeing not a single boat, admired the most beautiful day one could hope for, the first rays of a magnificent sun rising above the horizon, the two young boatmen rowing at full speed; and thinking at the same time of the cruel night I had spent, of the place where I had been the day before, and of all the coincidences that had been favorable to me, I felt something take hold of my soul, which rose up to merciful God, exciting the wellspring of gratitude, moving me with such extraordinary force that my tears rushed in an abundant stream to soothe my heart, choked with excessive joy; I sobbed and wept like a child who is taken off to school by force.

The coincidences of Fortune have just led Casanova to gain his freedom but lose his homeland. After fifteen tenacious months and several hours of courage, physical skill, and composure, he triumphs over the most ruthless authority, then breaks down in tears like an abandoned child. Afterward, he laughs. With undaunted enthusiasm, no protection, and an empty purse, he is about to jump merrily over two rivers, to escape the Inquisition's guards and to find immunity at the outer limits of the Most Serene Republic. His incredible escape confirms him in his euphoric certainty of being above the law, subject to no constraints, a child protected by Providence.

FOUR

The Stratagems of Voluptuousness

THE PLEASURE OF WOMEN

From his first amorous awakenings, Giacomo Casanova admits to being the plaything of women. As memoirist he does not hide this; his central character as he portrays him is at the mercy of feminine desires. Women call the tune. They can do as they please with him. He rarely challenges destiny, or does so only obliquely. He prefers to give in to circumstances without openly taking the initiative. With insatiable curiosity and the cunning patience of someone who knows how to wait for an opportunity and immediately seize it, Giacomo welcomes love's fortunes and calls them good fortune. He is an available man.

His happiest love affairs are those beyond his control—with Donna Lucrezia, who fears neither adultery nor incest; Henriette, his most mysterious and perhaps for this reason his greatest love; M.M., the nun from Murano, who initiates him into libertinage. These women run the show and set the rules: the time, the place, the situation, the beginning and end of the affair. The initiative is theirs. He submits to it, consents to it, rejoices over it. Beneath his conquering airs, Casanova has a

taste, even a need, for passivity. This may be a kind of stratagem, a tactic he uses with himself. Something happens, almost
without his realizing it. Something occurs without the interference of conscious will, as though he were letting chance, or the
other person's desire, relieve him of his own desire and let him
enjoy the sweet pleasures of irresponsibility. He refuses to know
why or how, and is delighted at the sleight of hand that offers
him voluptuous pleasure. He awaits the reward that will surely
turn up along the way:

*. . . when we find ourselves in those very free tête-à-têtes afforded by
travel, in a state of sweet idleness, which forces the mind and body to
do everything, to replace doing nothing. One wearies of talking, insisting,
reasoning, and even laughing; we let ourselves go, and we act, because
we do not want to know what we are doing. We think about it afterward, and we are very pleased that it all happened.*

SHIELDED FROM HATRED

Surrendering to the amorous pleasure of a woman protects Casanova from hatred. Never to harm a mistress, never to arouse
her anger or disappointment, never to make her suffer from their
affair in any way—this is what he consistently aspires to. Giacomo would never forgive himself for tormenting a woman with
the slightest hint of tragedy. Though on several occasions he
sincerely plans to marry a lover, he can never bring himself to
give up his freedom. He knows he would make a bad husband.
He dodges the law or only pretends to submit to it, he laughs
at authority and religion, but he respects his women friends and

he is careful not to be at fault where they are concerned. If he knowingly commits wrongs, he hastens to redress them. Death and misfortune, which had shadowed him in childhood, must be kept away at all costs. They elicit only disgust and loathing.

Casanova never forgives himself for being at fault or tactless with a lover. One of the saddest days of his life was the day he discovered that Lucia, the daughter of the Count of Montereale's concierge, had become a fallen woman, a madam in Amsterdam's most sordid cabaret. Twenty years earlier, when he was still a virgin himself, he had aroused, though respected, the naïve young maiden's desires. Without revealing his identity, he now gives money to the woman he once loved, and he leaves, devastated. That night, dire dreams assail him. There is nothing he dreads more than seeing a woman become his enemy.

The very sound of the two or three instruments that formed the orchestra plunged the soul in sadness. A room reeking with the bad tobacco being smoked, the stench of garlic coming from the belches of the men dancing, or sitting with a bottle or mug of beer to their right and a hideous tart to their left, offered to my eyes and thoughts a distressing image that showed me the miseries of life, and the degree of degradation to which brutality can make pleasure descend.

Several years later, he feels responsible for another misfortune, La Corticelli's:

I stood there transfixed, beside myself and under the mortifying necessity of recognizing that I was one of the causes of the dreadful abyss in which I saw that the unhappy woman had fallen. Pity prescribed I do something for her first.

Aside from these two downfalls for which he feels guilty, Giacomo believes he made the women he knew happy. A former mistress whom he meets again by chance several years later says to him, *My dear and tender friend, I owe you my good fortune and peace of mind.* One of his conquests exclaims, *You were born to make people happy.* When Henriette, the French noblewoman, calls him "the most honorable man I have known in this world," there is no sweeter music to his ears.

Giacomo showers his lovers with discreet care, kind attentions, elegant gifts, joyful surprises, and in his memoirs he respectfully gives the best-known among them anonymity. Generous, indeed prodigal, he gives without counting; he gives more than he owns. He likes to cause surprise, wonder, and happiness—organize a costumed ball, or a sumptuous and refined banquet; bring a theater troupe by boat, braving bad winds and corsairs; dress a lover from head to foot in the finest lace and softest, most exquisite fabrics, or have her portrait painted in miniature and concealed inside a valuable jewel with a secret pivot. He wants to dazzle. He will do anything to fulfill a woman's expectations, certain of making her pleased with him if he can make her pleased with herself. This is perhaps the most reliable way he has found of obtaining a lady's favors.

Casanova needs to be certain of his partner's consent. An obedient manner distresses him. He complains to the young Rosalie, whom he lifts from poverty: *Your submissiveness proves to me that you do not love me. Why do you not anticipate my wishes?* Several days later, when the young girl manifests only joy, instead of gratitude, she finally makes him happy.

He likes nothing better than a woman who shows signs of independence. But if she is dependent on him, he sees to it that she becomes the mistress of her fate: with money, employment, a protector, or even a dowry and a husband. Casanova likes the role of Pygmalion. Nothing amuses him more than making the rounds of stores and shopkeepers in order to refurbish a woman's wardrobe as a surprise for her. *I did not make a mistake in a single measurement*, he later notes with pride. Dressing a lover offers a delightful sight. It heralds the moment when he will undress her, but, especially, it arouses the enchantress's vanity and self-esteem. With eyes shining, deepened dimples, laughing mouth, she is ready for Venus' refined pleasures. Does Giacomo remember his mother's sudden interest in his hair and wig color? Isn't giving a person a beautified image of himself the most reliable way of making him fond of you? Casanova leads his lover before a mirror, encourages her to look at herself, and laughs on seeing her laugh. They are each enclosed in the rapture perceived in the pupil of the delighted partner's eye. *I adored them adoring me*, he admits.

He would like to see his female companions enjoy the same freedom he grants himself. Though only women carry the burden of maternity and have monthly "lunations," they are equal to men in intelligence and judgment. There is not a trace of misogyny in Casanova. In the great book of life, women are his masters. The feminine so fascinates him that he would like to merge with it.

The games of love offer a taste of the difference between the sexes, but at the moment of supreme pleasure, distinctions are obliterated. Casanova sees himself as having the same sex as his partner or her as having his; he no longer knows to what gender he belongs. A feeling of undifferentiation comes over him, proof of having regained a childlike omnipotence. Such is the price of rapture.

Giacomo cannot conceive of what he calls a love skirmish unless pleasure is completely shared. His partner must be his match, full of ardor and as valiant in combat as he, a beautiful warrior thirsting for exploits several times renewed. Allowing his lover the time to reach orgasm, he is careful not to come to the end of his own "career" too quickly.

I have been dominated all my life by the fear that my steed would be recalcitrant about starting a new race, and this economizing never seemed painful to me, for the visible pleasure I was giving always made up four-fifths of mine.

And so that love will remain a light sensual pleasure, the Venetian lover cautiously minimizes the risk of a *fatal plumpness.* With no hesitation he slips on a *little garment of very fine, transparent skin, eight inches long, closed at one end, but resembling a purse and having at its open end a narrow pink ribbon.*

Does his tireless "steed" measure eight inches, or is he using the common measurement of ancient erotic texts?

SEX AND CONVERSATION

The qualities that intrigue him in a woman are charm, a lively mind, a subtle way of expressing herself, gaiety and social grace, personality far more than beauty, facial features more than bodily perfection. He dislikes cosmetics but responds to the veils of modesty. For Casanova, a beauty who lacks intelligence offers only a physical pleasure derived from her bodily form, while an ugly witty woman captivates through the charms of her mind and delights the man she seduces.

Still, he is responsive to feminine beauty and contemplates some of his mistresses with an art lover's eye. The canons of classical beauty recur in his writings. He readily compares his women friends, whose beauty he is probably overstating, to figures painted by Raphael or sculpted by Praxiteles. But without words the pleasure of love is lessened by "at least two-thirds," notes the well-traveled lover, who dislikes making sacrifices to Venus in silence. He woos in Italian, and especially in French, the language used throughout Europe. He chooses not to approach the most famous English courtesan because he does not know the language of Shakespeare. He has bad memories of the young girls who speak "coarse Swiss" and became attached to Zaïre, a young Russian woman, only after having taught her the rudiments of Italian.

With Leonilda, he debates a La Fontaine epigram that exists only in the first edition of his *Contes*. With Clementina, he reads Fontenelle's *Conversations on the Plurality of Worlds*. He discusses transcendental philosophy with Helena. Henriette has more interesting things to say on happiness than Cicero in his *Tusculanae disputationes*. La Dubois, who "liked Locke," amuses him until midnight with philosophical questions. For him, there must be complete harmony between the mind and the senses. If there is no exchange of words, the prettiest face ceases to attract him. Sex and language go hand in hand. The joys of the bedroom are insipid unless accompanied by culinary and conversational delights. He loves abundance: wine, gold, talk, seed—giving of himself unstintingly, he expects no less from his women companions.

THE PROMISE OF IMMORTALITY

Casanova seeks a joyful love that is free of drama, sorrow, conflict, and antagonism—happy love. Lies or betrayal are excluded, also violence, liquor, or physical coercion. Only reciprocal desire, voluptuousness, lightness, happiness of the moment, and, after love, friendship. He wants to be sure that no conflict will arise. No drama must darken the lovers' good relationship even after they separate.

Casanova never breaks up with a woman. Separation is always by mutual consent, usually because of the circumstances of life, not the deliberate will of the protagonists. No rancor, no remorse, no revenge, no heartache. At most a bit of sadness, a few tears and sighs. There is laughter, too, and even joy, because what comes between the lovers is fate, not the will to break up, and there is no reason why they cannot believe that, if chance sees to it, they will meet again. Numerous reunions do take place in the course of his love life, furthered by his incessant travels throughout the courts and theaters of Europe.

He writes about La Valville, a French actress he meets in St. Petersburg, with whom he travels across Russia in a comfortable "sleeping carriage," first to Riga and then to Königsberg, where they part:

We separated very gaily, and none of the sad thoughts common to all separations such as ours came to trouble our good humor. We had been lovers only because we had attached no importance to love; but we felt the most sincere friendship for each other.

This is the way he tries to convince himself that sorrows cannot affect him and that no parting is definitive. He strives to protect himself from abandonment or bereavement. Yet sometimes pain prevails over lightness; he is gripped by a sense of emptiness; he loses the taste for life in the absence of the beloved. He takes to his bed, doesn't eat or drink, tries to lose himself in sleep. But life regains the upper hand—he can't help it. He acknowledges he has a "fortunate soul," not because it forgets, but because it substitutes a new feeling of wonder for an old one.

Forgetting is not a virtue but a weakness. Casanova takes notes all his life, keeps copies of his letters, saves those he receives, and writes down conversations and witticisms he wants to remember. Each encounter becomes a unique story, a small theatrical play. Some are brief; others include many episodes. After a twenty-, thirty-, or forty-year interval, the memory has not faded. Each face still has its outline; each voice its inflection; each skin its particular white glow; the gaze and the hair have lost none of their nuances; personalities and temperaments especially are rendered with all their unique features. He is an observant painter; his portraits are warm, precise, often deep and detailed; they capture the very breath of life.

Casanova does not draw up a catalogue of his beauties. He does not love all women, he loves one woman at a time, each for her uniqueness. He does not count or enumerate them on a cold list of conquests, or a sinister hunter's log. He remembers them with emotion. Their charms seem to be affecting him again. From a distance, through the passage of time, and sometimes beyond death, the memories of the women he loved remain intact within him. We sense the artist ready to surrender to his model. What would the old man not give to see one of them escape alive from his pages and join him in his sad exile!

After having desired and loved them, Casanova puts his lovers tenderly to rest on the page. It is his way of being faithful to them forever. The inconstant lover gives his lovers immortality.

THREATENING FIGURES

Inaccessible women frighten and fascinate Casanova. If they admit they are in love, why do they reject the incarnation of their passion? Angela in Venice, the Marchesa G. in Rome, or Signora F. in Corfu, and later, the culminating example, La Charpillon in London, make him suffer. Whatever the reason—excess virtue, spiteful coquettishness, or "unnatural impulse"—Giacomo fears the gentle sex when it takes on the menacing, incomprehensible shape of rejection. Yet he is unable to turn away. Something compels him to draw nearer, hoping against hope for a favorable outcome. A haughty woman who raises his hopes dazzles him. He will do anything to change the cold and distant mask into a tender, loving face.

Giacomo is seventeen when he is introduced to a renowned Venetian courtesan "as a young friar who was beginning to make a name for himself." Giulietta looks him over, with her aristocratic air, as if he were up for sale, which greatly irritates him. Later, she asks him to organize a ball at his house. He does not know what to make of this but accepts. After supper, while the guests are dancing the minuet, the beauty invites him to the bedroom.

I want you to dress me up as a friar, in one of your robes, she says to him, *and I will dress you up as a woman in my dress. We shall go downstairs disguised in this way and dance the quadrilles. Come, quickly, my dear friend, let's start by doing our hair.*

Giacomo sees her lock the door and thinks she has amorous intentions. He puts his stockings and shoes on her, adjusts the trousers and arranges the jabot, but Giulietta finds his hands too inquisitive. She then gives him her chemise and skirt to slip into and suddenly becomes angry when she notices "the too visible effect of her charms." The adolescent wants to give her a kiss, she refuses, and he becomes impatient. *Despite her, the stains from my incontinence appear on the chemise.* She insults him; he explains that she is to blame; she disagrees. They go downstairs to dance and are a great success, but the affair ends with the young friar receiving a violent slap on the cheek. He declares Giulietta her own worst enemy but does not fully learn his lesson.

In the spring of 1745, in Corfu, now a soldier in the service of his country, Giacomo meets a Venetian noblewoman five years older than he, Andriana Foscarini, whom he finds "well above all the women" he had seen until then. Though his position of adjutant gives him the honor of dining at her table, this wife of the galleys' commanding officer pretends to ignore him, which hurts him. Theater entrepreneur, sophisticated expert on Europe's princely genealogies, matchless storyteller, even chambermaid when the occasion arises, he is ready to perform any feat that will get her to notice him. Gradually, she lets him approach her.

His adoration for Signora F. is such that he even swallows dragées that contain a few of her hairs ground into powder! Alas, his adored one persists in believing that abstinence makes love immortal. She refuses to give him access to what she calls the "fatal vault." However, since he is unable to imagine what pleasures the soul would enjoy divorced from the senses, he puts all his eloquence into convincing her to welcome him into the "house of delights," the "sanctuary," the "true paradise." After several weeks of assiduous courtship, and unexpected intimacies alternating with hypocritical aloofness, the young man thinks he will finally be rewarded. He is overcome with happiness, but Signora F. keeps him for only an instant; she pushes him away from her and quickly withdraws, throwing herself into an armchair and exclaiming, eyes ablaze with love, *My dear friend, we were on the verge of ruin.*

Giacomo feels he is dying. He looks at her, trembling, "trying to understand the origin of this unnatural impulse." He runs away in the night, devastated by the cruelty of the experience. Yet she had put her cards on the table from the beginning and had announced after a first kiss that they would go no further: *Always like this, my dear friend, never any further. Love is a child that must be appeased with badinage, real nourishment can only make it die.*

In spite of this warning, Giacomo fell into the trap. He has become her marionette. *Being very young and needing to laugh, she had set her heart on entertaining herself with me as she would with a puppet.*

The low point in Casanova's amorous career comes in London in 1764. When La Charpillon—a prostitute whom he could have bought for a few cents but by whom he wanted to be loved—deliberately chose to hate him and make a fool of him, to the point of his losing his dignity, he wanted to die. Suicide seemed to him the only solution. La Charpillon had warned him; she wanted to laugh at him and punish him by making him fall madly in love with her, "with no solution."

—*It is the plan of a monster, and it is unfortunate for men that you do not look like one. I will profit from your frankness, and stay on my guard.*

—*In vain. Unless you cease seeing me.*

Casanova cannot resist seeing her again. The faithless woman spares him no rebuff, no humiliation, no calumny. He tries to satisfy her every whim, to no avail. A slow descent into hell begins. He ends up filling his pockets with a hundred pounds of lead and heading for the Tower of London to throw himself in the Thames. A young English nobleman diverts him from his fatal plan and persuades him to go out with him. This is when he finds La Charpillon dancing the minuet, though several hours earlier she had said she was dying because of him. Shaking, in convulsions, he breaks out in a cold sweat. This is the limit. The desire to die changes into a desire for revenge. A parrot provides the means. The rejected lover—mocked, humiliated, and financially ruined, in vain—trains the bird and places it in the midst of passersby, in front of the Exchange; he is thrilled to hear it repeat incessantly: *Miss Charpillon is more of a whore than her mother* . . .

This took place in London, the city where Zanetta Casanova had made her theatrical debut after abandoning her newborn infant in Venice.

"THE DUPE OF WOMEN"

Casanova-the-writer presents Casanova-the-hero as madly in love with the eternal feminine. He chooses to talk about himself as a man who seeks the eternal feminine as an absolute. The way is paved in Padua by Bettina, the sister of his schoolmaster, his first passionate love, chaste and unhappy. She is fourteen, he is twelve. She teases him with caresses that are "of no importance" to her but that he finds very arousing, though out of timidity and tactful consideration he does not dare reciprocate. She prefers to spend her nights with one of his schoolmates, Candiani, who has already reached puberty. Giacomo, seething with anger, feels betrayed, humiliated, abandoned, reduced to an object of contempt. His newly acquired virile honor is at stake. Afterward he refuses to accept an invitation to the ball that involves dressing up as a girl. But it is too late, for Bettina is seized with dreadful convulsions; she raves in Greek and Latin . . . Soon she is deep in scenes of exorcism that remind Giacomo of his own recovery at the hands of the Murano witch. He no longer resents her but rather feels close to her, as to a sister. Between two violent attacks of possession, she puts forth utterly shameless arguments to justify her betrayal. The more he is aware of being deceived, the more he lets himself be moved. When it becomes clear that her fever is from smallpox, Giacomo moves his table and notebooks to her bedside and watches over her.

It was in this dreadful state that she inspired in me all the tenderness which I showed her after her recovery.

Starting with this first impossible love, and with this young girl and her strong, disquieting appeal—all in trompe l'oeil, traps and tricks, which finally turn against her and consume her— Giacomo takes the only course he considers possible: he lets himself be deceived, identifies with the deception, establishes himself as the woman's indestructible ally, sides with her, makes her schemes his own, and merges with her desire. This original experience (perhaps it reminds him of his mother's amorous behavior) induces in him an infinite, forever unsatisfied curiosity about women. It brings him near to a part of himself that can identify with the feminine and therefore understand women so intimately that he almost always succeeds in being loved by them. It is as though, after feeling abandoned and betrayed by Bettina—a young mother figure as well as a beloved—he had let himself be won over rather than suffer, and sided with her. Casanova understands, as a very young boy, that one must never seek to take possession of a woman, since she will invariably escape, but must accept loving her by surrendering to her with the utmost sincerity. He has no desire to debauch a woman, lead her astray, or abandon her. The very idea repels him, for it would give rise to the intolerable thought of the abandoned woman's hatred.

The professional seducer, who has this as a project, he writes sternly, *is an abominable man, essentially the enemy of the person on whom he has designs. He is a true criminal who, if he has the qualities required to seduce, makes himself unworthy of them by abusing them to make a woman unhappy.*

Giacomo cannot help being sincerely infatuated by each woman he desires. Malice is never involved. Love intrigues him; for him, love is neither philandering nor vanity. It is a kind of madness, an incurable disease,

bitterness compared to which nothing is sweeter, sweetness compared to which nothing is more bitter. Divine monster which can only be defined by paradoxes.

If he seduces, it is because he is seduced. The first dupe is always himself, incorrigibly in love, open to any stratagem to preserve the illusion of infinite love, like the endless reflections cast by the beveled edges of Venetian mirrors.

In 1794, when revising the third chapter of the *History of My Life*, Casanova describes Bettina, old, sick, and dying at her brother, Doctor Gozzi's, house; he had taken her in after her unhappy marriage to a shoemaker called Pigozzo. His first love dies before his eyes twenty-four hours after his arrival there, in June 1777. He remained attached—in his own way faithful—to her to the day of her death. Nostalgic, the old man in Dux writes the following words:

Yet, despite such good schooling before attaining adolescence, I continued to be the dupe of women until the age of sixty. Twelve years ago, if my guardian genie had not come to my rescue, I would have married a young scatterbrain with whom I had fallen in love in Vienna. Today I believe I am safe from such madness; but alas! it grieves me.

THE SAGE OF DUX

Casanova refuses to end his life as an elderly seducer. He wants to avoid being ludicrous in old age. The decrepit figure of Senator Malipiero, in vain foisting his desires on the young Teresa Imer, protects him from such a decline. Giacomo prefers reliving the joyous excesses of his youth through the magic of his pen and his memory. What an implacable revenge on the impotence of old age! How appropriate a response to the passage of time! He who had been threatened with death since earliest childhood, and had shaped his life into a magnificent afterlife, he the man of the moment, madly in love with living, has now become wise. Presently his mind is on the past, reflecting over Fortune's surprising designs; he writes so he can rejoice and laugh again, delighted that in his imagination he is addressing his chosen public—the very best company. He writes in order to make his life an insolent demonstration of the reality of pure pleasure and, even more insolently, of the enduring existence of happiness in remembrance:

I loved, I was loved, I was in good health, I had a great deal of money, and I spent it, I was happy, and I would tell myself I was, laughing at the foolish moralists who say there is no real happiness on earth. It is the words on earth *that make me laugh, as if it could be sought somewhere else.*

To the end, he never deviates from his conception of life. He declines meeting his last female admirers, such as Elise von der Recke, in order not to present them with what he fears is a pitiful sight. But in their correspondence he exchanges ideas with Elise on Plutarch's poetry and Seneca's philosophy. A year before his death, he confides:

. . . if I need to die in order to find out if I am immortal, this is knowledge I am in no rush to attain. A truth obtained at the cost of life is too expensive; but if I should still have feeling after my death, I would never agree to say I am dead.

The next world is not his world. A whole existence is needed to quench all forms of curiosity and discover all sources of happiness. His materialism and sensualism lead him to believe that the only immortality is through literature. There is no other afterlife as far as he is concerned. This one is never guaranteed but it is worth pursuing. The exiled old man never puts down his pen. Yet he is still captivating, attracting attention by what was once his greatest talent—conversation. He describes, recounts, and bewitches with words. His beautiful voice, to his great regret now raucous with age, retains all its seductive inflections.

During a brief stay in Dux, Lorenzo Da Ponte's young wife is struck by the liveliness, volubility, and manners of this old man, whom she finds extraordinary. Henriette de Schuckmann, who met him briefly ten years earlier, writes to him in 1796 to ask him to "enlighten" her so that she may fight against the superstitions and stupidity that surround her: *I wish you to be my guide, do not say I am unwelcome when I am begging you to be my Apollo.*

And the young Cecilie von Roggendorf, his last epistolary friend, calls him in turn father, friend, lover, and dreams of meeting him, if only once, *to assure you of the esteem I feel for you, and so I can have the pleasure of dancing a small minuet with you . . .*

Casanova will never dance this last minuet, but he had the satisfaction of knowing that he was immensely desired to the very end of his life. Perhaps the supreme stratagem of this friend of women is that at the twilight of his life he knew not to give himself to women and, instead, pays them the brightest, most tender homage with his prolific pen. He knew to forsake their presence in order to make them live again in his memory, and love them again with the power of youth.

THE GOD EROS

After the first episode with Bettina in Padua, the scene switches to Venice, where Giacomo, as an adolescent, is initiated into the games of love. He discovers the sufferings that can be inflicted by coquettes, inaccessible women, and virgins whom he does not dare deflower or who want him as a husband. He tries to avert his fear of seeing the desired woman become hysterical or possessed by the devil, like the sad, frightening sight shown him by Bettina. He is prepared to fill the job of exorcist or to offer himself as a medication, but still fears using his erotic power openly. He has his first blissful taste of sensual enjoyment shared with two sisters. Under cover of darkness, Giacomo becomes Marton's "wife" and Nanetta's "husband"; in so doing, he is identifying with absent Angela, his beloved who will not give herself to him but who usually sleeps with the two girls. A confusion of sexes, roles, and identities supports their reciprocal initiation. He owes his taking the plunge to this odd arithmetic of desire. It is the first quartet in his amorous oeuvre.

Constrained by his sense of his mother's omnipotence and unable to free himself for lack of solid enough fatherly support, Giacomo has only two alternatives: to make a travesty of his virility, blur the differences between the sexes, and erase the contours of identity or, on the contrary, to show his virility vigorously, defy the wrath of heaven, and pass himself off as a sorcerer or omnipotent magician. In his first experiences in love, he tests both approaches. Masked or unmasked, in both situations, he tries to be, for each woman, the little god Eros in person. Or at least this is how Casanova, when writing his life history at the end of his life, presents his protagonist, the young and dashing Chevalier de Seingalt.

UNDER A STORMY SKY

A two-wheeled barouche crosses the countryside of the Veneto. Aboard is a young friar and a pretty farmer's wife. The friar, at seventeen, is impious; the farmer's wife, a nineteen- or twenty-year-old newlywed, can barely hide her jealousy about a husband who likes to banter publicly with her young sister, and she pretends to play at being *la disinvolta;* the friar encourages her to appear to be in love with him. She laughs freely in company but not in private; she resists, objecting that any caresses with a man of the Church would be a mortal sin and she fears for her soul.

A coldness comes between them; hence everyone suspects that the inevitable has occurred.

After a visit with Luisa Bergalli, a famous poet and wife of Gasparo Gozzi, and returning with all of the Count of Monte-reale's guests, the young friar Casanova insists that the young wife share his barouche. He instructs the postilion to take the shortest route, through the Cecchini forest, and break away from all the other carriages. The sky is of a disarming blue, but in less than half an hour a brief and terrible storm breaks out, the kind that seems determined to disrupt the earth and the elements.

—*Oh! My God!* says the farmer's wife. *We are going to ride out a storm.*

—*Yes*, the friar answers, *and although the barouche is covered, the rain will ruin your clothes, I'm sorry to say.*

—*I don't care about my clothes but I am afraid of the thunder.*

—*Stop up your ears.*

—*And the lightning?*

—*Postilion, take us somewhere where we can find shelter!* the friar orders.

—*The nearest houses*, comes the answer, *are half an hour from here, and in half an hour the storm will be over.*

The driver drives calmly on; soon lightning flashes repeatedly and thunder rumbles; the downpour begins. The young priest takes off his coat to cover his female companion and himself. After a big flash, the lightning strikes a hundred paces ahead of them. The horses rear. The farmer's wife is seized by convulsions. She throws herself on him and clasps him in her arms. He bends down to pick up the coat, which has fallen near their feet, and as he picks it up he raises the bottom of her dress with it. The young woman tries to pull her skirt back down but lightning strikes again and in her fear she is unable to move. Her companion wants to readjust the coat, but just then she falls most opportunely on top of him and, without hesitating, he quickly puts her astride him. The position couldn't be more fortunate. Losing no time, the young Casanova adapts to it as he pretends to tuck his watch into his trouser belt. She calls him impious; he tells her to pretend to have fainted to avoid having the postilion turn around and realize what is happening, and having her lose her honor. He clasps her "by the buttocks" and persuades himself that he procured "the most complete victory that ever a skillful gladiator won."

—*How dare you defy the lightning with such wickedness?* asks the good Christian wife.

—*The lightning approves of me*, he answers.

The young woman seems to calm down slightly and, after seeing and feeling his ecstasy, asks him if he has finished. He laughs and demands to have her consent before the storm is over.

—*Consent, or I will let the coat fall off!*

—*You are a dreadful man who will have made me miserable for the rest of my days. Are you happy now?*

—*No.*

—*What do you want?*

—*A shower of kisses.*

—*How unhappy I am! Well, there you are!*

—*Say you forgive me. Admit that I gave you pleasure.*

—*Yes. You can see, I forgive you.* Now, the pretty farmer's wife smiles brightly.

—*Say you love me.* Casanova is again insistent.

—*No, because you are an atheist, and hell awaits you.*

The clear weather has returned. The adolescent banters about the adventure, kisses her hands, and guarantees that he has cured her of her fear of thunder, but she should never reveal the secret of the cure to anyone. She answers that no woman has ever been cured by such a remedy before.

—*On the contrary. It must have happened a million times in a thousand years.*

—*I can believe it, but in the future I will travel with no one but my husband.*

—*You will be making an error, for your husband will not have the sense to console you as I did.*

—*True again. With you, one does acquire strange bits of knowledge.*

As soon as they arrive in Pasiano, the young woman runs off and locks herself in her room; Casanova hands the postilion a scudo; the man is laughing.

—*What are you laughing about?*

—*You know quite well!*

Thereby does the lightning's challenge end in laughter. Derision must prevail over tragedy. The adolescent Casanova confronts the storm to cure not just the young farmer's wife's fear but also his own. Fear of the lord and master of lightning, fear of woman: with his sexual organ erect like a magic wand, Casanova defies heaven and earth, the inviolability of the marriage laws, and the omnipotence of women. As a child, he was cured by magic; as an adolescent, he wishes to cure by the most magical of human practices: sexual pleasure.

Consent to the pleasure I am giving you before the end of the storm!

Casanova needs the woman's consent; he must be in harmony with her and she with him, for fear of being struck by lightning. Thunderous turmoil and sexual turmoil; the raging amorous passion breaks out like a storm upsetting the calm prospect of a beautiful Italian day. During his second sexual experience, the atheist friar no longer sacrifices to love in a confused night spent groping between two pretty sisters. He asserts his triumphant virility in full daylight, with the grandiose power of the entire sky raging above him. Behind the back of a complicit barouche driver, Casanova proclaims before thunder and lightning that he knows the secret of women: what women want is men. The universal remedy is called love as physician or love as magician. The only god worthy of respect is called pleasure.

Yet this triumphant staging of sexuality prevailing over terror does not protect the young friar from a heartrending loss. Upon his return to Venice, the adolescent finds his kindly grandmother ill. He sits by her bedside until death parts them. She leaves him nothing, for while she was alive she gave him everything she owned: unconditional love, a magical love capable of stemming the flow of blood and giving back life.

LOVE AS MAGICIAN, OR, THE PHALLIC CHALLENGE

During the summer of 1749, Giacomo, at twenty-four, meets "one of the strangest eccentrics," who invites him to visit his collection of curiosities. He shows him a rusted old knife which he claims was used by Saint Peter to cut off Malchus's ear; he tells him about a treasure that can be dug up with this knife. With his usual ability for slipping into the role expected of him, Casanova professes to be a magician. But he must find the sheath of the knife in order to succeed in the operation, for, he declares, the sheath without the knife, or the knife without the sheath, is useless. *Mitte gladium tuum in vaginam* (Put your sword into your sheath). No sooner said than done. Using the sole of an old boot, Giacomo creates a sheath that he rubs with sand to give it an antique look. He compounds this mischief by composing a very learned letter, signs a contract with the owner of the knife, then sets off with the owner's son to see the peasant who is the lord of the treasure they seek. There, with the help of Genoveffa, a young virgin of the house, he prepares all the objects and clothes needed for the job. He knows that his conjurations will have no effect and that no gnome will bring the expected treasure up from the earth. He nonetheless plays this part of magician, a part he "madly" adores. On the designated night, he rids himself of all secular garb and slips on the big surplice sewn by Genoveffa's pure hands, lets his long flowing hair hang loose, places the seven-pointed crown on his head, takes the Great Circle on which frightening characters and figures are painted in black, holds the famous relic in one hand and the olive-wood scepter in the other, walks three times around the circle, which he has spread out, then jumps into it.

A large, black cloud darkens the horizon, thunder rumbles, lightning flashes repeatedly in quick succession, a violent wind rises, followed by a torrential downpour. Giacomo feels panic grip him. Far from being a magician, he is now simply a *complete coward*, paralyzed with fear.

My philosophical system which I thought was equal to anything had vanished. I recognized a vengeful God who had waited for me there to punish me for all my misdeeds and put an end to my unbelief with death. What convinced me of the futility of repentance was that I found I had become unable to move.

The storm abates rapidly and the moon reappears more beautiful than ever in the serene sky. The fake magician picks up the circle and returns to his room, where he finds Genoveffa looking so pretty that she frightens him. Shivering in spite of the heat, he goes to sleep in a pitiful state. The following day, he wakes up "sick of this comedy." Everything has become muddled. He made light of acting the magician and magic made light of him. He did not believe in his antics and was caught in the trap of his own staging. Genoveffa's virginity seems sacred to him, and he feels guilty for having wanted to desecrate it. Is he still a man at least?

She no longer seemed of a different sex from me, since I no longer felt that mine was different from hers. A powerful superstitious notion compelled me to believe at that moment that this girl's state of innocence was protected and that I would be struck dead if I dared desecrate it.

No doubt, he has never been closer to seeing the precariousness of his dream of absolute power or felt such intense anguish before a thing that surpasses him and that he is unwilling to recognize: a superior force, a law, setting a limit on his desires. After the raging sky, Giacomo is afraid of finding the Inquisition's spies hot on his heels. He puts an end to the masquerade, encourages Genoveffa to get married, and gives her fine gold bracelets to make up for his deception. Other challenges and other adventures await him. He does not give up.

Most men abandon their childhood illusions along the road. Not so the child of Venice; as he matures, Casanova maintains his grand dreams almost intact. He gives nothing up. Great terror during the storm, a prison interlude, venereal disease, a huge gambling loss that leaves him without resources, are ways of erasing the traces of guilt. While he readily scorns authorities, rules, and boundaries, pokes fun at representatives of the law, denounces the hypocrisy of the powerful, and proclaims he is his own man, Casanova also regularly inflicts sanctions on himself, as well as disappointments and reversals of fortune or health. This is his own way of paying with his person—he is not afraid of being afraid—after which he bounces back with renewed vigor and the disarming confidence of a small child who was once loved unconditionally by his grandmother.

After his experience with Senator Bragadin, Giacomo's involvement with the occult sciences reaches its height with the Marquise d'Urfé. How can one resist a lady who is beautiful though old, who is rich and "allied with all that was noblest in France," and who thinks you are "the most powerful of all men"?

According to her, not only did I possess the stone, but I could confer with all the elementary spirits. She therefore thought I had the power to disrupt the whole earth and bring about the happiness or misfortune of France, he writes with voluptuous pride.

By now Giacomo Casanova is more than thirty; his escape from the prison in Venice and the protection of the Abbé de Bernis give him an assurance and fortune that he has never had before. Paris is the center of the world and it gives this son of actors the feeling of being on the most beautiful theater stage. The Marquise d'Urfé is a choice partner. For about six years, they will live a kind of folie à deux, an alchemical idyll. She believes in it, he does not, but he is unwilling to disclaim the omnipotence she ascribes to him.

Madame d'Urfé is learned in all the abstract sciences, owns an extraordinary library and a laboratory worthy of the best alchemists. She impresses Casanova. He seems equally well informed in alchemy; he makes an impression on the marquise thanks to his gift for cryptography, when he impulsively attributes the deciphering of a coded manuscript she gives him to read to a genie. *This false confidence is the one which made Mme d'Urfé my slave. On that day I became the arbiter of her soul and I abused my power*, he admits. In her fanciful expectations, the marquise thinks Casanova can "make her soul enter the body of a male child born of the philosophical coupling between an immortal man and a mortal woman, or between a mortal man and a divine female being." He plays along, prolonging the game as much as he can. He does not disabuse her, and they study the arcana of occult knowledge that deals with the mastery of time and generation—a delightful journey which leads him to hope, once again, to escape from the human condition by uniting his fantasies with those of a woman who is above everyone and everything. Gold, silver, precious jewels, letters of recommendation—Madame d'Urfé is a marvelous protectress and Giacomo likes his new princely life.

After several failed attempts, he decides to carry out in person the alchemical coupling with the marquise. On this occasion, he must simulate sexual pleasure, since the lady's aging charms are inadequate, despite the more stimulating presence of a third, extremely pretty partner:

The undine, caressing me in the most arousing way, preserved what was being destroyed by the old body I was obliged to touch . . . I decided to cheat a second time by an agony accompanied by convulsions and ending in motionlessness, the inevitable consequence of an agitation that Séramis [the marquise] found unparalleled, as she told me afterward.

When the marquise asks him if the procedure had come off well, Giacomo answers with some hesitation that "the word of the Sun was in her soul and that, in the beginning of February, she would give birth to herself with her sex changed." She suggests that they marry so he can be the tutor of their son, in other words of herself, for fear that this child be pronounced a bastard.

Her reasoning was very sound, but the heart of the argument being an absurdity, I could only feel pity for her.

"Paralis" or "Paralisée Galtinarde," alias Casanova, begins to weary of this tomfoolery, particularly since one of his accomplices seeks to unmask him in the eyes of Madame d'Urfé. She, far from complaining about the services of her good genie, is now solely preoccupied with her astonishing pregnancy. She is delighted at what her Paris physicians will say about the confinement, which they will find "most extraordinary at her age."

But Giacomo is now beginning to play the role of magician reluctantly. He had probably already lost his taste for occult games three years earlier, when he was with the gentle Esther in Amsterdam and when—with magical squares and cabalistic pyramids, amazing predictions and soothsaying oracles—he had seduced the young girl and her father, a rich Dutch merchant. Esther liked to think she would become as knowledgeable in the cabala as he. She asked him for books so that she could devote herself to studying the occult sciences. She was eager to astonish the ignorant. Giacomo, not wanting to deceive her, responded to her request, but grudgingly. Their speculative entertainments became mingled with more passionate games. Marriage was mentioned. Esther's father would have liked to give his daughter's hand to his Italian guest and include him in his business. Previously, in Constantinople, when he was only nineteen, a wise and honorable man had suggested that he become not only his adoptive son but his son-in-law, and that he would help him make his fortune, but Giacomo had been unable to make up his mind. At thirty-three, he had no greater inclination to give up his freedom. He was repelled by the irreversible. He wanted as always to preserve the possibility of future prospects.

Before leaving Esther, whose intelligence and mind he admired, he insisted on setting her straight concerning the occult power of his cabalistic pyramid. She nevertheless wanted to pursue the study of this "fanciful science," for, as clever as she was, she believed that "without charlatanism no science would ever be able to compel recognition": *Let us love each other, my dear friend, until death. We do not need to get married to do this.*

He returns to the inn, relieved of a "great burden"—the burden of feigning seriousness. Casanova likes women who expect no more from him than he can offer: the fullness of the present.

THE FIRST LOVE QUARTET

The first love scene takes place in Venice, probably in the autumn of 1742, in the San Samuele neighborhood, on the third floor of a bourgeois house. It is night. *There were four of us, we had been talking for three hours, and I was the hero of the play*, recalls the exile in Bohemia with delight.

Giacomo is seventeen, he is still a virgin and in love with Angela, the parish priest Tosello's niece. She is embroidering on a tambour with two sisters, Nanetta and Marton, who are organizing their nocturnal get-together. The young friar is eloquent but the young girl is deaf to badinage. She does not know Ariosto and prefers common sense to poetry. Occasionally, she "blurts out" a proverb, "the way the Romans fired a catapult." The rejected lover suggests playing blindman's buff, but only Nanetta and Marton allow him to catch them. Five hours later he still has obtained nothing. At dawn he discovers tears on Angela's cheeks and regrets having cursed her.

The young man then departs from Venice and spends two

months in Padua, where he receives his doctorate in civil and canon law. Upon his return, he accepts an invitation to try his luck a second night. Supplied with Cyprus wine and smoked tongue, he goes up to the little room. In spite of her promise, Angela does not show up. Only the two sisters come to the rendezvous. *She is making fun of me and triumphing*, Giacomo complains, and then decides to do without the faithless girl.

Nanetta and Marton having brought bread and Parmesan cheese, the threesome improvise a joyful feast and, kissing one another, pledge to be like brother and sisters. The innocent kisses soon arouse a fire that surprises them. Marton then reveals to him that when the three girls sleep together, Angela covers her with kisses and calls her my dear friar, and that then Angela, in turn, serves as a husband for Nanetta. Taking Angela's place in her absence, Giacomo slips into bed between the two sisters. Under cover of a barely feigned sleep, without knowing whom he is touching first, Nanetta or Marton, he has his first taste of sexual pleasure.

Little by little I uncurled her, little by little she spread out, and little by little with sustained and very slow movements, but marvelously natural, she adopted a position which was as propitious as she could offer me without betraying herself. I set to work, but in order to make it perfect I needed her to participate in a way that could not be disavowed, and nature finally compelled her to do so.

Giacomo then turns to the other sister, who also simulates sleep,

until, affecting a completely natural movement, without which I could not have reached my crowning achievement, she helped me to triumph; but at the moment of climax, she did not have the strength to keep up

*her fiction. Taking off the mask, she hugged me very tightly in her arms
and pressed her mouth on mine.*

The three accomplices, delighted with the experience, pledge
eternal friendship. Laughingly, they gaily splash water on themselves, heartily finish the rest of the smoked tongue, and partake
in varied frolics and games until morning. Two days later, the
sisters slip him a parcel containing the imprint of a key, asking
him to have a key made and to use it to come and spend his
nights with them.

His relationship with his "two angels" endures for almost four
years. It is interrupted—but he will meet them again later—
when the young friar has to leave Venice, at the request of his
mother, to join the Bishop of Martorano in Calabria. Before embarking at the little square of San Marco, probably in early October 1743, he notes the following:

*This love, which was my first, taught me nearly nothing about the ways
of the world, for it was a perfectly happy love, never disrupted by the
least discord or tarnished by any form of self-interest.*

Casanova's amorous life, shaped by this first sexual experience, brings together features that he will subsequently often
seek to reproduce: it incorporates lightness, cheerfulness, and
reciprocal pleasure, rules out tragedy and suffering, eagerly welcomes disguises or confusion of identity. The women, two sisters
or two friends, have a strong tacit understanding between them.
They willingly indulge in homosexual play or share the same
lover with great naturalness and no feeling of transgression. This
multiplicity of partners in the course of a single affair and the
diverse configurations it engenders favor the scrambling of identities and of genres, which Giacomo very much needs in order

to escape the threat of castration and loss and to remain on the safe side of a dangerous otherness.

This dream of uncertainty, confusion, and lack of differentiation sometimes takes on surprising guises, constantly renewed in the course of his adventures. Some of these seem too good to be true, as if reality were too responsive to his fantasies—for example, his meeting with a false castrato in 1744 when he is nineteen. Bellino—or "Teresa"—a person of uncertain sex, so fascinates him that he thinks he will go mad. In this case he is not dealing with a woman disguised as a man or a girl who plays the part of a boy in bed; Giacomo is thrown into turmoil when Bellino asserts he is a castrato and refuses his visit.

You are in love with me whether I am a girl or a boy, the hermaphrodite says to him ... *How can you, with your enlightened mind, imagine, or flatter yourself, that if you found I am a man you would cease to love me? ... You would persuade yourself that you could metamorphose me into a woman, or, imagining that you could become a woman yourself, you would want me to treat you as one.*

A short time thereafter, against all expectation, Bellino goes on a trip with his fervent admirer. Stopping in a posthouse, they share the same bed; they are scarcely under the covers when the false castrato, driven by a passionate transport, turns to her companion and reveals herself to be a most amorous woman. Angiola Calori—such is her name—then tells him her strange story. Her beautiful voice attracted the attention of one of the greatest castrati of the day, Felice Salimbeni, twenty years older than she; he gave her a musical education. When she became an orphan, he took her to a music teacher. There, a young castrato whose name was Bellino had just died and Salimbeni suggested the young girl substitute for him, board with Bellino's mother, and join him later in Dresden; there she could come not as a girl but as a castrato and they could live together without shocking anyone. Angiola accepted her benefactor's plan and learned how to fit onto her sexual organ a small device that could change her appearance in case she had to undergo an examination.

Casanova is curious to see "Teresa" put on this strange mask (this is the name the writer gives her in his account in order to protect the identity of a singer who became extremely famous). She fits it on, and he is plunged into ecstasy over this androgynous woman who so meets his innermost fantasies.

It is a kind of long, soft piece of gut, the size of a thumb, white and with a silky surface . . . This contraption was in the center of a very delicate, transparent oval-shaped piece of leather, five or six inches long and two inches wide. By applying this skin with some tragacanth gum in the area where the sexual organ is visible, she makes her femaleness disappear.

Struck by her story, her beauty, her talent, her candor, her feelings, and the extraordinary disguise she wears in reality as well as onstage—false sex and false name—Casanova wants to share her fate, or have her share his: he asks her to marry him. A (conveniently?) lost passport decrees otherwise.

Sixteen years later, the traveler meets her again, now *prima virtuosa* at the Florence opera. She introduces him to her husband, with whom she says she is in love, and to a false "brother," Cesarino, whom she says is the fruit of their former love. Casanova is proud of this son, whose paternity he cannot make legitimate but who resembles him uncannily. He listens to him sing Neapolitan songs and accompany himself on the harpsichord with all the desired vivacity. Teresa, who no longer toys with sexual ambiguity but with a kinship of convenience, allows her gaze to roam from one to the other, kisses her husband, and exclaims that only love brings happiness.

This is how I spent that day, one of the happiest of my entire life, concludes Casanova. For him, happiness is achieved only when identities are blurred, genders scrambled, filiations conceal mysteries, and families have secrets, and when the joy of reunion confirms that love knows a kind of constancy and fidelity that neither time nor separation can eradicate.

Throughout his life, Giacomo Casanova meets women who are his doubles, his accomplices. Like him, they cultivate a taste for erasing the differences that society is founded on. With strength and lightness, they live according to their own rules. They are above the prejudices, proprieties, and superstitions that obscure reason, and they assert themselves, in their daily lives, as free to think, free to act, free to love.

FIVE

Gardens of Love

UNDER THE SIGN OF THE SERPENT

In the spring of 1744, a beautiful twenty-nine-year-old Roman woman leaves Naples for Rome in the company of her husband, a Neapolitan lawyer, and her sister, Angelica. A despondent-looking young friar boards the coach with them. He dries his tears, looking out the window at his friends on the Strada di Toledo receding in the distance. He remains silent until the evening.

In Capua, where the travelers stop for the night, the lawyer declares: *I will therefore have the honor of sleeping with the Signor Friar.*

—*I leave you in charge, signore, of arranging things as you wish.*

Donna Lucrezia, the wife, smiles at this sally. The ice is broken. The journey continues, enlivened by cheerful banter. Various subjects are touched upon, for example whether beards should be considered as excrement or hair.

—*Well*, Giacomo asks, *do I have a beard or not?*

—*I thought so*, the lawyer's wife answers.

—*Then I will start being shaved in Rome*, the young friar answers, surprised.

His elder by ten years, Donna Lucrezia shows an interest in this appealing young man who has not yet entirely relinquished the privileges of adolescence; he shifts from tears to laughter and from gaiety to grief, owns some valuable jewelry and snuff-boxes, proves generous, is an excellent conversationalist, and obviously enjoys badinage. She encourages his nascent attraction, grants him a kiss as a token of affection, and casually plays foot-sie with him in the carriage.

Thanks to the innkeepers' accommodating attitude and the way they routinely make travelers into roommates or even bed-fellows when their only connection is that they happen to be journeying together, Friar Casanova plans to slip into bed with the two sisters, on the side of the beautiful married woman, at the next overnight stop. Alas, the bed he lies in next to the sleeping husband is so noisy that he all but gives up his plan. Then in the middle of the night there is the sound of gunfire and people rushing up and down the stairs, an alarm is sounded, drumbeats roll, there are cries and shouts—confusion has been sown by a skirmish between German and Spanish troops. The lawyer wakes and goes to fetch a light. The young man takes advantage of his absence to steal some favors from his beloved, but when he clasps the object of his desires with too much ardor, the bed gives way and collapses. He retires; meanwhile, the husband returns and bursts out laughing when he finds the two sisters buried at the bottom of a broken bed.

On the following day the travelers reach Rome, where the young women's mother lives, in the Minerva neighborhood. The friar is invited to visit and to consider himself a friend of the family. Hired into the service of Cardinal Acquaviva, Giacomo soon gets to know the world of Roman clergymen; he finds them flexible, ingratiating, and great dissemblers, in control of their facial expressions, having but one tone of voice, gentlemanly and clever politicians. He escapes between lessons in French, which he has been strongly urged to learn, to make innocent visits to Donna Lucrezia's family.

During a walk in the Roman countryside, at the Villa Ludovisi in Frascati, thanks to her mother's discretion in taking the arm of Lucrezia's husband while Angelica strolls off with her fiancé, Lucrezia contrives a fortunate "vis-à-vis" with her young lover. As they embrace on a garden lawn, Giacomo is worried they might be caught.

—*Do not be afraid. Our genies are watching over us*, the intrepid young Roman woman answers. *Look! Did I not tell you that our genies are watching over us?* she adds suddenly. *Ah! How he stares at us! He wants to reassure us. Look at him, the little demon. This is the most mysterious thing in Nature. Admire him. He is certainly your genie, or mine . . . Do you not see that beautiful snake, with his flame-colored slough and his raised head, who seems to worship us?*

Giacomo turns his head and is hardly pleased to see a yard-long snake of variegated color. Lucrezia watches the animal with no trace of fear, and when she sees the snake go away she declares that it was trying to warn them of the arrival of unknown people. They straighten their clothes and start walking along slowly, when they meet the lawyer and Donna Cecilia coming down a nearby path.

The young man asks Lucrezia's mother whether her daughter fears snakes. *In spite of her intelligence, she is afraid of thunder to the point of fainting and runs away shrieking when she sees a snake*, the mother answers.

Giacomo thinks he has witnessed a miracle of love. He is dazzled by so much determination. It is the first time he has loved a married woman who not only responds to his ardor but anticipates, encourages, and orchestrates it. Though Casanova's deep incentives are the magical omnipotence of desire and derision of the established order, he is always eager to maintain the appearance of proper social behavior. He likes to prove the tactfulness of his feelings, the purity of his intentions, the innocence of his actions. His subversion resembles a commedia dell'arte farce: he aims to deceive with the complicity of the very people whom he derides. Whatever happens, Casanova remains a man "of no importance." He likes to make others believe—and entertains the belief himself—that he is a mere instrument in their hands, an irresponsible actor, content with taking his cue from others, which he does with grace and brio because he adores applause.

In Lucrezia he has found his master. She fulfills all his desires on that morning in paradise and even gives him pleasure beyond anything he could imagine. For the time being, he experiences voluptuousness, in broad daylight, amid flowers and fountains, with a delightful woman who makes no demands on him other than pure momentary pleasure. It will take twenty-six years for the three-act play to be completed and reach its final denouement. The question is, does Lucrezia already know how this ardent young man will fulfill her expectations? The Roman beauty pursues the affair with the complicity of her sister, who cannot "forget the collapsed bed," of her husband, "who pays no attention to certain badinages," and of her mother, who "is probably aware of everything but knows it is none of her business." Married for ten years and childless, perhaps Lucrezia is quite innocently seeking to provide her obliging husband with an heir?

After a refined meal, during which the lawyer encourages his wife to accept Casanova's snuffbox in exchange for a ring (could this be his way of showing he consents to another exchange, which must remain secret?), the merry group goes to the magnificent gardens of the Villa Aldobrandini. Lucrezia leads Giacomo into an arbor of greenery, a shelter for their lovemaking. There they feel as innocent as Adam and Eve before the Fall.

And if the Pope comes with the entire Sacred College, let us not move.
His Holiness will give us his benediction, the lovers whisper to each
other.

After several detours, we entered a rather long covered walk which,
midway down, had an arbor with grass-covered seats, each differently
shaped. We saw one that was striking. It had the shape of a bed which,
aside from the usual bolster, had another one, three-quarters the size,
lying parallel to the first but a few feet farther down. We looked at it
and laughed. It was an eloquent bed. We immediately decided to test its
suitability. From this bed, we enjoyed the sight of an immense, empty
lawn, where even a rabbit could not reach us unnoticed. Behind the bed
the walk was blocked, and we could see the two ends of it to the right
and left, at equal distance. Without running, no one who entered the
walk could reach us in less than a quarter of an hour. Here, in the
garden at Dux, I have seen a similar arbor, but the German gardener
didn't think of the bed.

A last country outing brings Donna Lucrezia and Giacomo
together in Tivoli. After visiting all its wonders, the group
spends the night at Francesco's, Angelica's suitor's house. The
two sisters choose a room that gives on the orangery, adjacent
to the room assigned to the young friar. The lawyer sleeps with
his wife's brother, and Donna Cecilia with her youngest daughter. Everyone is pleased with the arrangements. When Lucrezia
has extinguished the night lamp and blown out the candles, Giacomo pushes the door and falls into the welcoming arms of his
beloved, who says to her sister: *It is my angel, hold your tongue and*
go to sleep. The two lovers embrace, then fall asleep until the
first light of dawn. As soon as they wake, they take up their
"combat" anew.

   —Mind your sister, she could turn and see us.

—No, my sister is charming; she loves me . . . Turn, Angelica, kiss your sister who is possessed by Venus and behold what awaits you when love makes you its slave.

Lucrezia, entreating me to kiss her, climbs over to the other side of me, and enjoys seeing her sister languishing in my arms and showing not the slightest sign of resistance . . . Wiping the drops of sweat from my brow, Angelica finally expired for the third time, so tenderly that it sent my soul into rapture.

Just before leaving for Naples with her husband, Donna Lucrezia suggests to Giacomo that he keep her sister as a mistress. He turns the offer down, almost shocked, and answers in all seriousness: *I must beware of troubling domestic harmony.* End of act one. The next act takes place seventeen years later.

THE FACE OF HAPPINESS

In a repeat of the Judgment of Paris, Casanova chooses from among the three Graces Aphrodite, goddess of beauty and love. After sampling an ecclesiastical career and then a military one, he chooses a life of love. Protected since the age of twenty-one by the Venetian nobleman Matteo Bragadin, he behaves like a young man with money, free in his movements and with his purse. The State Inquisitors having got wind of the cabalistic practices that bind the two men, Giacomo prudently leaves Venice at the beginning of 1749. He travels in northern Italy—Padua, Verona, Milan, Mantua, Bologna, and Cesena, where he spends the summer. "With an empty heart," eager to "be face to face with Teresa and Donna Lucrezia," he is preparing to leave his inn and go down to Naples, but the chance occurrences of travel decree otherwise.

Awakened at daybreak by a great uproar in the adjacent room, Giacomo finds that a gang of police has knocked down the door. They want to verify if the occupant, a Hungarian officer who speaks only Latin, is really the husband of the person accompanying him. The *shirri* threaten the officer with prison or a fine of several zecchini. Realizing these foreign travelers are victims of an odious plot, Giacomo takes the matter to heart and raises a great row with the authorities to obtain reparations for them. As a reward, he hopes to discover who the person is hiding in the bed. Is it a man or a woman disguised as a boy? The only thing the Hungarian officer says is that his companion is French. Giacomo invites them to lunch and sees a tousled head emerge from under the blanket, laughing, fresh-faced, and attractive. A little later, he finds the lady very elegantly dressed in a "whimsical" military uniform. Her beauty immediately "makes a slave of him." He offers to accompany the couple to Parma.

The Frenchwoman intrigues Casanova. Why is she with a sixty-year-old officer who does not speak her language, who is neither her father nor her husband, and with whom she does not seem to be in love? Her behavior is that of an adventuress; she has audacity and courage, but she is too clever and her manners and sentiments are too refined for her not to have received an exquisite education. Who can this girl be, Giacomo wonders, who combines nobility with an appearance of great libertinage? And why does she demand to remain alone and independent, after arriving in Parma, though she has no money or resources?

The young man also wants to know what awaits him in that city. Will he have to ignore the young woman, or can he hope to conquer her heart? Burning with passion, Giacomo, clumsily insistent, demands an unequivocal answer:

—*If you tell me to accompany you to Parma, you must assure me, madame, that you will make me happy in the possession of your heart; no less. I wish to be your only lover, on condition, however, if you wish, that you will make me worthy of your favors only when I shall have succeeded in deserving them through my care and attentions, and through all the things I will do for you with a submission unequaled by anything you have ever seen.*

—*Let me laugh, I pray, for I have never in my life imagined an irate declaration of love. Do you understand what it is to say to a woman in a declaration of love, which should be all tenderness: Madame, one or the other, choose this instant?*

—*The word "choose" cannot seem harsh to you: on the contrary, it honors you, making you the arbiter of your fate and mine.*

The young Frenchwoman does not remain impervious for long to the intensity of desire that she arouses in the young man. No doubt she can already sense all the qualities that are part of his irresistible charm—his ardor, generosity, and taste for surprises, his availability, his desire to be loved, and his fear of being made a fool—but also what makes his company delightful for a limited time: his impulsiveness, his changing moods, his immoderate spending. Henriette finds out everything about her lover very soon; she has no illusions concerning his social station, his financial resources, his fickleness. But it gratifies her to be allied with him for several months, for the duration of a pleasurable love story. She does not make him wait long for her answer: *Yes, come to Parma.*

Once in his father's native city, Giacomo chooses to use his mother's maiden name, Farussi, for fear of being recognized by the many spies roaming the town, Parma having just come under the government of the Infante Philip of Spain and his wife,

Louise-Elisabeth, Louis XIV's oldest daughter. The French-woman, who requests that Giacomo call her Henriette, signs the registry *Anne d'Arci* and refrains from revealing her real identity.

All the elements of Giacomo's amorous scenario are here intermixed: a woman disguised as a man, a borrowed name, an aristocratic education, intellect and beauty, a strong personality with a clear taste for independence, the promise of a violent but transitory passion. The Venetian announces he is free, but Henriette cannot say as much; she knows her Provençal family is trying to track her down. She does not reveal the reasons for her "running away" to Italy. She is the one in charge; it is she who sets the rules in this game of love. The affair's location, duration, beginning, and end are all up to her. Because from the onset their union is at the mercy of a sudden, unpredictable conclusion, independent of their wills, it has the taste of happiness.

The two lovers never part for a minute. Henriette learns Italian, Giacomo rents a box at the Opera and takes her there every night. They are in love when they go to bed and even more in love when they get up.

People who believe that a woman is not enough to make a man equally happy all the twenty-four hours of a day have never known a Henriette.

At a private concert, a symphony and several duos are performed, followed by a cello concerto; Henriette stands up and with a modest, serene air offers to play the cello herself. She invites the orchestra to play the concerto again, places the instrument between her knees, and begins to play. Her lover, astonished, initially thinks it is only a joke, but when he sees her make the first stroke of the bow, he suffers such violent heart palpitations that he thinks he will die of emotion. The audience's applause is deafening. Casanova disappears to go and weep in the garden, where he cannot be seen.

Who is this Henriette? What is this treasure whose master I have become? It seemed to me impossible that I could be the lucky mortal who possessed her.

Fata viam inveniunt: Fate knows how to guide us. Virgil's maxim, for which Giacomo has a special fondness, just happens to be one of the mottoes of the Albertas family, likely the family of the mysterious Henriette. It is particularly well suited to their romance, the fruit of an awkward chance encounter. Several weeks of happiness are still granted them before the beginning of the last act.

During a walk in the gardens of the Dukes of Parma's summer residence, a member of an illustrious Provençal family recognizes the young woman. Her relatives get in touch with her by mail. Giacomo knows nothing about what is being transacted but can guess that their liaison is drawing to an end. He reproaches himself bitterly. Why did they stay so long in Parma? How blind of him! Henriette, wisely, says, *Let us simply prepare ourselves to be superior to any event that may occur.*

To drive away feelings of sadness, they spend two weeks in Milan, with no thoughts other than for themselves. Giacomo gives his beloved two winter dresses and a lynx pelisse. On returning to Parma, they learn that their separation is now inevitable. Giacomo accompanies Henriette to Geneva, a five-day journey by sedan chair and mountain sleigh. They stay in the hotel A la Balance. The Frenchwoman leaves at daybreak the following day with a lady's companion by her side, a footman seated next to the coachman, and another ahead on horseback.

Casanova watches the departure of this woman whom he will hold particularly dear in his heart forever. She mingled nobility and daring, passion and wisdom, peace and happiness. She knew how to take the best Giacomo had to offer and never demanded anything he was unable to give. She neither burdened his life nor coerced him in any way. She conducted their affair as though they were living a pure fiction, almost a work of art, outside space and time. Giacomo follows the carriage with his gaze, then stares dreamily in its direction long after it has disappeared from his sight. On the following day, he receives a letter from his beloved with just one word: *Adieu*. He spends one of the saddest days of his life. On the window of the room, he sees words Henriette had inscribed with the point of a small diamond he had given her: *You will forget Henriette, too*. What did she mean? That the wound would heal?

As he considers this episode of his life, the wise man of Dux confides his thoughts to paper:

No, I have not forgotten her, and it is balm to my soul each time I remember her. When I think that what makes me happy in today's old age is the presence of my memory, I decide that my long life must have been more happy than unhappy, and after thanking God, cause of all causes and sovereign orchestrator—we know not how—of all chance happenings, I congratulate myself.

Two days after Henriette's departure, Giacomo sets off for Italy. Even though it is the bad season, he crosses the Saint Bernard Pass by mule in three days. He is overcome with grief; nothing seems arduous to him. He feels neither hunger nor thirst nor the cold which freezes that part of the Alps. He is in the grip of a despair "which also has a kind of sweetness." He deliberately chooses to stop in an inferior inn. In Parma, the Pro-

vençal gentleman hands him a long and noble letter from
Henriette:

*It is I, my only friend, who had to desert you. Do not add to your grief
by thinking of mine. Let us imagine that we have had a pleasant dream,
and not complain about our fate, for never did such a pleasant dream
last so long. Let us boast that we knew how to make each other perfectly
happy for three consecutive months; there are few mortals who can claim
as much. So let us never forget each other and recall our love often so
that we might renew it in our souls, which, though separated, will take
pleasure in it with even greater intensity. Do not inquire about me, and
if chance should make you succeed in knowing who I am, act as though
you did not know it. You should know, my dear friend, that I have so
well arranged my affairs that for the rest of my life I will be as happy
as I can without you. I do not know who you are; but I know that
no one in the world knows you better than I do. I will have no more
lovers in all my life to come; but I hope that you do not intend to do
the same. I want you to love again, and even to find another Henriette.
Adieu.*

After reading this, the disconsolate lover goes to bed without
eating. He is prostrate, languishing, for two days. He does not
want to die but has no great desire to live. Sadness prevents
him from thinking. A neighbor, a chance acquaintance, is worried about him and makes him drink some broth to break his
fast. After several days, persuaded to go to the theater, he
meets a very flirtatious actress who leaves him with a nasty case
of the pox in exchange for several coins. *I considered I was justly
punished for having so shabbily debased myself after having belonged
to a Henriette,* he notes, distressed at having to resort once again
to the "great cure." It is not the first time that the Venetian
catches Venus' ailment when he has a broken heart. He himself

noticed that he spent a large part of his life trying to make himself sick and then trying to recover his health. A six-month mercury treatment puts him back on his feet, but in the meantime he falls victim to another disease. Under his neighbor's influence, Giacomo now becomes devout, so great is his despair at having lost his divine Henriette. Certainly he never knew such great happiness with a woman, or suffered a similar loss.

THE LIBERTINE NUN

What inclination, fancy, or whim led Marina Maria Morosini, a nun in the convent of Santa Maria degli Angeli in Murano, to write to a stranger and request a lovers' meeting with him? The nun, who conceals her identity, leaves it up to the man to choose the site of their first rendezvous: the visiting room of her convent; a *casino*—a small, usually extremely luxurious, house or apartment intended for pleasure; or should they meet for supper in Venice? She begs him to deliver his answer on the following day to the same woman who gave him her letter, an hour before noon in the Church of San Canziano, next to the Rialto bridge, first altar on the right.

The letter is white and sealed with aventurine-colored Spanish wax imprinted with a slipknot. A woman messenger lets it drop at Giacomo Casanova's feet; he picks it up, unseals it, and discovers the following words:

A nun who has seen you in her church on every feast day for the past two and a half months would like you to become acquainted with her.

Consider, she adds in conclusion, *that if I had not supposed you to be kind and honest, I would never have taken such a step, which might have led you to judge my character negatively.*

Giacomo is surprised by the tone of the invitation. The request seems that of a madwoman and yet he finds a dignity in it which makes her respectable. She seems too well versed in romantic intrigue for him to believe she is a novice or inexperienced. Above all, he finds he is very surprised by the great liberty of these "saintly virgins who could so easily breach their enclosure." With curiosity prevailing over the fear of being caught, he accepts this singular adventure. He is probably not displeased that the libertine nun suspects he understands French. Without revealing his own identity, he declares himself "Venetian, and free in the fullest sense of the word."

Does the nun know the name of this handsome stranger who hears Mass in her church without ever looking at the recluses behind the railing? Does she know he is Senator Bragadin's adoptive son and the "fiancé" of another nun, Caterina Capretta, her own protégée? What aroused her interest in this tall twenty-eight-year-old man with a dark complexion?

Marina Maria Morosini, born into one of Venice's great patrician families on September 11, 1731, is twenty-two in the fall of 1753. Beautiful, rich, witty, intelligent, very cultured, and above all a freethinker, how can she have chosen to become a bride of Christ? Yet this does not prevent her—in an arrangement, though scandalous, that is known to be practiced by several Venetian nuns—from having a powerful and wealthy lover, who, thanks to the complicity of several people and plenty of gold, has her periodically scale the convent wall and spend the night in the temporal world. Giacomo suspects a protector of high rank, whose identity intrigues him:

So much boldness at her age surprised me, and I was unable to understand so much freedom. A casino *in Murano! At liberty to go to Venice! I decided that she had to have an acknowledged lover who liked to make her happy. This idea put a check on my sense of triumph.*

The amorous intrigue begins with a misunderstanding; Giacomo, who believed in his good luck, feels humiliated, demeaned, scorned. Time and several letters are needed to dispel the storm.

Who could have guessed that you would react to this with the incredible violence which your letter put before my eyes? asks M.M., surprised and hurt that this man could see her as a shameless monster of the kind that does not exist among women who, like herself, have "birth and education." This is precisely Giacomo's sensitive point. He is of lowly birth, the son of actor parents, the grandson of a shoemaker from the lagoon. He is merely a man "of no importance"; he does not have a noble lineage, even if he knows the genealogies of all the European princes by heart. Burned by several bad experiences in the past, he fears lest this noble nun deceive him and hold him up to ridicule, lest a hideous person lurk behind her angelic traits. It is hard for Casanova to believe what is happening to him. Joy and impatience make him unable to eat or sleep for three days prior to their first rendezvous.

Aside from M.M.'s birth, and her beauty and mind, which constituted her real merit, prejudice played a part in making the greatness of my happiness incomprehensible. She was a vestal virgin. I would be tasting a forbidden fruit. I was going to infringe the rights of an omnipotent husband, taking possession of the most beautiful sultana of his divine seraglio.

As always when the emotion of love holds Casanova in thrall and he idealizes the object of his passion, he fears that an obstacle will arise at the last moment, that a patriarchal law will suddenly be invoked against his desire—desire being synonymous with transgression. At the very moment when she offers herself to him, Casanova feels ill. He throws himself on the sofa and cries out: *I have lost all confidence; you will never be mine; this very night some fatal contretemps will tear you away from my desires, perhaps a miracle performed by your divine husband become jealous of a mortal. I feel I am being crushed. In a quarter of an hour perhaps I shall no longer exist.*

—*Are you mad? I am yours this very moment, if you wish,* the sister answers with wonderful serenity.

Who will the beautiful sultana clasp in her arms? What does she find desirable in this man six years her elder? His elegance, his above-average height, his reputation? But is she aware of it? It can be assumed that she was serious and wise enough to gather information before throwing herself into a compromising adventure, or that her acknowledged lover—a foreign ambassador—had made discreet inquiries. The memoirist, on the other hand, stresses their reciprocal anonymity but, being a good stylist, knows that this enigma reinforces the mystery of the intrigue.

Their first tête-à-tête takes place in a Murano *casino* that belongs to M.M.'s protector. The choice, exquisite supper is served on Sèvres porcelain. To keep them hot, the dishes are placed on silver boxes filled with boiling water. They drink only Burgundy and champagne. Giacomo admires his hostess's knowledge, skill, and grace. Such social and amorous ease intrigues him. Among her watch charms, he notices a small rock-crystal flask exactly like one he has on his watch chain. They both contain a rare rose essence whose creator is the King of

France. Giacomo guesses the nationality of the acknowledged lover. He recognizes in the divine M.M.'s refinements the art of living, loving, and thinking of French libertinage that he had discovered during his Paris stay between the summer of 1750 and the fall of 1752.

For their first night of love, Casanova rents, in the San Marco area, the most luxurious *casino* there is, the one that had belonged to the English ambassador. It consists of five rooms furnished in exquisite taste: mirrors, chandeliers, a magnificent pier glass, wainscoting embossed with gold or painted with flowers and arabesques, a boudoir with a bathtub and "English-style premises" (water closets), an alcove with two secret exits, small Chinese porcelain tiles representing erotic motifs—the setting is lacking in nothing. The day before, to make sure that everything will be perfect, he instructs his cook to prepare an eight-course supper for two; he comes to taste it and comment on it in the presence of the chef. Game, sturgeon, truffles, and oysters, served on Meissen porcelain, are declared excellent. Casanova's one complaint is that the chef forgot to set out hard-boiled eggs, anchovies, and vinegar mixtures for the salad. He also requests bitter oranges and rum for the punch, and for dessert, all the fresh fruit he can find as well as ice cream. He asks that the *casino* be very well lit.

On the following day, after nightfall, he sees a man in a mask step out of a gondola; he becomes alarmed, but the person comes up to him and calmly holds out his hand; it is his "angel" dressed as a man. She laughs at his surprise, clings to his arm, and, without speaking, they cross the Piazza San Marco to go to the *casino*. M.M. appears delighted to see herself infinitely multiplied and from a hundred different angles in the candle-lit mirrors. It is a new sight that makes her "in love with herself." While she gazes at herself, Giacomo admires her elegance, her rich finery and jewelry, and he praises her protector. She tells him that he had insisted on bringing her to Venice himself and had wished her a good time, convinced that the one she would be making happy deserved it.

It is unbelievable, my dear friend. A lover of this quality is unique, and I can never deserve the happiness that already dazzles me.

In this intrigue, is M.M. innocent or consenting? In extending an amorous invitation to Giacomo, is she aware of her French lover's desires? The nun is the one to have made the first move. It is a desire, an order. Perhaps a trap as well. Does she know how the play continues? Is she herself a performer in a plan that eludes her, or does the story progressively take shape as the protagonists act? Is Casanova the nun's plaything, while she is manipulated by her protector? At the next rendezvous, in the Murano *casino*, the acknowledged lover, hidden in a secret closet, takes pleasure in watching the nun and the ex-friar's amorous frolics.

Shortly thereafter, Giacomo learns by letter that M.M. has initiated C.C. into Sappho's mysteries and the great metaphysics. Then, one night, Caterina Capretta comes to the *casino* instead of M.M. Giacomo is astounded. This is hardly the way he expected to resume his relationship with his gentle fiancée from the Zuecca garden, whose father had placed her in a convent until she reached marrying age. They spend the night in conversation. He believes M.M. has betrayed him. There is an exchange of letters and a reconciliation. The nun tells him that her acknowledged lover is the French ambassador to Venice and that he would like Giacomo to invite them both to supper in his *casino*. He receives them like "a commoner to whom a king and his mistress would have done the greatest of honors."

The Venetian foresees that he will be the dupe and also that they will *have a taste* of C.C., his dear friend. He has no control over the plot developments of the play in which he is performing. On the appointed night, he goes to the *casino;* the Frenchman has asked to be excused. Giacomo spends the night between his two sweethearts.

All three of us—intoxicated by voluptuousness and its frustratoires, *and transported by continual fits of rapture—wreaked havoc on everything visible and palpable given to us by Nature, openly devouring everything we saw, and finding that we had all three become of the same sex in all the trios we performed.*

Confusion of the sexes—but to which same sex do the three belong?—reaches its height in this libertine quadrille. Yet Giacomo is bitter. He knows that the next time he will have to yield his two lovers graciously to the ambassador. The party is drawing to a conclusion. He can play, as he once did with Marton and Nanetta, the roles of wife with one and husband with the other, and vice versa, but he is not prepared to do this with the ambassador, and perhaps the ambassador is not willing either.

The two nuns spend a voluptuous night with the ambassador. M.M. gives Giacomo a detailed account of it as soon as the two are alone together again. Casanova finds no pleasure in this, for he is not feeling as free-spirited and casual as his libertine friend. He notices that she is still as beautiful, gay, playful, and amorous; she is still the same. But for him nothing is the same anymore. Casanova does not have a taste for orgies when he is in love.

The curtain falls. In M.M., the Venetian has met his mentor in voluptuousness. She made him discover all the refinements of literature, food, the bedroom, luxury, transgression, and philosophy. She taught him that the greatest happiness is to live and die peacefully. He will remember this in his old age.

LOVE LETTERS TO THE ADORED VENETIAN

Maria-Magdalena Balletti was born on April 4, 1740, into a family of actors. Casanova makes the most flattering portrait of her mother, Silvia, Marivaux's favorite interpreter. Maria-Magdalena, called Manon, is ten during Giacomo's first stay in Paris, in 1750, and seventeen during his second. Her parents welcome him, a friend of her brother's, like a member of the family, and he comes to the house at the rue du Petit-Lion-Saint-Sauveur, near the Comédie-Italienne, almost every day. The young woman soon breaks her engagement to a musician, and then has eyes only for Casanova, who is fifteen years her senior.

Silvia's daughter loved me, and she knew I loved her, even though I never plainly told her; but she was very careful not to let me know it. She was afraid of encouraging me to demand favors, and not knowing if she would be strong enough to turn me down, she feared she would lose me afterward.

For three years, Manon lives through a touching, chaste passion for this brilliant, amusing, extremely fickle man and is ready to forgive him all if he will marry her. But Giacomo still feels unable to give up his freedom for the love of one woman.

The friendship and esteem which bound me to her family kept any idea of seduction away from me; but feeling more in love with her every day, and with no thought of asking her to become my wife, I could not conceive what my aim was.

At night the young girl writes letters in her room, behind her parents' back. They are tender, lively, impatient, full of doubt, naïve love, and romantic hope—like this one of April 1757:

I shall reply scrupulously to your last letter. You begin by greatly exaggerating your love, which I believe is sincere; it flatters me and I have no other desire than to see it last forever. Will it last? I know that you will rise up against my doubt; but after all, my dear friend, does ceasing to love me depend on you? Or loving me forever? . . .

May this tender friendship we feel for each other be happy! It can be the cause of our happiness or our misfortune; what a difficult alternative! It is cosi *awkward to love! But good night, my dear friend, I am ready to drop with sleep . . . I dream that I tell you that I love you!*

And this one on a Monday at midnight (around mid-May 1757):

. . . I derive infinite pleasure from conversing with you in whatever manner, and it will always be so . . . I would do almost anything for you, I feel it: what about you, my dear friend, would you do anything for me? Yes, I believe you would, you love me, and I want you to be assured that I love you as well, and I will change only when I can be certain of your infidelity (which will never happen, I hope), and even then, I believe I could never stop loving you. Goodbye, good night, my dear, my very dear friend . . .

Then Sunday evening at midnight (late August 1757?):

I am aware more than ever of the tender friendship I feel for you, my dear Casanova; the present occasion persuades me of it more than ever. Your being away causes a distress that I am unable to describe for you; the despondency I feel does not give me the strength to do so . . .

And September 1 (1757):

. . . You will also tell me, oh my dear Casanova, if you still love me, if you think of me as often as I think of you. Ah! I think this is hardly possible, for you never leave my memory for a moment; I desire you always . . . How time seems to drag! How insipid and gloomy the evenings seem to me! How different from the ones I spent with you, oh my dear Casanova! They always seemed to me too short, and the evenings now seem to me eternal. When will you return? . . .

Coming back from Dunkirk, where he was sent on a secret mission, Casanova brings magnificent presents for the Balletti family.

I was fêted as though I had been a child of the house, and in turn I convinced the whole family that I wanted to be considered as such. It seemed to me that I owed all my good fortune to the family's influence and constant friendship. I made the mother, the father, the daughter, and the two sons agree to accept the presents I had got for them. I had the richest one in my pocket and I presented it to the mother, who immediately gave it to her daughter. These were earrings that had cost me six thousand florins . . . I gave Mario, who liked to smoke, a gold pipe, and my friend a beautiful snuffbox . . . But was I wealthy enough to give such costly presents? No, and I knew it. I gave them only because I was afraid of never becoming rich enough. If I had been sure, I would have postponed it.

Casanova wants to make a fortune. He participates in the creation of the first lottery with the powerful support of the Abbé (soon Cardinal) de Bernis, the accomplice of his Venetian nights with the lovely Murano nun. He meets the Marquise d'Urfé and Madame du Rumain. On September 16, 1758, Silvia dies. Giacomo goes to Holland for several months.

For Manon, time crawls. Sunday evening (October 1758):

... I was delighted to find you so tender, saddened to know you were absent, overjoyed by the hopes you give me, and disheartened about their uncertainty ... I have no news regarding my allowance; as for the convent, I am quite certain that I will be there before you return, and this distresses me ...

October 14, 1758:

... In saying I know what power I have over you, *you are greatly mistaken, for I have never thought I had any ... But, by heaven (if it is true that you love me), you would feel very sorry if I sulked ...*

Back in Paris, Casanova establishes a workshop for manufacturing printed silk and hires twenty young girls to do the work.

But Manon Balletti shuddered when she saw me as head of this seraglio. She was dreadfully sulky with me, even though she knew that in the evening they all went home to eat and sleep.

Manon distresses him with her jealousies and her "just reproaches." She cannot understand his postponing marrying her if he truly loves her. He has rented a little "folly" called Cracovie-en-Bel-Air, in the district known as Little Poland, behind the Madeleine barrier. Two gardens, three master apartments, a twenty-horse stable, baths, a good wine cellar, and a large, well-equipped kitchen—the Venetian has never had such royal lodgings. But soon troubles proliferate and he prefers to leave Paris to make his fortune once more in Holland. He invites Manon to come and stay in his house; she does briefly and then leaves, hurt by the malicious rumors that are spread about her.

To Mr. Casanova, in the Douleerstrat at Rondeel in Amsterdam [October 23, 1759]:

My dear friend, I feel an anger, indignation, and a grief that cannot be described (but not against you, have no fear). I come from Paris where I was pained to hear that a rumor is circulating that I am here with you and that you are hiding. Is this not shameful, horrible, the most dreadful calumny? What monster is so wicked as to have invented such a falsehood? Listen, my dear friend, I am dying of grief, I am assailed on all sides, I can't hold out anymore; I must give in, with heart broken, with the honor that people want to rob me of! . . . Oh! my dear Casanova, avenge me, avenge yourself on these unworthy accusers by arranging to marry me in spite of their jealous malice. And console me; for I will die if you do not give me some hope.

It is already December 16, 1759. Things are taking a long time!

But my dear Casanova, haven't I made it clear enough to you that my feelings are unvarying? Why would you think me changed so suddenly? Why do me the injustice of thinking that calumny is capable of cooling the infinite tenderness I have for you? Oh! my dear Giacometto, you were wrong to allow yourself to be pained for so little cause . . .

But my dear Casanova, my dear Giacomo, lover, husband, friend—whatever you wish—please believe for once and for all that I love you with all my soul, that you are my only treasure, that I wish to live only for you! . . . that I await with an impatience equaled only by my love the moment when I will be united with you! that the beginning of my life will be dated from the moment when I have the happiness of pledging you my troth! that I will miss this life only because it separates me from that which I love more than life! . . . You are my first true passion.

On February 7, 1760, Manon sends Giacomo one of her last letters:

My dear husband . . .

You remember that I love you, do you not? Well, never forget it, dear friend. Goodbye, I kiss you with all my heart and think ceaselessly of you, even when studying my parts. 3 baci per Giacomo.

The letter of separation following this one has never been found. On July 29, 1760, Manon Balletti marries François-Jacques Blondel, architect to the King and member of the Academy of Architecture, thirty-five years older than she. They will have two children. In 1761, Casanova declines a dinner invitation at the painter Vanloo's so as not to find himself in their presence. He will preserve the letters of this tender, chaste, impetuous "fiancée" all his life. Forty of them were found in the castle in Dux. She offered him her heart, which he dared not take.

Good night, good night, I shall go to sleep filled with thoughts of you, caressing you, calling you by the most tender names, and to encourage my tenderness, I shall imagine that you hear my endearments and like them. Goodbye, my only friend, I kiss you with all my heart.

AN UNEXPECTED TURN OF EVENTS IN A
CHINESE ROOM

Happy to be back in Naples after an eighteen-year absence, Giacomo Casanova goes to visit the Duke of Matalona, as he had
promised when they had seen each other in Paris. The Duke
takes him to the Opera, where a gala performance is staged in
honor of the King's birthday, January 12, 1761. He introduces
him to all his friends, including his acknowledged mistress,
Leonilda, who fills Casanova with the most intense admiration.
She is beautiful, full of grace and wit, and speaks not just with
her lips but with her hands, her elbows, her shoulders, and often
with her chin, which surprises and delights him. Two days later,
the Duke invites his mistress, "whom he loves as a father loves
his daughter," and his Venetian friend to lunch in a room decorated with erotic Chinese motifs. The three play "a delightful
little game intended to tease a nascent love, laughter and play
being the real nectar that makes it immortal." Casanova tells the
Duke that he will no longer see his mistress unless he relin-
quishes her to him, declaring he is prepared to marry her and
provide her with a dowry of five thousand ducats.

The love she had inspired in me was of the kind that could bear neither
rivals nor delay nor the least suggestion of later inconstancy.

The marriage contract is prepared; the young girl's mother,
who lives in the country, a day's journey from Naples, is summoned. Casanova, very much in love, comes to Leonilda's at
suppertime. He sees the Duke standing between the mother and
the daughter, facing away from him. They turn around, and the
mother lets out a cry and sinks onto the sofa.
—*Donna Lucrezia!*

—Let us catch our breath, my dear friend. Sit down here. You are going to marry my daughter.

I sit down, I understand everything; my hair stands on end, and I lapse into the gloomiest silence . . .

—Leonilda is your daughter, I am certain of it; I have never considered that she might not be; even my husband knew it; it did not anger him; he adored her. I will show you her certificate of baptism, and after seeing her date of birth, you will make the calculation yourself. My husband never touched me in Rome, and my daughter was not born prematurely . . . This marriage, my dear friend, is loathsome to me. Yet, as you can imagine, I will not oppose it, for I would not dare give the reason. What do you think? Will you still have the courage to marry her? You hesitate. Might you already have consummated the union?

—No, my dear friend.

Lucrezia has lost nothing of her calm determination or her former disposition. She still greets love without prejudice, shame, or false modesty. And if incest is a crime in the eyes of society, she accepts the restriction only because of convention, giving herself the right to set her own limits on it. After she has bid her daughter recognize Giacomo as her father, she sees no transgression in welcoming them both into her bed.

She was content to be the one in the middle, and content that it was only upon her that I put out the fire which she saw was consuming me.

Leonilda proves to be extremely curious about the scene performed by her parents: *So this is what you did, eighteen years ago, when you conceived me?* asks the ingenue libertine.

But the moment which brings Lucrezia to the death of love is precisely the moment when, out of consideration for her, I think it my duty to withdraw. Leonilda, all sympathy, with one hand helps the passage of her mother's little soul and, with the other, places a white handkerchief under her father, who spurts into it.

In the morning, the "innocent" Leonilda describes their nocturnal labors to the Duke of Matalona. He does not seem disconcerted by such a trio; on the contrary, incest, the eternal subject of Greek tragedy, tends to make him laugh. After paying his respects to all the Naples nobility, Giacomo takes leave of his daughter, promising to return when he learns that she is married. He keeps his word.

End of act two.

A CHANCE MISHAP

Casanova is several miles beyond the intersection of the Chemin du Bouc and the road between Aix and Marseilles when the shaft of his carriage breaks and he has to call upon the occupants of the closest house in order to get a cartwright. He is greeted by three ladies and two aristocratic gentlemen, who offer their hospitality to him and to his female companion, the young Marcolina, whom he introduces as his niece. Because the Provençal wind is blowing violently that day, the ladies wear their hoods drawn far forward and the traveler cannot distinguish their faces. One of the ladies sprains her ankle; she goes to lie down and receives her guests in her room.

She was lying in a large bed in an alcove made even darker by crimson taffeta curtains. She was without a hood; but it was impossible to see her well enough to know if she was ugly or pretty, young or getting on in age.

After supper, Marcolina goes to sit at the edge of the Countess's bed, *without fuss*, notes Casanova, who is hurt at being excluded from the increasingly tender scene taking place between the new friends. Their laughter, hugs, and kisses make him realize he should withdraw. He wishes his hostess good night and tells her he is not responsible for the sex of the person whom she is admitting into her bed. She answers that she only stands "to gain." The next morning, the carriage is repaired, the travelers take their leave; the Countess still does not show herself to Giacomo, who feels aggrieved and upbraids Marcolina:

—*You are a strange person. You cuckolded me with a woman and let me sleep alone. Perfidious wench, you prefer a woman to me.*

—*It was a passing fancy. But bear in mind I owed her this compliance, for she was first to declare she was in love with me.*

They set out on the road again in the direction of Avignon, where they arrive at the end of the day. They stop at the Hôtel de Saint-Omer, where Marcolina carries out the Countess's assignment and hands her companion a letter from her.

My heart was pounding, Casanova recalls. *I unseal it, and I see the address in Italian:* "To the most honorable man I have known in this world." *I unfold the sheet and at the bottom I see:* Henriette. *That was all. She had left the sheet blank. The sight paralyzed me, body and soul.* "Io non morii, e non rimasi vivo" [I did not die, and I did not remain alive; Ariosto]. *Henriette! It was her laconic style . . . Henriette, whom I had loved so intensely and whom I felt I still loved with the same ardor. You saw me, and you did not want me to see you? Perhaps you thought your charms might have lost the power with which they secured my soul sixteen years ago, and you did not want me to see that in you I had loved only a mortal. Oh, cruel Henriette, unjust Henriette! You saw me, and you did not want to know if I still love you. I did not see you, and I could not find out from your lovely lips if you are happy. It is the only question I would have asked you. I would not have asked you if you still love me, for I know I am unworthy of it, since I was able to love other women after having loved in you Nature's most perfect creation. Adorable and generous Henriette! . . . Let me imagine that you are happy. My dear, my noble, my divine Henriette!*

SUCH LASTING FIDELITY

Since he wants to spend the carnival of 1769 in Aix-en-Provence, Casanova stops at the Auberge de Saint-Jacques, a few steps away from the Cours Mirabeau. The next day, he goes immediately to visit the Marquis d'Argens in his country property, at the Eguilles castle. There he is introduced to all the nobility of Provence. A play is performed in the little theater, a good meal is served, the guests stroll outside regardless of the season's chilly weather. Some time later, returning to Aix in an open sedan chair without an overcoat, he is exposed to a very strong north wind and arrives chilled to the bone. He goes to bed with a pain on his right side; several hours later he is clearly afflicted with pleurisy. He coughs violently and spits blood. His condition worsens, and six or seven days later, he is thought to be dying. On the tenth day, the elderly physician caring for him vouches he will recover. A week later, he is out of danger. During the whole of this acute illness and the ensuing convalescence, a woman whom he does not know waits on him day and night. No one can tell him who she is or who had sent her to nurse him.

After his recovery, as he takes leave of the Marquis d'Argens, they discuss literature. The Marquis urges him never to write his memoirs. Casanova assures him that he will not commit such a folly. On the road to Marseilles, he stops at the door of the castle where he thinks he might see his noble Provençal friend again. She is not there, but to his great astonishment, he finds the servant who had cared for him so devotedly. So the guardian angel who had looked after him discreetly, without wanting to disclose her identity, was Henriette! Marveling at this fidelity of more than twenty years, Casanova chooses not to annoy his friend by returning to see her in her house in Aix. He sends her a letter and goes to wait for the answer in Marseilles, poste restante. He soon receives an extremely long missive in which she enjoins him not to return to Aix immediately:

But if you return at a later date we shall be able to see each other, though not as old acquaintances. I feel happy when I think that I might have helped prolong your life by placing with you a woman of whose kindness and fidelity I was certain . . . If you want to have an epistolary relationship with me, I will do my very best to write regularly. I am very curious to know what you did after your escape from the prison in Venice. I promise, now that you have given me such strong proof of your discretion, that I will tell you the whole story behind our meeting in Cesena, and of my return to my country . . . Adieu.

On reading these lines, Casanova recognizes his former lover's wisdom. The force of her ardor, it seems to him, has diminished, as has his own. In seeing her again, he is afraid of letting people glimpse things that should remain secret. And then what would he do in Aix-en-Provence? He could only become a burden to her, a thought which repels him. Besides, former lovers pursue their liaison by writing letters; they share their lives by recounting them to each other. In this way they preserve the perfection of the happiness they once enjoyed.

Faithful and discreet to the end, the old man in Dux resolves to add Henriette's letters to his memoirs if his noble friend dies before him. He knows she is old and happy, and he certainly would not want to offend the woman who was and is his greatest love.

PARADISE ON EARTH

In Salerno, in August 1770, Casanova, now forty-five, meets Donna Lucrezia for the third time. When he asks for news of their daughter, he learns that she is waiting for him with her husband, the Marchese della C., a respectable old man who wants to meet him. The two men, delighted, discover that they are both Freemasons and converse at length. At the end of the afternoon, the Marchese asks Lucrezia to take their guest to the garden:

There were all the greatest delights one could desire: flowers that perfumed the air, fountains, rooms whose walls were covered with shells and which were furnished with down settees, softer than anything in the world. A large pool more than ten fathoms deep contained twenty different types of fish in all colors that quivered as they swam and that—being intended only for the pleasure of contemplation, and not fearing the rapacity of the greedy who might have liked to catch and eat them—came intrepidly to frolic almost in the hands of those who reached below the surface of their element. In this pretty paradise the covered walks had ceilings of vines, with bunches of grapes as wide as the leaves between them; fruit trees right and left formed the colonnade supporting them.

While they are walking in this enchanting spot, Lucrezia informs him of her daughter's happiness and describes the merits of the Marchese, who, aside from gout, enjoyed perfect health, and whose only misfortune is not having an heir.

—*But is our daughter really happy?* Casanova asks.

—*Very happy, even though she cannot find in her husband, whom she adores, the lover she would need at her age.*

—*This man seems to me incapable of jealousy.*

—*Indeed he is not jealous, and I am certain that if she had found among the nobility of this city a man who was attractive to her, the Marchese would have showered him with friendship and, deep down, would not have been displeased to see her conceive.*

—*Is it the case that if she gives him a child he would be absolutely certain that he could not possibly be its father?*

—*Not absolutely,* Lucrezia answers, *for when he is feeling well he comes to sleep with her, and from what my daughter has told me, he could flatter himself that he had done what in fact he had not done.*

Casanova understands the barely disguised hints. He admires Lucrezia's elegance and independence of mind, and he is prepared to live up to her expectations. Nothing pleases him more than to take on the other person's desire and gratify it. As they converse about one thing and another, the young Marchesa appears, followed by a page holding the hem of her dress.

We went and sat in a grotto where, when we were alone, we indulged in the pleasure of calling each other by the tender names of daughter and father, which justified certain liberties that, though imperfect, were nevertheless delinquent.

Donna Lucrezia advises them to be good and wanders off to the other end of the garden. Her exhortation, followed by her departure, produces the opposite effect.

Determined not to consummate the alleged crime, we came so close to it that an almost involuntary movement forced us to consummate it so completely that we could not have done more if we had acted as a result of a free and rational premeditated plan.

In the evening, the four dine in high spirits, with a clergyman who does not understand French, which sparks a merry and uninhibited conversation. As they wish each other good night, the Marchese promises his young wife a visit, thanking his Venetian guest for having made him feel ten years younger. Casanova slips away wishing them "a handsome son in nine months."

Over the next two weeks, Casanova continues to pay homage to Leonilda, at night in her room and during the day in a garden arbor. He leaves this noble family after an exchange of words expressing the most delicate feelings. Six months later, while he is living in Rome, he receives news of the Marchesa's pregnancy; she asks him to send his congratulations to the Marchese.

When he relates this episode of his life—probably in 1792—Casanova's comment on his incest contrasts sharply with his account of it: *Whether because of nature or education, this news made me shudder.* Where are the lightness and joyful complicity that he described before? Here he seems to want to erase the transgression, delete the "double crime," so that the social need for a universally condemned act becomes apparent. Yet once again, as throughout the history of his life, the writer demonstrates that his hero is exempt from the common laws of mankind. He not only flouts the taboo on sexual relations between father and daughter, feeling no obligation to respect it, but instead of being punished for it, is congratulated.

As Casanova was leaving, the wise old Marchese, in the presence of his wife and mother-in-law, gave him five thousand ducats (the sum Casanova had offered Leonilda as a dowry when he wanted to marry her, which he left her as a gift when Lucrezia revealed their filiation). This sum was a way of thanking him. But thanking him for what? Clearly for allowing a descendant to inherit the nobility of the Marchese's name. Since neither God (in whom superior minds do not believe), age, nor health confer fertility, why not accept—indeed, encourage—the intervention of a brother in enlightenment?

Casanova, though he might shudder, seems to take pleasure in transgressing the laws, a pleasure that is magnified because he is doing so with authority's approval.

He performs a last sidestep two decades later: when he is in Prague for the coronation of Emperor Leopold on September 6, 1791, he arranges to be introduced, at Prince Rosenberg's, to the twenty-year-old Marchese della C. Father—and grandfather—of the young man, he enjoys his conversation and praises a wisdom which few men attain at sixty. But what enchants him particularly is "the boy's resemblance to the late Marchese, his mother's husband" and the joy this resemblance must have caused him. Appearances have been saved. Life can continue unperturbed. The anonymous parent is even invited to the young Marchese's wedding!

Casanova never wished to give his name to a child. He can be only a play-father in a social farce, a father for whom the very idea is a joke; he knows he is fertile, but accepts no responsibilities and none of the consequences; he is a father of no importance.

I laughed to myself that I found sons of mine all over Europe.

The father of sons and daughters who do not bear his name, Casanova believes that he himself is the son of a father who did not give him his. Since childhood, Giacomo has fabricated a story that makes him the son of the beautiful Zanetta and her noble lover Michele Grimani—the Venetian patrician who was his family's protector after the death of Gaetano Casanova. Was not Abbot Alvise Grimani, Michele's brother, designated as his tutor in order to divert suspicions? Is the effervescent Casanova the son of the commedia dell'arte or the illegitimate son of one of the patricians? Is his father a dancer and actor from Parma or Michele Grimani, member of one of Venice's noblest families?

Is there a secret surrounding his birth? Is this why he always enjoys scrambling genealogies and showing that the distance between legitimate and illegitimate is often only a matter of words? As for incest—imagined, suggested, or actualized, depending on the many different occasions when it occurs in his narrative— does it not represent the most absolute and provocative way of expressing the uncertainty of filiation, supreme generational confusion, the disorderliness of social roles?

Combining mother and daughter in the same love annuls the irreversibility of aging. Incest is one of the last cards Casanova plays in his race against time. And it is probably not coincidental that the prohibited act takes place in an extremely beautiful enclosure.

The garden is an image of paradise. There, impunity and wrongdoing, the Fall and happiness prior to sin, are intertwined in a single site; it is the meeting place of innocence and transgression, culture and Nature. The garden is a green metaphor for a moment suspended in time, for an infinite and perfect present, for an area of cosmological harmony where all differentiations are eliminated, where human destiny suddenly seems a pure mental fabrication—a game of appearances subject solely to desire. Situated at the boundary of dream and reality, the garden outlines the contours of a utopia.

SIX

On the World's Stage

Casanova paces back and forth on the European continent. His life is a journey; his life is theater. He feels at home everywhere—in Rome, St. Petersburg, Madrid, Constantinople, Vienna, Amsterdam—like an actor on the boards. He belongs to that vast country without frontiers where people speak and think in French: the Europe of conversation and gallantry.

He travels simply to get from one place to another; landscape is nonexistent, and the journey holds no interest in itself. The important thing is arriving somewhere. Comfortable conveyances and good inns contribute to the pleasure of the journey, and Casanova readily distributes zecchini, ecus, ducats, thalers, and piastres.

To travel agreeably, it is necessary to go to considerable expense: this is the way to be respected by everyone, to gain admission everywhere, and to take full advantage of the journey.

Sometimes his plans change because of chance encounters; he lingers somewhere or strays from his route and enjoys an unexpected stay in a country residence where he is invited by pleasant company. Circumstances determine his availability. A carriage stops in front of his inn: four well-dressed women step out. The third, Marie-Anne-Louise von Roll, a young baroness dressed in a riding habit, has salient black eyes under intrepid eyebrows, a lily-white complexion, and a quality that Casanova finds striking. Though he had just been contemplating taking up the monastic life at Einsiedeln, he is now ready to discard this plan so he can follow the beautiful foreigner and pay court to her.

Protect yourselves, mortals, against such an encounter, if you have the strength. Persist, fanatics, if you can, in the mad idea of burying yourselves in a cloister after seeing what I saw at that moment in Zurich on the 23rd day of the month of April [1760].

For Casanova, travel involves anticipating events, bringing chance constantly into play, testing his seductive power, his gifts, his stratagems. And after his credit and charm are expended in one place, he sets off for another. He turns over a new leaf, treats himself anew to untried, unblemished circumstances. To leave is to forget, to abandon the past—to try to escape the concatenation of acts and words. Travel becomes a way of avoiding duration. Casanova journeys in space in order to escape time. He roams the courts and cities of Europe, not because he is on a trip, but because he is perpetually starting a new one. The scenario is repeated, but always with new sets. In every new place, he has hopes of a fresh start, sometimes even of rebirth. For instance, after his Spanish trials, he is relieved to be on French soil once again: *I breathed more freely, being in France after so many misfortunes had tormented me in Spain; I seemed to be reborn, and indeed I felt rejuvenated.*

Travel involves putting one's body on trial, testing it against the strains of the road, disease, and accidents. Travel also involves thinking about destiny. In the course of his life, the meaning of travel changes for Casanova. At first, it is an initiation into the world; under Senator Bragadin's protection, when he journeys with the ease of a son of the nobility, it offers the pleasures of discovery; after his escape from prison, it becomes synonymous with flight and exile. Downfalls and successes, expulsions and applause succeed one another with a rapidity that seems to affect him only slightly. However, with the onset of age, the adventurer is losing his stamina and fortune becomes miserly. His journeys show a futile restlessness, a derisory and pathetic quest for employment, lodgings, a moment of respite. It becomes harder and harder to preserve freedom and lightness intact, and repeatedly to jettison the past. After disappointments in Berlin, St. Petersburg, and Warsaw—where Providence failed to appear in the guise of Frederick of Prussia, Catherine the Great, or even the King of Poland—he confesses to being discouraged, to wanting to end the unfulfilled expectation, to needing a truce. The year is 1767:

Tired and reeling from the pleasures, misfortunes, sorrows, intrigues, and troubles I had experienced in three capital cities, I prepared to spend four months in a free city like Augsburg, where the foreigner enjoyed the same privileges as the canons.

During the last thirteen years of his life in the Dux castle, he still escapes—to Dresden, to Prague, to Leipzig. He cannot resist the urge to go elsewhere.

LOGBOOK

Giacomo sets out on his first trip on foot, at eighteen, with a picaresque Recollect friar in whose company he travels to Rome. Father Steffano, a thirty-year-old redhead with a peasant's complexion, guarantees that if Giacomo wears his heavy coat, he will see to it that, in exchange, he is provided for all along the road by the holy men of his order. The young friar accepts the offer.

His coat was indeed a load for a mule. It had twelve pockets, all stuffed, not counting a large back pocket that he called the batticulo, *which by itself contained twice as much as all the others: bread, wine, cooked, fresh, and salted meats, chickens, eggs, cheeses, hams, sausages; there was enough to feed us for two weeks.*

Soon finding his mentor a nuisance, a thief, a fool, a liar, and a loathsome impostor, Giacomo gives him the slip. Continuing the journey on his own, he loses his purse, sprains his ankle badly, is almost raped by a drunken sodomite policeman who offers him board, and ends up regretting having abandoned the Recollect friar—at which moment he sees the latter suddenly come into view, laughing like a madman. He had taken five days to travel the same distance that Giacomo had covered in a single day, before his misfortunes. Steffano pays his young companion's debts and brings him along, in exchange for the protection of the Venetian ambassador. A few drinking scenes, some coming to blows when trying to escape a rape—female this time—and the trip is complete. Casanova is relieved to reach Rome. Though indigent, he does not look like a beggar and is determined not to endure Steffano's company any longer. From now on, he will carefully present himself as a young man who, though perhaps not wellborn, is well educated and whose bearing, at least, is proud.

As he grows older and more affluent, Casanova uses more rapid and less fatiguing means of transport. In his life history, the writer of Dux mentions a rowboat, a frigate, a tartan, even a small ice boat on runners, like a sleigh with sails. Barouche, sedan chair, hackney cab, "chamberpot," berlin, sleigh, diligence, or coach are his various means of conveyance. At times he boards a mail coach; at other times, when he feels his purse is well lined, he hires a six-horse four-seat carriage and arrives wherever he is going in grand style. When he is rich, he invariably treats himself to a private carriage, a privilege available to few. He crosses France in this way, from Lyons to Paris.

I had bought a carriage called a solitaire, *almost new, with three glass windows, two wheels, shafts, Amadis springs, and a crimson velvet lining. I got it for forty louis. I sent two strong trunks to Paris by diligence, keeping only what I needed in my* portmanteau, *and I was going to leave the next day in a dressing gown and nightcap, determined not to come out of my* solitaire *until after fifty-eight stages on the most beautiful road in all Europe.*

He often prefers to sleep in his carriage rather than the bad beds found in some roadside inns. On August 19, 1765, the *St. Petersburg Gazette*, as it customarily does when a foreigner leaves the country, announces the departure of Knight Jakob Casanova Farussi. Two weeks later, Vice-Chancellor Golitsyn signs the passport of Count Giacomo Kasanow de Farussi, who takes into his service an Armenian merchant, Rafaïl Ivanov, a good cook of Oriental cuisine, and then boards his "sleeping carriage" with the French actress La Valville and sets off for Königsberg. Not forgetting to take an ample supply of food and good wines.

Having put a good mattress and blankets in my sleeping carriage, I lay down with La Valville, who found this way of traveling as pleasant as it was comical, for we were actually in bed.

With the roads ruined by rain, the travelers take eight days to arrive in Riga and another four to reach Königsberg, where they part, since the actress was expected in Berlin and the adventurer wanted to go to Warsaw. Casanova lets her have the Armenian cook, sells his sleeping carriage, and goes on to the Polish court alone, and economically. He rents space in a four-seat carriage and, in the company of three Poles whose only other language is German, is terribly bored for the six-day journey.

Practical comments on the art of travel abound in the *History of My Life*. When Casanova mentions his means of transport, he often tells us its price as well, says a word about the comfort and speed, and reports on performances and delays. *Because of the sandy roads it took three days to travel a mere eighteen leagues in Germany*, he notes with precision. He also complains about the Old Castile road that he takes to get to Madrid: *Uneven, stony ascents and descents, nowhere the least sign indicating that carriages passed that way.*

In England, he appreciates the cleanliness and the beauty of the countryside and its main roads:

I admired the beauty of the carriages provided at the post for people who travel and do not have their own; the reasonable fares, the ease of payment, the pace of travel, always at a trot and never at a gallop, and the configuration of the towns I passed through between Dover and London.

He has occasional carriage accidents. He is overturned at midnight in the middle of the main road on his way from Naples to

Rome, beyond Francolisi, four miles from Sant'Agata, where the inn is a known place of ill repute—as Winckelmann and Goethe later confirmed. His valet, riding ahead of him on horseback, retraces his steps to warn Casanova that the two postilions have fled, perhaps to get highway robbers who will strip them of their possessions. He goes off to find several strong peasants to put the carriage back on its wheels. While waiting for the postilions to return, Casanova crawls out of the door above him, unharnesses the four horses, ties them in a circle to the wheels and shaft, and stations himself behind them with his five firearms. He is proud of having come out of the fall unharmed, unlike the man accompanying him. *I was accustomed to being overturned and had not been hurt at all. It depends on the position one takes. Don Ciccio may have broken his arm because he extended it outside.*

The darkness and the strong north wind make the situation very unpleasant. At the least sound, Casanova cries out, "Who goes there?" threatening death to anyone who dares advance on him. Two hours later, a band of peasants finally arrives with guns and lanterns. They put the carriage back on its wheels and harness the horses. They reach the next posthouse at daybreak. Casanova raises a great row and calls for a notary to draw up a statement. He accuses the postilions of having overturned the carriage on purpose and demands reparations. A wheelwright examines the axle, which is broken, and requests that the travelers stay a day to give him time to make a new one. They accept the hospitality of the Marchese Galiani, brother of the famous diplomat Abbé Galiani, whom Casanova has met in Paris. The next day, he sets off again, with only fifteen stages, each about two hours apart, before reaching Rome. The carnival awaits him.

ROOM AND BOARD

Leipzig lark, fish from the Lake of Morat, mullet from Marseilles, partridge and turkey pâté with truffles in Angoulême, ratafia from Grenoble, white truffles from the Piedmont, mushrooms from Liguria's chestnut groves, good wine from La Mancha, oil from Lucca, and "four-thieves vinegar" with its herbal flavorings, a Jewish family's compote, and goose liver . . . Casanova the traveler likes to discover his hosts' gastronomical specialties. In London, he tries to get used to the beer but finds it unbearably bitter. He is surprised to see the English eat so much lamb and so little bread, and since they readily do without soup or dessert, he feels their dinners have no beginning or end. When he takes a young Italian woman to the rural environs of Paris, he has her taste matelote, *boeuf à la mode*, an omelet, and squab *à la crapaudine*. With the Marquis d'Argens, he enjoys a delicious stuffing made of *andouillette*, sweetbreads, mushrooms, artichoke hearts, and foie gras. In his opinion and for his palate, nothing surpasses French cuisine.

Casanova stays in the best hotels except when he wants to remain incognito, when he stays in mediocre lodgings of no repute and makes his presence known to no one. In Aix-en-Provence, he stays at the Auberge de Saint-Jacques, a venerable abode two minutes away from the Cours Mirabeau. In Ancona, he lodges at the Carnation Inn, the *osteria del Garofano*, where it is not unusual to see princes traveling incognito. If we retrace Casanova's footsteps, we enter into a world of charming, well-known eighteenth-century residences: the Cheval-Blanc in Montpellier, A la Balance in Geneva, the Al Pellegrino in Bologna, the Santa Marta in Genoa, the Tre Re in Milan, L'Epée in Zurich, the Saint-Omer in Avignon. In Dresden, he stays at the Stadt Rom hotel, opposite the Hotel of Saxony, where his mother, Zanetta Casanova, resides, as well as his brother Giovanni, director of the city's Academy of Fine Arts.

When he wants to stay on in a city for a while, he usually rents rooms or an apartment in a private house. In St. Petersburg he lives a minute away from the Winter Palace, on the elegant Bolshaya Morskaya street, at the merchant Toulier's, who gives him two furnished rooms, with two beds, four chairs, two small tables, and magnificent, huge stoves. Once he has come to an agreement with his host about the price of heating and food, Casanova completes these furnishings by buying a chest of drawers and a large table which he can use for writing and for his papers and books.

In Spa, he moves into the Fontaine-d'Or, at 45, rue de l'Assemblée. In Rome, during his stay in 1770, he spends six months in a pretty apartment at number 32 Piazza d'Espagna. In Paris, his lodgings vividly illustrate the state of his finances and his social connections: in a modest little room very close to the Comédie-Italienne at the beginning of his stay; when he becomes a millionaire, he lives in high style and treats himself to a small princely "folly" where he holds sumptuous receptions. He has chickens fed in a dark pen so their flesh will be snow-white and exquisitely tasty. On rue du Bac, he lives in an apartment which the Marquise d'Urfé furnishes especially for him with studied elegance and refinement; the walls are decorated with magnificent tapestries representing different procedures in the grand enterprise of alchemy.

In Soleure, Switzerland, in the spring of 1760, in hope of pursuing his romance with the young Baroness von Roll, Casanova rents a beautiful, spacious country house with a ballroom, a print room, many bedrooms, a big garden, a fine vegetable plot, fountains, and a central building convenient for taking baths prepared by an apothecary. (It may have been the castle of Rienberg, located not far from the French ambassador's summer residence.)

When on June 14, 1763, he arrives in London, where he intends to stay for several months, the Chevalier de Seingalt (in London, he never went by any other name) rents a three-story house in the most fashionable area of the city, near Pall Mall. Porcelain, mirrors, bells, linen, silverware—nothing is lacking. As domestic help, aside from his personal valet, he hires an English governess and an Indian, called Jarba, who can speak French. An English cook with his entire family also comes to live with him. Casanova is very pleased with the cook, for he prepares not only his country's specialties but also *poularde* and the most refined French ragouts. Now lodged, served, and fed, the Chevalier drops off a few letters of introduction, then makes the rounds of the theaters and taverns to become acquainted with and accustomed to English ways.

THE SIGHTS

Though he never mentions a guidebook, Casanova is surely familiar with certain *Tableaux, Wonders, Guides*, or *Delights* of Europe. If he did not read them earlier, he has certainly consulted some of them in the library at Dux castle. Some of his comments seem inspired by one of the most famous guidebooks, Misson's *Nouveau Voyage d'Italie [New Journey in Italy]*, which describes nearly all the regions of western Europe. In Amsterdam, for example, he stresses the city's cleanliness and wealth; the sight of the Stock Exchange, where millionaires are dressed like villagers; the skaters on the frozen Amstel and the *speel houses*—taverns where people dance and listen to music. In Switzerland, Casanova describes a Latin inscription on a historical chapel in the same terms as a guidebook of the period but does not seem to notice the mountains and lakes. What strikes him more is the separation of men and women at concerts, or the custom of *Kiltgang*, whereby young village girls grant their boyfriends a trial night on the eve of the wedding.

In Spain, the memoirist describes the taste for tobacco and bullfights, a spectacle he finds cruel and sad. But he also notices the contrast between people's devotion to statues and paintings of the Virgin and the women's libertinage. He admires the Spanish language, which he finds resonant, energetic, and majestic, though less musical than Italian because of its guttural sounds. He makes a point of wandering around the ruins of the ancient city of Sagunto, the remains of its amphitheater, and the recently discovered road paved in mosaic. He visits Valencia, its five great bridges over the Guadalaviar, its twelve gates, its churches, and its magnificent gothic-style Silk Exchange. He praises the excellent climate but deplores that the roads are as yet unpaved.

Poor Spaniards! The beauty of their country, its fertility and richness are the cause of their laziness, and the mines of Peru and Potosí are the cause of their poverty, their pride, and all their prejudices.

Casanova shows no special liking for picturesque tourist attractions. Landscapes, historical monuments, ancient ruins never detain him for long.

I saw that everything in the world that is famous and beautiful, if we rely on the descriptions and drawings of writers and artists, always loses when we go to see it and examine it up close.

His geographical descriptions often end abruptly. Of Constantinople he writes only: *A view of this city from a league's distance is astonishing. Nowhere in the world is there such a beautiful sight.* In relating his arrival in St. Petersburg during the winter solstice, he merely specifies that it was at the moment when "the first rays of the sun were gilding the horizon." Struck by the white nights, he adds that he saw the sun appear at the far end of an immense plain at "twenty-four minutes after nine," and that the longest night in that region lasts "eighteen hours and forty-five minutes." We learn nothing more. He prefers commenting on the way Russian masters have the habit of beating their servants to prove their attachment and that the tsars use the language of despotism at the slightest opportunity. He says the following about Moscow in a single sentence:

In a week, I had seen everything: manufactories, churches, old monuments, exhibition rooms, including natural history collections, libraries (which did not interest me), the famous bell [the Anna Ivanovna bell was the largest in the world], and I noticed that their bells are not hung to swing like ours, but are immovable.

However, though he likes "to have seen all the sights" wherever he goes, he has a special interest in the customs and way of life. He does not describe his first impressions of Dresden, Prague, and Vienna, being far more interested in the personalities of their governing princes. He is struck by the prodigality of August III, King of Poland and Elector of Saxony; his court is dazzling, the arts are flourishing, the only thing missing is gallantry. He finds Vienna beautiful and luxurious, but difficult to live in for those who are dedicated to Venus, since the Empress Maria-Theresa zealously persecutes intemperance and debauchery.

Villainous spies, who were called commissaries for chastity, were the merciless tormentors of all the pretty girls; the Empress, who had all the virtues, did not have the virtue of tolerance with regard to illicit love between a man and a woman.

During his first stay in Paris, in 1750, what holds his attention, here as elsewhere, are bed and table manners. He prefers to sketch portraits of princes and actors and everyone whom people talk about than describe the environment. The walk in the Palais-Royal is the only thing to give him pause for a few lines: beautiful garden, straw chairs rented for a cent, sale of booklets, perfumed water, toothpicks, trinkets. His attention soon focuses on the behavior of the gawkers. He sees men and women with their noses pointed upward, staring at the dial of a clock so they can set their watches at noon. Then, finding a long line a few feet away, he is surprised that no one wants any other tobacco than La Civette's, a boutique made fashionable by the Duchess of Chartres. He quickly realizes that fashion and novelty are the only gods worshipped by Parisians. And since "one must live like the Romans when in Rome," Casanova hastens to conform.

In traveling he is a moralist and man of letters. He takes notes on what he observes wherever he goes. He likes to grasp the peculiarities of the peoples and nations he gets to know, seeking to capture the spirit of the times as well as each country's distinctive characteristics.

The island called England is a different color from the one seen on the surface of the continent . . . The water of the Thames has another taste, different from any of the other rivers in the world. Horned animals, fish, and everything edible has a different taste from what we eat, the horses are of a particular species even in their shape, and men have a character of their own common to the whole nation, which makes them

think they are superior to others. It is a belief common to all nations;
each one thinks it is preeminent. They are all correct.

In London, Casanova soon learns to use paper money instead of
gold and to carry two purses at all times, a small one to give to pro-
spective thieves and another with the money he needs. He discovers that the common people, those "democratic animals," are
capable of tearing down an entire theater in anger at being misled
about the play performed, and that a noblewoman who responded
to his advances in the darkness of her barouche is too haughty to
recognize him later in a well-lit drawing room.

—*I told you my name, madame. Do you not remember me?*

—*I remember you quite well; but such follies are hardly a claim to*
acquaintanceship, the noble Englishwoman answers, without
flinching.

He finds equally surprising that when he asks someone in the
City who So-and-So and So-and-So are, he is told that one is
worth twenty thousand pounds and the other a hundred thousand.

—*But I want to know their names*, he retorts.

—*The name is meaningless*, is the reply. *For what is a name? Ask*
me for a thousand pounds and make out the receipt in my presence
under the name of Attila and that will satisfy me. You will reimburse
me not as Seingalt but as Mr. Attila and we will laugh.

Casanova wants to be initiated into all the "enchanting sin-
gularities," like cockfights and betting clubs, of the proud English nation. He spends several hours at the British Museum and
soon knows all the London spots where it is fashionable to walk,
dine, applaud plays, or dance. He witnesses the birth of a new
women's hair style worn by Lady Grafton; first considered mad,
absurd, and fit to be hissed for being unbecoming, less than six
months later it crosses the Channel and spreads all over Europe.

In the case of spectacles, initial opinions are not to be trusted. They are often unsound.

A FEW DAYS IN THE TRAVELER'S LIFE

Departures are also a way of dismissing the repercussions of one's errors and thoughtless blunders—a way of remaining a man of no importance whose actions are of no consequence. One place resembles the next. Casanova does not move; he repeats himself.

In Florence, toward the end of 1760, the Venetian stops at Doctor Vannini's hotel, an establishment with a very good reputation where all the distinguished foreigners stay. He chooses an apartment on the Arno embankment with a view and a beautiful terrace. He rents a town carriage and a footman, whom he dresses, as well as the coachman, in the blue and red livery of Senator Bragadin. The next day, he goes out alone on foot, wearing a simple redingote, to see the city without being seen. In the evening, he goes to the Teatro del Cocomero, to hear Arlecchino Roffi and Pertici, who is already old.

The next day, he goes to see the banker Sasso Sassi, with whom he has a large letter of credit and, after dining alone, dresses in a suit that is new and appropriate for the season and goes to the Opera, via della Pergola. He takes a seat in a box near the orchestra, "more to see the actresses than to hear the music," which has never really captivated him.

The opera, theater, or comedy are ideal places to meet town nobility as well as the most beautiful girls to be courted. "Not knowing where to go, and wanting amusement, I went to the rehearsal at the Opera" is a virtual refrain in his life history. Though one comes to see the spectacle, one comes primarily to be seen. Casanova likes to attract looks and is pleased when a pretty woman's lorgnette is focused on him. His lace, charms, and rings compel interest. He loves to dress up and knows how to adjust the splendor of his clothes and jewelry to the degree of attention he wants to attract.

How great is his surprise, that night, when he sees the *prima virtuosa* come out on the stage! It is Teresa—or Bellino—his strangest conquest. Angiola Calori has become one of the best singers of her time. As she looks out at the spectators, her gaze lingers on Casanova. She recognizes him. When she finishes her aria, she goes back to the wings, turns, and, gesturing with her fan, invites her former lover to join her in her dressing room. It has been sixteen years since their last meeting! They have so many adventures to tell each other about! She introduces him to Cesarino, their son, who is presented to everyone as her brother. And, to her young husband, she says of her erstwhile lover, *You see my father, and more than my father, for I owe him everything.*

Momentarily tongue-tied, the "father" goes one better: *Yes, signore, she is my daughter, she is my sister, an angel with no sex, a living treasure, and she is your wife.*

When he wants to be forgiven for not having answered one of her letters, she interrupts, *I know everything. You were in love with a nun, you were locked up in prison; I heard about your miraculous escape when I was in Vienna. Later I heard about your experiences in Paris and Holland; but after you left Paris I was unable to get news of you from anyone. But here we are . . .*

At rehearsals and dinners they become inseparable. The mood is joyful. Actors, actresses, and music lovers all drop by to kiss the singer's hand and court her, among them an affable old man who recognizes Casanova; it is Abbot Gama, who had initiated him into Roman life when he was an adolescent. An eloquent as well as inquisitive person, he reports on common acquaintances, then urges Casanova to narrate his adventures. As a token of friendship, the abbot introduces him to the Marchese Botta-Adorno, Governor of Tuscany, who, in turn, invites him to meet Sir Horace Mann, English resident of Florence. Casanova describes him as a rich, amiable man, a great art lover with excellent taste. When he is summoned cordially to the Englishman's house, he admires everything—his garden, his furniture, his paintings, his choice of books. Some time later, Mann will subscribe to Casanova's translation of the *Iliad*.

Thus one recommendation leads to another, and salon doors open. The guests engage in conversations and Casanova shines. One morning, Mr. Mann takes him to view the paintings in the Great Gallery of the Uffizi. Between two dinner invitations, or after savoring a perfectly whipped, frothy hot chocolate, Casanova shuts himself up in his apartment to write letters or take notes on the various observations and conversations he wants to remember. He is also engaged, at the time, in an amorous intrigue with a young dancer who has minor parts at the Opera.

A mysterious adventurer compromises him in a matter involving a forged bill of exchange, and Casanova is obliged to leave Florence within three days if he does not pay; he refuses, feeling he was unjustly accused. His friends support him, but to no avail; he must leave. He enjoys the intoxication of glittering banquets and cheerful company to his last evening. Then he departs, prepared to resume the same kind of life elsewhere, as if nothing had happened.

When he arrives in Rome at nightfall, after thirty-six hours of travel, he goes to the customs office, the *dogana di Terra*, at Piazza di Pietra. Every foreigner is required to show his trunks and books. Casanova has about thirty books, all critical of religion and its required virtues. He is prepared to relinquish them in his haste to get to bed. But the clerk who examines his equipage merely asks him to count them, then promises to return them at his inn the next day. Pleasantly surprised, Casanova goes straight to the Albergo di Londra, on Piazza d'Espagna, where he is given something to eat while a fire is made in the apartment intended for him. He goes to bed and sleeps until noon, dreaming about the innkeeper's daughter, of whom he had caught a glimpse.

When he wakes, his valet announces he has located the house of his brother Giovanni; it is only a few minutes away, at 54 via della Vittoria. He is living with the painter Raphael Mengs, his teacher and friend. The two brothers have not seen each other for ten years; they tell each other their adventures and stroll around the city, as Giacomo asks for news of old acquaintances. Afterward his brother brings him to a house of the "highest class," the Countess Cherufini's, Cardinal Albani's mistress, where the most fashionable receptions—*conversazioni*—are held. But Giacomo becomes annoyed and impatient; people do not gather around him, his worth goes unrecognized, his witticisms fall flat, and no one responds to his bons mots. He blames his brother, whom he considers too inconsequential to inspire respect: *I saw that in this house I would lose some of my intrinsic value, and the reason for this was the status of the person who had introduced me.*

He cannot bear hearing people say, "He is Casanova's brother." He strikes up a lively conversation with a priest and soon they are good friends: it is Winckelmann, then librarian to Cardinal Albani and responsible for his collection of antiquities. The next day, the three men pay a visit to Mengs, who is painting his *Parnassus* on the ceiling of the gallery in the Villa Albani. Casa-

nova also goes to see Monsignor Cornaro, one of Rome's ecclesiastical judges, "with the goal of making my way into the best
circles after succeeding in being introduced to His Holiness."

Zuane Cornaro, being Venetian, is afraid of compromising
himself by recommending a man who has fled his homeland; he
prefers to ask Cardinal Passionei to introduce Casanova to the
Holy Father. The Cardinal asks him to tell the story of his escape.

—*Should I sit on the floor?*

—*Oh! No, your suit is much too handsome.*

Cardinal Passionei rings and has a footman bring in a stool
with no arms or backrest. This irritates Casanova and he tells
the story badly. The Cardinal gives him a funeral oration to read,
telling him that he writes better than his guest speaks, but that
the Pope will see him the next day. As Casanova leaves, he
reflects on this man's strange character, highly intelligent,
haughty, vain, and talkative. Since he wants his protection and
is aware of his passion for books, he sends him a copy of the
code of *Pandectes*, a rare Roman volume. The next day at the
appointed hour he presents himself before Clement XIII, who
warns him that Cardinal Passionei will want to pay for his gift.
In that case, Casanova says, *I will send back his funeral oration!* The
Pope laughs and asks to be discreetly informed of the end of
this incident.

Coming out of his audience, he meets a man he knew as a
Venetian gondolier who is now a *scopatore santissimo*, a sweeper
of the pontifical chambers. Delighted to be reunited with a compatriot, he accepts an invitation to share a meal of polenta and
pork chops with the sweeper's modest family. He takes his
brother along and arranges to have his valet bring six bottles of
Orvieto wine and an entire ham. They eat heartily and discuss
the lottery to be held the next day. Mariuccia, a young girl who

is as pretty as an angel, urges Casanova to bet on number 27. He agrees. They part at midnight, promising to meet again the following evening. In the meantime, the Cardinal has sent back the valuable Roman book but Casanova has obtained the Holy Father's permission to donate it to the Vatican Library. The Pope promises him tokens of his "special affection."

In the evening, the gathering celebrates the lucky Venetian, winner of the lottery. He squeezes Mariuccia's hand under the table and she responds. Stealthily, he asks her where they can meet. At eight o'clock at the church of Trinità dei Monti, she whispers. As the price of her favors, she asks Casanova to rescue her from poverty by giving her, through her confessor, four hundred scudi which she needs as a dowry to marry a nice wigmaker. He goes to see the father confessor immediately and settles the marriage; then he rents a little room and makes arrangements to furnish it with a bed, a table, four chairs, and a coal stove. In the evening, he dines with Mengs and then goes to the Opera, to the Aliberti theater, but his impatience about the next day interferes with his enjoyment and later with his sleep. In the morning, he initiates the dazzling young beauty into the pleasures of voluptuousness. He promises her that he will see her again before her wedding, when he returns from Naples, where he plans to stay for about ten days. Several hours later, he receives the token of Clement XIII's "special affection": the cross of the Order of the Golden Spur, which he immediately hangs around his neck on a broad dark red ribbon. His vanity is rewarded, but five years later, in Warsaw, Czartoryski, Prince Palatine of Russia, will dissuade him from wearing it and says: *It is rubbish that only charlatans still wear.*

THE THEATER OF THE WORLD

I did not want to command respect, but I wanted to play a part.

These words betray Casanova's wounded pride and social insecurity. The admission that he wants to be onstage and exist in the eyes of those who count can only be a pale reflection of his true ambition, his deepest wish and perennial pursuit: to command respect, and to do so conspicuously in a society where he does not belong by birthright. Beneath the appearances of wealth, worldliness, and volubility are his modest origins and his shame at being the son of actors and the grandson of a shoemaker from the Venetian lagoon.

Prestigious letters of introduction, eminent patronage, gold zecchini placed with the best bankers in town, a sumptuous lifestyle, literary conversation, gifted writing—nothing can erase the precariousness of his station: he is a free spirit, inquisitive and independent, in a century where an individual does not yet exist unless he is wellborn. He proclaims he is his own man, but he depends on society's opinion for recognition, and his freedom hinges on his good or bad reputation. Playing a bit part is surely mortifying, for Casanova likes to have the main part, but if he must choose, he would prefer a bit part to exclusion from the world's stage.

A threatened childhood, ephemeral wealth, the fear of passing time, being a déclassé spectator of the social theater—Casanova's vulnerabilities nourish his appetite for living. His life is a race of desire, a conjuration, an obstinate way of rejecting anything that prevents enjoyment. He has a stubborn taste for happiness, and amusement and lightness are his favorite weapons. When old age catches up with him and he sees death approaching, ready to dislodge him from the great theater of life, he turns to his last recourse, literature, to set down forever the evanescence of happiness, before it is too late.

THE TEMPTATION OF IMMOBILITY

Immobility frightens Casanova. To settle down would be to renounce omnipotence. To safeguard open prospects and the entire spectrum of possibilities, he tries to escape from the march of time. He rejects the irreversible: a residence, a job, a wife, wealth, social prestige, security. He is offered all these things in Rome, Constantinople, Amsterdam, Paris, and Naples. He does not want them.

I could not resolve to renounce the bright hope of becoming famous . . . , either in the fine arts or in literature.

When Esther's wealthy father offers his daughter's hand and invites him to share his house, Casanova admits quite frankly: *It was not love for Manon Balletti but a foolish vanity, a desire to play a part in Paris, that made me leave Holland.* The beautiful Lucrezia, many years later, will be no more successful at tying him down:

I could have lived happily with that charming woman, but I loathed the idea of settling anywhere. In Naples I could have bought property which would have made me rich; but I would have had to adopt a wise way of life which was absolutely contrary to my nature.

Marriage and studious retreat are two temptations that periodically preoccupy him. The quest for a quiet—indeed, monastic—happiness runs through his life. Perfect peace is the greatest of all fortunes; such is his conviction when he considers becoming a monk. This is in 1760, at the monastery of Einsiedeln, in Switzerland.

I thought I saw that I was truly in the place where I could live happily until my final hour, no longer at the mercy of Fortune . . . To be happy, it seemed to me, I needed only a library.

Four years later, at thirty-nine, he spends a perfect week in the palace of the Duke of Brunswick, in Wolfenbüttel, where the Duke has assembled one of Europe's most beautiful libraries:

I spent a week without ever leaving it except to go to my room and without ever leaving my room except to go to it. I did not see the librarian again until the eighth day, to thank him an hour before leaving. I lived in the most perfect peace without ever thinking about the past or the future, since my work prevented me from being aware that the present existed. I see today that to be a true sage in this world I would have needed only some minor combination of circumstances, for virtue always held greater charms for me than vice.

For the present time, it is still too early to renounce the world. Casanova will remain onstage.

THE CARNIVAL OF THE IMPOSSIBLE

Dressing up in a costume or wearing a mask is a way of cutting through the weight of society and escaping a foreordained destiny. Casanova wants to choose his position in society, not accept one assigned to him. He seeks a nobility that no one can question, a nobility of personal talent and *savoir-vivre*, of a wit and man of letters. He tosses off repartee wherever he is, to attract, interest, amuse, astonish, lose himself, and communicate his joie de vivre. His life unfolds as a series of intrigues, coups de théâtre, denouements in which he is both actor and author. Inwardness and appearance are not at odds, but related, intermixed, excited by one another. The performer is guided by a single moral principle: Raise the curtain! May the show begin and may it continue until the curtain falls! Casanova also enacts his life by recounting it, a tactic he began to use probably when quite young.

His favorite repertory belongs to the time-honored commedia dell'arte—the comedy of masks—in which his mother performs at the court of Saxony's Italian theater. In improvised comedy, success depends not on the story structure but entirely on the actors' performance. They must invent on the spot, wed their actions to their words, and enter into their partner's acting style, making it seem as though they had worked it out together. *Arte.* A comedy of art and savoir faire, of quick intelligence, vivacity, verve, and knowledge of the human soul. Casanova respects and admires these improvisational actors, finds inspiration in them— for example, in the immensely talented Harlequin whom he describes so marvelously:

His refined witticisms, the beautiful sentences he strings together, his graceful way of twisting them, his unusual erudition and learned blun-

ders are so many momentary and ephemeral images, flashes of fantasy, shadows, sparks, and quasi-dreams that arise out of true reminiscence. These are disorderly and undigested kernels which he gathers right there and gives to the audience; they would no longer be what they are if he wanted to polish, compose, and improve them with thought; they would lose the grace of their elegant neglectedness. To be such a Harlequin, I think one must have read a great many books, heard a wide variety of people talk, have a wonderful memory, a unique mind, and a deep practical experience of the human heart.

Like him, Casanova has more than one trick up his sleeve. Wearing his valet's clothes so he can be allowed to remove the boots of a beautiful unknown woman; rewriting in a night the part of an actress who cannot pronounce the letter *r;* learning the fandango so he can escort a Spanish woman to a ball—nothing stops him; everything amuses him. He is always ready to play opposite his interlocutor, whoever he may be—Voltaire, Frederick of Prussia, Catherine the Great, Benedict XIV or Clement XIII, the naturalist Haller, Count Bonneval, Lorenzo Da Ponte, perhaps even Mozart. Be his companion a prince or a soubrette, he is never at a loss. He converses about poetry, literature, gardening, calendars, lotteries, minerals, religion, music, as the circumstances require.

Crébillon the Elder, to whom Silvia introduces him, becomes his language teacher during his first stay in Paris, when he is twenty-five years old. With his knack for sensing what is appropriate, as soon as he meets him Giacomo recites his own Italian translation of a scene from Crébillon's *Rhadamiste et Zénobie.* Charmed, Crébillon urges him to improve his knowledge of French.

—*But, monsieur, how am I to find a teacher? I am an unbearable student, inquisitive, curious, troublesome, insatiable. I am not rich enough to pay for such a teacher, even if I found one.*

—For fifty years, monsieur, I have been looking for a pupil such as you depict yourself, and it is I who will pay you if you want to come to me to take lessons.

Casanova makes a perpetual carnival of his life. Like his incestuous utopia, the carnival suspends time and derives from a will to create one's own laws. At the carnival in Cologne, he attends a ball where all the guests are dressed as peasants—the Peasant Wedding feast, a baroque masquerade very popular in Germany and Russia. In Milan, he invents a new, daring disguise which transforms the best nobility into false paupers. Is there any better image of an inverted society than these *pitocchi*, these luxury beggars? On the last day of the Roman carnival, he goes to the Corso on horseback, dressed as Pulcinella, generously throwing sweets into prams with babies and emptying his basket on Momolo's daughters.

People go masked, or unmasked if they like; they stage all kinds of masquerades on foot and on horseback; they throw the people sweets, they distribute satires, pasquinades, and pamphlets. All the noblest people in Rome mix with all the lowliest; there is a great deal of noise . . . At nightfall all these crowds fill the theaters—operas, comedies, pantomimes, tightrope acts—where all the performers must be either intact men or castrati. People also go to hostelries and taverns, where all the rooms are packed with people eating voraciously, as if they ate only during carnival.

In Aix-en-Provence, on May 25, 1769, he attends a surprising procession on the feast of Corpus Christi. What astonishes him are the masquerades, follies, and buffoonery that take place:

The devil, death, the deadly sins, comically dressed, fighting with one another, angered at having to pay court to the creator on that day; the shouting, booing, whistling of the people scoffing at these characters, and the din of the songs with which the crowd mockingly acclaims them and plays all sorts of tricks on them—these create a spectacle that is much more frenzied than the Saturnalia or anything we read had taken place anywhere amid even the most extravagant paganism.

When he disguises himself for a carnival, there are two commedia dell'arte characters whose costumes he favors: Pedrolino, with his naïve, candid, and elegant grace, his sleepy, gauche bearing (immortalized by Watteau), and Pulcinella, a double hunchback, with a bird-like hooked nose, a flowing white gown and big white skullcap, a powerful character (whose temperamental and sensual gluttony is well captured by Tiepolo). These two impersonations, he feels, are especially good camouflage when he wants to avoid being recognized by certain people. He chooses to appear in the visiting room of the Murano convent disguised so that his nun friends, M.M. and C.C., cannot identify him.

I decided to go masked as Pierrot. There is no better disguise so long as a person is neither hunchbacked nor lame. Pierrot's ample costume, with its long, wide sleeves and wide pants that flow down to the heels, conceal anything that might be distinctive in a person's body by which someone who knew him very well could recognize him. A cap covering his whole head, his ears, and his neck hides not only his hair but also the color of his skin, and gauze over the eyeholes of his mask prevents people from seeing if his eyes are black or blue.

Respecting the character of the mask, Giacomo takes on a simpleton's gait and dances the minuet with a female Harlequin, appearing to be constantly on the verge of falling, which frightens the company and makes them laugh. Afterward he dances twelve furlanas with extraordinary vigor, then lets himself drop and pretends to fall asleep. Everyone respects Pierrot's slumber. But a little while later a Harlequin, with the impertinence allowed by his character, comes up and spanks him with his stick. Having no weapon, Pierrot grabs the Harlequin by the waist and runs all about the room with him; the Harlequin continues to hit him, and soon his female companion comes to help him. But then an impertinent Pulcinella comes up from behind, trips him, and makes him fall. Much provoked, Casanova fights so well that his antagonist begs for mercy; Pulcinella's costume flies open and he loses his hump and his false belly. *To the sound of applause and laughter from all the nuns, who had probably never before enjoyed such a spectacle, I seized the moment, cut through the crowd, and ran away.*

In his thin white cotton costume, Pierrot takes a gondola to the *ridotto* where he will gamble before meeting his beautiful nun at the Murano *casino* at two in the morning. He loses, then wins, and is wildly extravagant:

In complete freedom of my body and soul, certain that no one recognizes me, enjoying the present and mocking the future, as well as all those who have nothing better to do than keep their reason sadly employed at foreseeing it.

Did not Montesquieu write that the mask, in Venice, is not a disguise but an incognito? An incognito offers the freedom of enjoying the present moment without consequences.

PORTRAIT GALLERY

Angiola Calori, Anna Binetti, Ancilla, Silvia, Carlino Bertinazzi, dall'Oglio, Teresa Imer, Vincenzo Campioni, La Denis—Casanova keeps company with most of the Italian dancers, actors, musicians, and singers of his time. Traveling incessantly like them, he crosses their paths again and again, as determined by his peregrinations and their contracts . . .

I remember Carestini and the noble Salimbeni, well-known castrati who laughed quite merrily when they encountered innocent souls who pitied them.

Among his portraits of performers, the most heartrending comes from his meeting in Mantua, in 1749, with the aged La Fragoletta, his father's former love, whom he describes as almost a witch, with the dreaded face of decline and old age.

In spite of her wrinkles, she used white powder and rouge, and she dyed her eyebrows black. She exposed half her flabby bosom, repellent precisely because it showed what might have been, and two dentures which were quite obviously false. Her hairdo consisted in a wig that adhered quite badly to her forehead and temples; and her trembling hands made mine tremble when she pressed them. She smelled of ambergris, as did her entire room, and the simpering way she tried to let me know she found me attractive almost made me lose the strength I was summoning to keep from laughing. Her attire was very studied and belonged to a fashion that was probably outdated twenty years earlier. I saw with horror the traces of hideous old age on a face that must have attracted many a lover before being withered by time.

Italian actors are like one big family: this first mistress of his father happens to be the grandmother of his best friend, Antonio Balletti (hence of Manon, his chaste fiancée). When he comes to Paris with him in 1750, he is introduced into the inner circles of the Comédie-Italienne. Antonio introduces him to his father, Giuseppe Balletti (known as Mario, his name as leading man), his aunt Elena Riccoboni, and his uncle Lodovico Riccoboni, actors and writers; and to Camilla and Corallina Veronese, actresses known for their talent and love affairs. The Harlequin Carlino Bertinazzi remembers Giacomo, having met him as a child in Padua, when he and Casanova's mother were returning from St. Petersburg. Casanova soon becomes friends with everyone, particularly Silvia, his friend Balletti's mother, of whom he paints an especially flattering portrait, in stark contrast to the one of his father's mistress, La Fragoletta. Is he describing the actress-mother he wished he had had?

I found her above everything that was said about her. She was fifty years of age, her figure was elegant, and her bearing aristocratic, as were her manners; she was graceful, affable, cheerful, a subtle speaker, obliging to everyone, full of wit and with no sign of pretension. Her face was an enigma: it was interesting and pleasing to everyone, yet on examination it could not be considered beautiful; but no one ever dared pronounce it ugly . . . An actress capable of replacing her has never been found and never will be, for she would have to have in her the same combination of traits that Silvia applied in the most difficult art of the theater—action, voice, physiognomy, intelligence, deportment, and knowledge of the human heart . . . Her morals were pure. She wanted to have friends, never lovers . . . By unanimous opinion, Silvia was a woman beyond her station.

The Italian actors in Paris wish to show their compatriot their lavishness and invite him to elegant dinners. He is taken to the Opera, where he attends a performance of André Campra's *Fêtes vénitiennes* and sees the two greatest dancers of his time, Dupré and the renowned Camargo. At the Comédie-Française, he happily applauds the plays of Molière—*The Misanthrope*, *The Miser*, among others—and returns every chance he can get.

The morals of the performers seem to him freer in Paris than elsewhere. When he goes into ecstasies over the beauty of a young actress and expresses the desire to make her acquaintance, an elderly actress tells him that it will not be difficult; the parents will gladly invite him to supper and afterward leave him alone at the table to converse with the young girl. And when Casanova expresses surprise at this freedom, the matron answers:

You are in France, monsieur, where the price of life is known and people try to enjoy it to the full. We love pleasures and we consider ourselves happy when we can initiate them.

When he is introduced to the famous opera singer Marie Le Fel, he sees three young children gathered around her:

—*The appearance of each of the three presents a different kind of beauty.*

—*I should say so*, she answers. *The oldest is the son of the Duke d'Ancenis, that one is by the Count d'Eguemont, and the youngest is the son of Maisonrouge, who just married La Romainville.*

—*Oh, oh! Please excuse me. I thought you were the mother of all three.*

—*And so I am*, the singer answers, bursting into laughter.

The student in gallantry is a fast learner; he wastes no time mastering the ground rules. Seven years later, during his second stay in Paris, he moves with great ease in the world of actresses kept by high-ranking protectors.

Theater foyers are a noble marketplace where enthusiasts go to exercise their talents in embarking on love affairs. I had known how to profit well from this pleasant school; I started by becoming friends with the official lovers, and I succeeded by never showing the least pretension, and especially by seeming not just inconsequential but of no importance. It was always necessary to have one's purse available for the occasion, but since small amounts were involved, the pain was not as great as the pleasure. I was certain that in one way or the other I would be repaid.

Thus does Casanova go forward on the world's stage, prepared to play a small part as long as he can hope to command respect later.

A MAN OF THE THEATER

For Zanetta's child, the theater—a family, a picture of life, a place of intrigue and amusement—also gives him the opportunity to exercise his many talents. Theatrical entrepreneur, librettist, translator, adapter, director, prompter, amateur actor, publisher and editor of a theatrical journal—Casanova is part of the eighteenth-century history of the stage.

In 1745, at twenty, as a soldier posted in Corfu, he becomes a theatrical entrepreneur to please the company he is with, especially the inaccessible Signora F., who had complained that no theater performance was scheduled for the forthcoming carnival. He therefore sets sail for Otranto, where he assembles a troupe of actors—Pantalone, Pulcinella, Scaramuccia, lovers. He leaves in the evening with twenty actors, the record book of their repertoire, and six huge boxes containing costumes, sets, props, and everything they needed to perform farce. This once, Signora F.'s attentive suitor sets down the following—for him rare— remark, *Throughout the carnival my absorption in theater prevented me from thinking about love.*

A year later, having renounced a military career (he found the wait for promotion too long), he decides to play the violin in the orchestra of the San Samuele theater. He had been taught to play the instrument by his schoolmaster, Doctor Gozzi. He earns a scudo a day, enough to support himself but not in a way he considers honorable.

Seeing myself reduced to this after so many fine titles, I was ashamed, but kept it to myself. I felt humiliated, but not degraded. Since I had not repudiated Fortune, I thought I could still count on her. I knew she exercised her power over all mortals without consulting them, as long as they were young; and I was young.

When he is in Paris in 1751, the ambassador of the court of Poland and Saxony instructs Casanova to translate a French opera into Italian. He chooses *Zoroastre*, with a libretto by Cahusac and music by Rameau. His adaptation is performed in Dresden on February 7, 1752, in the large opera house at the Zwinger Palace—an honor for the Italian actors at the court. Zanetta Casanova, his mother, plays one of the main parts, Erinice, and his sister, Maria Maddalena, is a nymph in the corps de ballet. *Le Mercure de France* praises the adaptation: "The spirit of the work is everywhere rendered either with a strong or a pleasant coloring, and its author, Monsieur Casanova, makes it quite clear that he is capable of producing works of his own worthy of being read." He himself is not really satisfied with his poetry, but he writes in his memoirs: *Nevertheless, I received a lovely gold snuffbox from the generous monarch; and I gave my mother great pleasure.*

Casanova writes a play in collaboration with François Prévost d'Exiles, *Les Thessaliennes, ou, Arlequin au Sabbat [The Thessalonian Women, or, Harlequin at the Revels]*, which is given four performances at the Comédie-Italienne in Paris; at the opening night, on July 14, 1752, Parfait's *Dictionnaire des théâtres* states the author "enjoys an honest fortune, which allows him to satisfy his taste for literature and travel."

Casanova develops a fondness for theatrical writing. His parody of Racine's *The Thébaïde, or, The Enemy Brothers*, transcribed into Italian, is performed in Dresden at carnival time in 1753, on February 22. *The only thing I did was to please the actors with a tragicomedy in which I used two characters to play the part of Harlequin.*

He collaborates on the first French oratorio, *Les Israélites sur la montagne d'Oreb [The Israelites on Mount Horeb]*:

I wrote it in Italian lyric verse, and my friend the Abbé [de Voisenon] wrote it in French verse, not by translating me, but by imitating me and embellishing my ideas in combination with his own. He gave it in a concert of sacred music during Lent [March 14] in the year 1758.

And in 1761 Casanova translates Voltaire's comedy *L'Ecossaise* for Pietro Rossi's troupe of actors at the Sant'Agostino theater in Genoa. To stimulate the audience's curiosity, the troupe has the following announcement printed on the poster: "We will be presenting Monsieur de Voltaire's *L'Ecossaise* in a translation penned by an unknown, and will be performing it without a prompter."

When he returns to his homeland in 1774, Casanova devotes himself to sundry literary labors, including a translation of the *Iliad*. In the summer of 1780, he becomes an impresario and recruits a troupe of French actors, including a certain Clairmonde, boosting this initiative by publishing a weekly, *Le Messager de Thalie*, which he writes himself in French; he puts out eleven issues and arranges to have them distributed free of charge in cafés and other public places. He also revitalizes theatrical practice by launching substantial publicity campaigns and using tickets with stubs. The first performance takes place in the Sant'Angelo theater on October 7, 1780. In spite of the breadth of the repertoire, which includes Corneille's *Cinna*, Destouches's *The Conceited Count*, Marivaux's *The Surprise of Love*, Voltaire's *L'Indiscret*, and Lesage's *Turcaret*, they do not have the success Casanova anticipated and he has to give up his theatrical and publishing activities for lack of funds.

Many years later Casanova writes a tragicomedy in French, *Le Polémoscope, ou, la Calomnie démasquée par la présence d'esprit [The Polemoscope, or, Calumny Unmasked by Presence of Mind]*, not for money but for pleasure, as an obliging neighbor, and knowing this would probably be his last endeavor of the kind. The play is performed during the summer of 1791 by an amateur group assembled by the Countess de Clary, daughter of Charles Joseph, Prince de Ligne, in her castle in Toeplitz, a few miles from Dux. The plot is centered on a "fibbing" lorgnette that enables people to see to the left or right of the object they appear to be focused on, and involves a bet that offends a lady's virtue, so she is prepared to lie to avenge the affront. Finally, thanks to a spirit of graciousness, outraged wisdom triumphs over impudence.

EPILOGUE ON TIPTOES

In the summer of 1764, the Chevalier de Seingalt attends a performance of the Italian opera in the small theater in Charlottenburg, outside Berlin. He is especially moved by one of the dancers onstage. When he is told her name he remembers that he met her in Venice when they were both children. She was called Pantaloncina.

This little ten-year-old dancer was the first girl to inflame Giacomo's heart. He was only twelve or thirteen at the time. One evening, his mother had sent him to the theater with his teacher, Gozzi, and at the end of the play the daughter of the actor playing Pantalone danced the minuet with a graceful charm that enchanted the young boy. He went to the little Giovanna Corrini's dressing room to compliment her. Her father, one of Zanetta's old acquaintances, instructed his daughter to stand up so Giacomo could embrace her. She did so graciously. Giacomo felt awkward but was so filled with happiness that he bought a small ring which the girl had found pretty from a woman who was selling jewelry backstage and gave it to her as a present. Pantaloncina kissed him once again. Giacomo returned to his box, his heart in a pitiful state. He knew he had just done something doubly foolish, for not only did the zecchino he paid not belong to him—he owed it to Doctor Gozzi—but also he had spent it, he later wrote, *like a dupe, to obtain only a kiss*. He spent a troubled night, wondering how he would repay the borrowed money. The next day the jewelry vendor, summoned to Zanetta's at dinnertime, praised the prodigal, love-smitten youth. Exposed, the young Giacomo asked his mother to forgive him and explained that he had committed the misdeed out of love and that this was the first and last time it would happen. At the word "love," the gathering broke into unfeeling laughter, wounding the young boy, who vowed to himself that he would never let love upset him again.

Twenty-six years later, Giacomo Casanova is taken to his compatriot's house. She and her husband, J.-B. Denis, are now among the most renowned Italian dancers in Germany. Frederick the Great commissioned a portrait of her for the palace of Sans-Souci before she left the Berlin stage to retire in Florence. Casanova reminds her of their meeting long ago, the ties that link their two families, and the emotion she had aroused in him: *You were the first to have inspired amorous thoughts in my soul*, he admits. The next day he becomes La Denis's "tender friend," "the just reward for a constancy of twenty-six years," he adds ingenuously.

In theater, too, time suspends its course and love endures.

SEVEN

The Backstage of the Body

"THE COUNTRY IN EQUILIBRIUM"

Casanova's body is always effusive. He burns, overflows, explodes. Fluids, humors, fevers run through the stories of his life. Words referring to the body spell out in their raw nakedness the passions of his soul—eruption of bile caused by rage; bitter saliva; vapors from anger; sweat filtering through his epidermis and streaming down to the prison floor to the left and right of the armchair where he sits, naked; sweat mixed with powder and an ointment wiped from his forehead by the Marquise d'Urfé midway through an alchemical coupling...

Casanova is a body. Whether healthy or sick, it is vibrant, excessive, immediate. His emotions, his feelings, his desires are instantly incarnated in his veins and stomach; they poison his blood and alter his face. Restrained indignation makes him tremble all over; boredom makes him lose weight; great surprise and impotency are diuretic. Thinking he is being enlisted by force, he experiences "such a strong orgasm" that in less than an hour, it seemed to him, all the fluids in his body "were seeking an outlet to evacuate the place they were occupying." Angered to learn that Manon Balletti will marry François Blondel, architect to the King, a man he does not know but who is now daring to "marry a girl who belonged to me and who people believed was my wife," he is ready to kill him, and he loses sleep.

My empty stomach sent vapors to my head that made me drowsy, when I came to. I raved, talking to myself in fits of anger that lacerated my soul.

He has no doubt that "anger kills if a person does not succeed in purging himself of it in one way or the other." A woman who hates him provokes an attack of vomiting; a desire for revenge, as well as news of unexpected good fortune, deprives him of sleep. An excess of amorous ardor drains the blood from his lips; his last orgasm is tinged with blood. The libertine nun from Murano discovers, aghast, spattered on her breast, "his soul diluted with drops of blood." *Do not be afraid, my angel, it is the yoke of the last egg which is often red*, he says calmly.

His body is ablaze. His words carry the humors that move him and his lady friends: blood, sweat, saliva, milk, tears, sperm, female fluids. The body is liquefied, it pours out, receptive to all forms of circulation. He is unafraid of describing its juices and miasmas. The linen stained from a miscarriage; the livid color of a wound; a lover's resonant farts; the spatter of his "incontinence" as he tries on English redingotes in a hovel in Marseilles—Casanova notes all the outward signs of bodily life. None is repellent or indifferent to him. When he goes out to meet the world, his senses are on the alert. When as a writer he reconstitutes a scene, he invokes the memory of odors, tastes, tactile and visual impressions. For him, there is no other life but that of the body; reason is incarnated in it, not dissociated from it. His sensualism is a life principle, a philosophy of pleasure.

Oddly, in describing sex, his style often becomes elusive, precious, or even turgid. He seems to be obeying the advice given him by the prudish Signora F., when he was only twenty years old and she demanded that he tell her his amorous adventures: *Tell, but do not call things by name; that is the main thing.*

The unnamable female organ is designated as the temple of Venus, the sanctuary, the arena, the tomb, the jewel, the delicious "little that." When the Countess de Bonafede invites him to admire her drawing of Adam, whom she has endowed with every single muscle, the young Giacomo assures her that he will prefer her Eve.

—*It is a figure,* she says, where nothing is visible.

—*But it is precisely that nothing that will interest me.*

This "nothing" that arouses him Casanova adorns with vocabulary from the hunt, from architecture, and from the sacred: to go off to conquer the ebony fleece; to catch the tender prey; to get close to the cornice, altar frieze, or church square; to spread the columns apart; to devour love's chamber; to perform the gentle sacrifice . . . Woman faints like a dove; goes from life to death; expires, submerged in voluptuousness. Casanova attributes to the female sex the power of having climaxes twice as often as he. At pleasure's height, the numbers are fabulous: seven male climaxes against fourteen moments of female bliss.

His own sexual organ is called, in turn, lightning, steed, the weapon that wounds to death without taking life, the main agent of humanity, the little fellow (dead or revived), or the masked personage (if clothed in a skin frock coat from England). When he spills his seed, he offers a liqueur, a nectar, a humid radical, the word. But after spending several hours with a beauty who has made him languish, he must "put the country back in equilibrium." When a hand comes to the rescue of virtue or abstinence, he talks about the "manustupration" of a schoolboy. *And without that relief,* says Hedwig, the pretty Genevan theologian, *I read we would have dreadful diseases.* For when they increase, the humors must flow out of the body. Love owes love its recompense.

He is enchanted by the battle between a weakening modesty and the expectation of voluptuousness, yet, though Aretino's thirty-five positions inspire him, he mentions only one, the straight tree position, and the joy of props, the hors d'oeuvres prior to satisfaction, which are set on stage with lightness and insouciance. With M.M. in Venice or, much later, with the two Roman novices Armellina and Emilia, his words celebrate the same feast of the senses:

After making punch we amused ourselves eating oysters, exchanging them when we already had them in our mouths. She gave me hers on her tongue while I brought mine to her lips; there is no more lascivious or voluptuous game between two lovers, it is even comic, but comedy does not spoil anything, for laughter is meant only for the happy. What a sauce, the sauce of an oyster which I suck out of the mouth of the woman I adore! It is her saliva. The power of love can only increase when I crush the oyster and swallow it.

THE INVALID IN SPITE OF HIMSELF, AND THE IMAGINARY DOCTOR

Tall—five feet nine inches—built like a Hercules, a slender and imposing figure, very dark skin, an "African" complexion, a candid face, a head held high, alert wide eyes with a lively and intense gaze, greedy lips: Casanova enjoys vigorous good health until very late in life. *Someone with your heart, your genius, and your stomach is never old*, writes the Prince de Ligne, who knew him when he was advanced in years.

During a walk in the gardens of Sans-Souci with King Frederick II of Prussia, after discussing hydraulic engineering and the theory of taxes, the monarch looks him up and down and says: *You are a very handsome man.*

Casanova is indignant, hurt at being lowered to the rank of someone with a pleasant appearance instead of being praised for his ideas, wit, and intelligence: *Is it possible, sire, that after this long, exclusively scientific disquisition Your Majesty sees in me the most trifling of the qualities that distinguish his grenadiers?*

He does not see himself as handsome "but as having something more valuable," though he "cannot define it": energy perhaps, petulance, youth, health, courage, a witty volubility, feelings of honor, a reputation as a "fine talker," and something in his face that disposes people to regard him favorably. The Greeks, speaking of charm, call it *charis. My great treasure is that I am my own man, I am not dependent on anyone, and I am not afraid of misfortune*, he explains to the singer Teresa, alias Bellino.

His last Venetian mistress, the seamstress Francesca Buschini, writes to him on Wednesday, March 10, 1784: *You are afraid of nothing, not even death.*

Whatever his activity, he lives it to the full: love, dance, sleep, appetite, revenge, gambling, conversation. He is generous with everything he can give, excessive in all his passions. Words, money, sperm, movement—he spares nothing, then suddenly reverts to wiser proportions. After a night of orgies, he restores his strength with long, sound sleep. He makes up for overindulgence by dieting, resting, and abstinence. He knows the laws of equilibrium and the precepts of Hippocratic medicine. He goes from one extreme to the other, aware of the benefits of temperance but unable to resign himself to it. His body lives in a perpetual present, and it has no scars, marks, or wrinkles. His health is his most precious possession, resiliency being indispensable for a life of travel and adventure.

In the morning, when I wake up, I take stock of my physical and mental state, and consider that I am happy; I examine my sensations and perceive them to be so well founded that I do not complain about not mastering them.

In all his self-portraits, he stresses both his satisfactory physical state and his independence, his freedom. He is his own man, primarily because he is in good health and can count on his own strength.

I could not refrain from scrutinizing myself and finding myself happy. I was in perfect health and in my prime, I had no obligations and no need to plan ahead, I was provided with ample funds, dependent on no one, lucky at gambling, and favorably received by the women who interested me.

Casanova must therefore maintain his vigor and physical wellbeing as a duty to himself. Though in love with an impecunious young Florentine dancer, he does not dare undress in her little room, where there is no fire and only one blanket on the bed; he is afraid of catching a cold. He promises to spend the next night with her on condition that she heat the room with a brazier and add another blanket to the bed; he leaves her fifty zecchini for these things.

You have robbed me of my only treasure, my health, the Chevalier de Seingalt complains to young Maton, referring to her "gallant gift whose symptoms were quite nasty."

Having contracted venereal disease several times, he has learned how to recover by following a strict diet of nitrate water for six weeks. He seems to have acquired the rudiments of medicine very young and then refined his knowledge. When he is sick he refrains from transmitting his "incense" to any woman. In describing his seventh venereal illness, contracted in Dresden from a beautiful Hungarian woman, the exiled old man notes, with regret, that he was forever making himself ill when he was in good health, and seeking to regain his vigor when he had lost it:

I succeeded very well and equally at both, and today in that respect I enjoy perfect health, which I would like to ruin again, but age prevents me. The illness which we call the French disease does not shorten life when one knows how to cure it; it merely leaves scars; but one can easily be consoled if one considers they were acquired during pleasure, just as soldiers enjoy regarding the scars from their wounds as evidence of their virtue and sources of their glory.

The pox, gonorrhea, "Celtic humors," or other venereal diseases put their stamp on different periods of his life, marking symbolic passages; they frequently accompany a heartrending separation or put an end to futile amorous desires for an inaccessible woman. Sickness is almost always a way of turning over a new leaf.

He contracts his first love diseases in adolescence, when he parts with childhood and with Venice, his native city. Inexperience drives him to gamble with dreadful scoundrels and to give himself to an "ugly destitute strumpet." He loses everything down to his shirt, and discovers with horror the marks of a shameful disease. Stripped of his resources and his health, Giacomo considers letting himself die. He is in such a sorry state that he does not even have the strength "not to want something." He surrenders to fate; then, regaining hope, he scrupulously follows a strict diet to recover from his illness.

In Corfu, one evening, frustration over the hopelessness of fully conquering the beautiful and haughty Andriana Foscarini drives the twenty-year-old youth into the arms of a clever courtesan. Punishment is quick to follow: three days later, a "burning sensation" warns him that the poison has infected him. A diet is not enough, so he calls upon an old Corfu physician, who cures him in two months. But nothing is the way it was before. Hope of advancement in his military career fades along with the hope of making a Venetian noblewoman fall in love with him. A stage of his life is irretrievably over. Time no longer passes quickly; painful pauses intervene. There is suddenly a before and after. Illness introduces him, against his will, to the passage of time.

Before knowing Melulla I was in good health, I was rich, lucky at cards, wise, liked by everyone and adored by the prettiest woman in the city. When I spoke, everyone sided with me. After knowing this fatal creature I quickly lost health, money, credit, good humor, consideration, wit, and the ability to express myself, for I was no longer persuasive . . . What I found odd was that when people saw I had grown thin and had no money, they no longer showed me the least respect. They did not listen to me when I spoke, or if they did, they found everything I said dull though they would have found it witty if I had still been rich. People avoided me as if my rotten luck were contagious; and perhaps they were right.

Ailments of the body are moments of apprenticeship. They have the bitter and painful taste of loss. Mantua, Parma, Paris, Dresden, Solothurn, Munich, London—his spells of amorous repentance carry the names of the cities where he experiences them during his peregrinations throughout libertine Europe. In his view, London—where he experiences bliss with Pauline and a disastrous entanglement with La Charpillon—marks the beginning of the twilight of his life. At thirty-eight, he feels the onset of death. He leaves England, because he is accused of having delivered a false bill of exchange, in appalling health. The night before crossing the Channel, he is seized with convulsions and a burning fever, complicated by the venereal poison. The physician despairs of saving him. Weak, distressed at running away like a thief, with no future prospects, Casanova experiences an unprecedented physical decline. Thin, ill-looking, sallow, his glands swollen, he enters painfully into the age of full maturity.

Having arrived in the town of Wesel as well as could be expected, he is treated by a Doctor Peipers, one of Boerhaave's disciples, who lodges him in his house and administers the "great remedy" for six weeks—mercury pills, sweat-inducing herbal teas, rigorous diet. When boredom overcomes him, the physician allows him to invite several young girls to do needlework in his room and keep him company. In bed, hidden in a curtained alcove, Casanova slowly recovers. Never has he been so patient and so sensible. *To judge a man, his behavior must be examined when he is healthy and free; ill or in prison he is not the same,* remarks the old man of Dux, driven by illness to take up the pen and recount his past adventures. Illness is a way of restoring a broken equilibrium, of trying to regain one's well-being, a form of creation.

CHANGES IN HUMOR

Casanova recognizes in himself each of the four temperaments in turn: phlegmatic in childhood, sanguine in youth,
bilious in adulthood, melancholic in old age. Four humors for
the four seasons of life. Four fluids: lymph, blood, yellow
bile, black bile. Four parts of the body: head, heart, gallblad-
der, spleen. Four characters: phlegmatic—the cold, moist humor characterized by prostration, lethargy, and lack of
curiosity; sanguine—the hot, moist humor, characterized by
intimacy; bilious—the hot, dry humor, characterized by
voraciousness, passion, and ambition; melancholic—the cold,
dry humor, heavy with sadness, distinguished by having few
desires and movements.

The beginning of his life is an anemic childhood, devoid
of energy and desire. He is deathly pale, nonexistent. First
when bewitched by the gestures and words of an old woman,
then when sent to Padua for a change of air, Giacomo wakens
to the life of the senses and becomes effervescent, craving
to discover all the pleasures and knowledge of which he had
hitherto been deprived. He now becomes a sanguine temperament, responsive, by his own description, "to the attractions of
any voluptuous pleasure, always cheerful, eager to move from
one form of enjoyment to another, and ingenious at inventing
them."

Occasionally, however, a surprising, exceedingly intense pleasure, about which he feels strangely guilty, casts him back into
the great malady of his childhood: hemorrhaging from the nose.
When he is about to find himself alone with a lovely young
peasant woman whom her uncle, an extremely naïve priest, is
unafraid of committing to his care for a day and even a night,
Giacomo is overwhelmed:

I found I was so astonished by this arrangement, which was so unex-
pected and so easily made, that the blood rushed to my head; my nose
bled copiously for a quarter of an hour, which did not frighten me, for
this had already happened to me a long time ago, but did frighten the
priest, who feared a hemorrhage. He went off on his business, saying he
would return at nightfall.

For the Ancients, perfect health depends on the four humors
existing in the right relative proportions of both quality and
quantity, and the combination must be perfect. Disease occurs
when one of the humors exists in too great or too small a quantity
and becomes isolated within the body instead of being mixed
with the others, when heat, cold, dryness, and moistness are no
longer in the proper balance.

Casanova, faithful to Hippocratic medicine, primarily a medicine based on diet intended to maintain or reestablish the equilibrium of the different substances, preserves his well-being by
adapting what he eats to the condition he feels he is in:

In adjusting my nutrition to my constitution, I have always enjoyed
good health; and having learned that what impairs it is always an
excess of food or abstinence, I have never had any other physician but
myself.

He likes to show that he is dependent on no one, especially
not on professionals; when at times he has to call on them, he
makes a point of representing them as dangerous charlatans. He
wants to show he is perfectly capable of doing without their
services so long as he practices a few simple principles of hy-
giene. His father's death, for which he blames Doctor Zambelli,
has given him the desire to exercise the healing art. He confides
as much at the very beginning of his *History of My Life:*

My vocation was to study medicine so that I could practice a profession for which I felt a strong inclination, but no one listened to me; they wanted me to study law, for which I felt an insurmountable aversion. It was maintained that I could make my fortune only by becoming a lawyer, and still worse, an ecclesiastical lawyer, because they believed I had a gift for speaking. If they had given it more thought, they would have satisfied my wish by letting me become a physician, a profession where charlatanism is even more effective than in law . . . I never wanted to employ lawyers when I happened to have legal claims in court, or summon physicians when I was sick . . . People who die at the hand of doctors are far more numerous than those who are cured.

The Chevalier de Seingalt enjoys recounting the episodes in his life when he supplanted several physicians by publicly proving their incompetence. Nothing delights him more than making people laugh at their expense. The doctor is a preposterous authority figure who must be flouted, overthrown, and triumphed over, resoundingly and uninhibitedly. After a picnic in Schönbrunn, bad indigestion brings him to the edge of the grave in less than twenty-four hours and gives him a chance to tell a tragicomic story in which he is the hero. A physician summoned by a well-meaning friend appears at his bedside:

This physician, thinking he was free to exercise the despotism of his art, had sent for a surgeon and they were about to bleed me against my will and without my consent. Half dead, I don't know what inspired me to open my eyes and see the man with the lancet about to pierce my vein. No, no, I said, and languidly drew back my arm; but the doctor claimed that the executioner was going to make me live despite myself, and I see my arm being grasped. I quickly reached for one of the two pistols which I had on my night table and I fired on the man who had sworn to obey the doctor. The bullet unraveled a curl in his hair, and that was enough to make the surgeon, the physician, and everyone who was by my bedside leave. The maid was the only one not to abandon me, and she gave me water to drink whenever I asked for it, and in four days I was in perfect health. This story became known throughout Vienna, and Friar Grossatesta assured me that if I had killed him nothing would have happened to me, for two gentlemen who were present had been witnesses that I was about to be bled by force. Furthermore, everyone told me that physicians in Vienna were saying that if I had been bled I would have died. It is true, however, that I had to beware of falling ill, for no physician would have dared call on me ever again. This incident was the talk of the town. I went to the Opera, and many people wanted to make my acquaintance; I was seen as a man who had defended himself from death by firing a pistol at it.

Where did he acquire such self-confidence, such calm assurance? How can he bet on his own life this way and risk dying? Is this the sangfroid of a gambler who knows how to take calculated risks? Or is he motivated by the fear of being bled, cut, and wounded in his bodily integrity? Is this the conviction of an experienced person who has often suffered indigestion and collected reliable remedies in response to the trials of life? Or does he have enough medical knowledge to know what he is talking about? Another suggestive story shows that while all these suppositions may be valid, when it comes to this eighteenth-century man, infinitely curious about everyone and everything, the last is as plausible as any other.

"I WAS THE MASTER OF MY HAND"

The scene takes place in Warsaw, on March 5, 1766. At the
theater, two rival women are performing, La Binetti and La Ca-
tai; the nobility has its favorites. Casanova tries to make a quiet
exit, but a Polish courtier calls him a "Venetian coward." Honor
demands he respond; the duel will take place in a green arbor
outside the city. As he prepares, Casanova orders a tasty meal
and drinks some excellent Burgundy to put himself in good spirits. The two men fight with pistols. The news appears in the
papers and becomes known throughout Europe:

*Last Tuesday, Count Branicki, Podstoli [Chamberlain] to the Crown,
fought an unexpected duel with the famous Venetian gentleman Casanova, who has been living here for several months. The duel took place
at Wola. Mr. Casanova's abdomen was grazed by a bullet and his left
hand wounded; but Count Branicki, though still alive, has a bullet
lodged in his body; the former, for his safety, has taken refuge in a
convent.*

Casanova describes with precision how the bullet wounded
his opponent: it entered his stomach at the seventh true rib on
the right and exited under the last false rib on the left. The two
holes were ten inches apart; the sight was alarming; the intes-
tines were thought to be pierced and his life in danger. As for
his own wound, he describes it with equal precision:

*Branicki's bullet had entered my hand through the metacarpus under
the index; it broke my first phalanx and remained lodged there; its force
had been weakened by a metal button on my jacket, and by my abdomen,
which had been slightly wounded by it near the navel.*

The first surgeon to be found removes the bullet. During this clumsily performed operation, Casanova tells the princes who had come to see him what had happened. The whole court is agitated. The King, though extremely alarmed by his uncle's condition, promises to pardon Casanova should Branicki die.

On the fourth day my badly swollen arm and my wound, which had become black and threatened gangrene, made the surgeons decide, after consulting among themselves, that my hand had to be cut off. I learned this odd news early in the morning by reading the court gazette, which was printed at night after the King had approved the text. This made me laugh heartily. I laughed in the faces of all those who came in the morning to express their sympathy to me.

Three surgeons appear at his bedside.

—*Why three of you, gentlemen?*

—*Because before resorting to amputation I wanted to have the consent of these professors. We shall presently see what condition you are in.*

He lifts the splint, pulls out the drain, examines the wound, its color and the livid swelling; they speak among themselves in Polish, then all three of one mind tell me in Latin that they will cut off my hand at nightfall. They are all three cheerful; they tell me I have nothing to fear and that thanks to this I could be sure of my recovery. I reply that I am the master of my hand and that I will never allow them to perform this ridiculous amputation.

—*Gangrene has set in and tomorrow it will make its way up the arm and then we will have to cut off the arm.*

—*Good. You will cut off my arm, but in the meanwhile, from what I know of gangrene, I have seen none in me.*

—*You are not more knowledgeable in this matter than we are.*

—*Go away.*

Visitors rally round the rebellious patient; the King is surprised by his lack of courage. Furious, Casanova writes the sovereign an impertinent letter calling all doctors ignoramuses and executioners; he says that he would not know what to do with his arm without his hand but he will let his arm be cut off when the gangrene becomes visible. The letter is read to everyone at court. The foreigner's conviction is surprising and shocking: how could the three best surgeons in Warsaw be mistaken? *To curry favor with Count Branicki, who is very ill and might need this consolation in order to recover,* he replies, as clever in seeing into the hearts of men as in protecting his body from the executioner.

In the evening, four surgeons come to examine his arm, which is now twice its normal size. Casanova, who obviously has the sharp eye of a medical observer, notes: *I see it is livid to the elbow; but when the drain is lifted from the wound, I see it is red at the edges, and I see a substance: I say nothing.*

He is secretly convinced that his arm is healing. Tired of arguing, he agrees to having the surgeons return the next day to amputate the limb; the news spreads, everyone rejoices, but he summons Prince Sulkowski's French surgeon, who, finding the wound not gangrenous, prevents the operation from taking place. *So ended the story. I kept my hand,* the old man proudly concludes, still amused by this valorous recollection.

To make his triumph perfectly clear to all, on Easter Sunday, Casanova goes to Mass at the court church with his arm in a sling. *My firmness did me immortal honor, and the surgeons had to acknowledge that they were all either completely ignorant or very imprudent.*

LOVE AS DOCTOR

The Venetian is not afraid of disease. The body—and not just where love is concerned—sharpens his curiosity and his thirst for knowledge. Medicine and alchemy, unclearly demarcated, fulfill his urge to heal and the dream of omnipotence which he has never surrendered. Even as a child, he does not balk at approaching his first love, the coquette Bettina, when she is covered with smallpox pustules. She looks ghastly—head swollen, sunken nose and eyes and a puffy face, her shriveled pimples turning black, suppurating, and infecting the air—but Casanova the child stays by her side without flinching, despite her foul-smelling perspiration and his fear of seeing her die.

In the course of his very first trip, he meets a man who is subject to uncontrollable laughter and fears he will die of it, like one of his uncles. The young man quizzes him: *Death by laughing?*

—*Yes. This illness which was unknown to Hippocrates is called* li flati.

—*What do you mean? The hypochondriac affections, which make everyone else sad, make you cheerful?*

—*But my flati, instead of affecting my hypochondrium, affect my spleen, which, according to my physician, is the organ of laughter. It is a new discovery.*

—*Not at all. It is actually a very old idea*, replies Giacomo, confident of his facts.

How did he acquire this knowledge, these rudiments of medical knowledge? From reading Greek and Latin texts? From associating, during his stay at the Sant'Andrea fortress, with a Spagyrist physician, practitioner of a hermetic medicine developed by Paracelsus? Or from some other source? Casanova does not say. Going from self-healing, which he practices at a very early age, to wanting to heal others is tempting for one who dreams of being a son of Aesculapius. Particularly if the patient is unusually pretty and the apprentice-physician is in love with her and ready to administer himself as a medication. When Signora F. sustains a deep gash on her ankle, her suitor feels her leg, making sure there are no hard lumps and that her thigh is not red. *I licked her wound,* he recalls, *firmly believing that my tongue would anoint it; but the chambermaid's return compelled me to put an end to this sweet remedy, which my love as doctor had made me believe was infallible at that moment.*

The first truly extraordinary healing scene takes places a short time later, in Venice. By chance, and thanks to his foolhardiness (had he been a mere amateur), he is given the opportunity to save the life of a senator of the old Venetian nobility. His determination to contradict the prescriptions of a licensed physician cannot be explained by common sense alone, nor the ease with which he replaces the physician in curing the patrician of his apoplexy. With his talents confirmed by success, the young Casanova starts to enjoy them. He dons the mantle of a professional, like a character in Molière.

Now I had become the physician of one of the illustrious members of the Venetian senate. I was truly delighted. I then told the patient that all he needed was a proper diet and that Nature would see to the rest over the summer months, which were drawing near . . . The patient was feeling better every day [and] listened to me as though I were an oracle. His two astonished friends lent me the same attention. Emboldened by this subservience, I spoke as a physician, dogmatized, and cited authors whom I had never read.

As on a great number of occasions in his life, Casanova takes advantage of chance circumstance to show that he has as much cheek as intellect and charm, and to discover a talent he was unaware of. He feels he owes his success to his bold, enterprising spirit, his sound reasoning ability, and his interlocutors' secret desire to see him play this role. Eighteenth-century European nobles, infatuated with cleverness and rationalism, are also readily amused by superstitious games and the abstract sciences. Senator Bragadin, filled with wonder at this young violinist's medical talents, ascribes occult powers to his new protégé: *You possess a treasure and you alone can decide whether to take full advantage of it.*

Giacomo Casanova thus gains from a benevolent paternal, not to say obliging, figure permission to combine medicine and alchemy, scientific knowledge and superstition. He immediately makes the most of it: *I congratulate myself on possessing something which I had not appreciated until now, but which I would value in the future, since it could make me useful to Their Excellencies.*

In Paris, the Duchess of Chartres asks the young Venetian (who is madly in love with her but never dares declare it) to use his talents to cure her of her unsightly, disfiguring pimples. After a cabalistic calculation, the oracle prescribes a diet and a purge, forbids all ointments, but recommends the use of plantain water morning and evening. When the Count de La Tour d'Auvergne is wounded in the thigh in a duel, he administers an amalgam of nitrate, flower of sulfur, mercury, and a small amount of fresh urine. He pronounces a magic spell as he applies the mixture and traces a five-pointed Star of Solomon on the wound. The Count, soon back on his feet, sings the praises of his healer, whom he then introduces to his aunt, the famous Marquise d'Urfé. What Casanova regarded as mere "farce" leads to collaboration with a "giddy" woman infatuated with alchemy and ready to do anything to attain "supreme knowledge."

More prosaically, he returns the hues of health to a young

Venetian who has lost her monthly "benefits"; spends a night by the bedside of the dancer La Denis when she suffers convulsions; assists Charlotte during childbirth, and then cares for her day and night as a fever takes her to the grave in a week.

Medical science interests him; it is the subject of many conversations in the course of his travels. With Tadini, in Warsaw, Casanova delves into ophthalmological questions—in particular, corneal lens implants for the treatment of cataracts. With Doctor Algardi, physician to the Prince-Bishop of Augsburg, he discusses whether a physician should tell his patient the truth or lie in order to spare him knowledge that might further shorten his life. *You practice a wicked profession*, he concludes.

At the end of his life, he enters into a polemic with the practitioner who is caring for him in his Bohemian exile concerning the anatomy of the digestive system. (A sixteen-page manuscript among his papers in Dux is entitled: *Letters of a Ubiquitous Scholar Addressed to Doctor O'Reilly, Irish Physician.*) Casanova displays great learning in anatomy and physiology, as well as sound clinical reasoning; to give weight to his argument, he makes the doctor suppose that he himself was afflicted with the illness in question:

You are free to believe, sir, that anatomical questions are irrelevant to useful medicine—the latter being founded only on experience, knowledge of a patient's temperament, and very simple remedies properly administered—and free to treat anything else as a pure curiosity and sometimes as quackery. But you must honestly admit that if you were sick with a persistent diarrhea for three years, you would not readily submit to a physician who would not know the canal through which your food must first pass before being reduced by your stomach to chyle and excrements and conveyed to the pylorus, then to the duodenum, and finally to the rectum, after having moved through the jejunum, the ileum, the cecum, and the colon.

Eager to be cured of your diarrhea, you would not want a doctor who would be ignorant of the process of digestion which the Ancients called chylopoiesis. Such a physician could only cure you as an empiric, and as you know, the word empiric is often synonymous with charlatan.

THE PLAY OF APPEARANCES

The body does not merely consist of internal organs, effusions, and suffering. It involves primarily the quest for pleasure and social appearance. Casanova refuses to accept anatomy as destiny. For him, sexual difference implies no barrier. Both sexes have a gift for pleasure, and both are capable of reasoning. Woman is no more a prisoner to her uterus than man is a prisoner to his sperm. In his pamphlet disputing two Bolognese doctors, *Lana Caprina*, he breaks with the prejudices of his time by asserting: *When their uterus is active, women are agitated, irritable, and deserving of pity. But that this influences the source of their faculty for thought is no more credible than that sperm influences the nature of the soul.*

It is true that women endure "the discomforts of bleeding at the full moon" and the "burdens of motherhood," but added to this female condition are, more important, the weight of upbringing and the "despotism" of men. For Casanova, an adventurer who has suffered mysteriously sudden, unexplained bleeding spells since childhood, the common destiny of man and woman is obvious. It is essential to an appetite for pleasure devoid of shame and hatred. In the games of love, he desires free and inquiring women who, like him, delight in amorous sensual pleasures. And since these contain no mystery for him, the "emptiness" of the female sexual organ never frightens him; on the contrary, he fills (and fulfills) it.

Tiresias, the arbiter in Jupiter and Juno's quarrel over which of the two sexes experiences the most pleasure, declared it was the female sex. Casanova reopens the age-old discussion and considers the argument that says "woman's pleasure must be greater since the feast takes place in her own house," and finds it inadequate. More convincing to him is that since women are subject to many evils which men are spared, they deserve to be compensated by a pleasure which is at least equal, if not superior, to their pains:

The pleasure I have felt when the woman I loved made me happy was certainly great, but I know I would not have wanted it if, to obtain it, I had had to incur the risk of pregnancy. Women take the risk even after experiencing pregnancy several times; therefore, they must feel that the pleasure is worth the pain.

Though he is prepared to concede that the sexes are equal, and even that the female sex is superior in its ability to enjoy much greater sexual pleasure than the male sex, he who likes to play on sexual ambiguity is nonetheless unwilling to give up being a man:

After all this inquiry, I ask myself if I would want to be reborn as a woman and, apart from curiosity, I say no. I have enough other pleasures as a man, which I could not have as a woman, which make me prefer my sex to the other. However, I admit that to have the extraordinary privilege of being reborn, I would be happy, and commit myself, particularly today, to being reborn not only as a woman but as a beast of any species—provided, of course, that I be reborn with my memory, he hastily adds, *for without my memory it would no longer be me.*

Both man and woman, face to face, adorned, powdered, perfumed, wearing valuable fabrics and glittering jewels, stand ready to seduce each other: it is only after the French Revolution that men wear mourning clothes. Cosmetics hold no secrets for Casanova. He leaves beauty spots, white powder, rouge, black mascara, and eyeliner to women, but he uses pomades, scented waters—rosewater on his handkerchief—and *poudre à la maréchale* (a variety of strongly perfumed, white hair powder), and before going to bed at night, he asks his valet to set his hair in curlpaper. He vividly remembers a very gentle and amusing old man—a French Chevalier to whom he was introduced by the Marquise d'Urfé—who used rouge on his aged, quivering cheeks, who wore a large bouquet of tuberoses and daffodils in the upper buttonhole of his coat jacket, and whose hairpiece (and eyebrows and teeth) exuded such a strong scent of ambergris that Casanova found social intercourse with him trying.

His trunk of undergarments follows him everywhere; every morning he expects to find a shirt, a waistcoat, a collar, underpants, and two handkerchiefs washed and ironed. The Venetian knows the code and protocol governing how to dress under different circumstances. He dresses in black for his conversation with King Frederick II of Prussia and for his first meeting with Leopold, Grand Duke of Tuscany. Black is worn to indicate that a person is either not wealthy or unwilling to mix with "high society." When he goes before King George III of England, by contrast, he dresses elegantly. The first time he goes to the Italian theater in Paris, wearing his fine coat jacket, the young Casanova realizes immediately that he stands out as a foreigner, for open sleeves and buttons all the way down to the bottom are out of fashion. This will not happen to him again. For the adventurer and social chameleon, clothes make the man. The body's appearance is his first visiting card. Man is judged by his demeanor, by the outward trappings of wealth: finery, jewelry, coach, servants. In his *History of My Life*, the memoirist is very attentive to these details. He places every protagonist—particularly himself—in a setting, a situation, a conversation, and, first of all, a costume. A person's social role, the rank he claims in good company, depends directly on his attire. Casanova learns this very early in life through his mother—so beautiful and so upset by a wig that clashed with his complexion and eyebrow color. The lesson has left its mark. A person's first and best letter of recommendation is his demeanor and dress.

As a young ecclesiastic of fifteen received in Venice's polite society at the Palazzo Malipiero, in the midst of "fashionable" ladies who make him want to cut an attractive and elegant figure, Giacomo is reprimanded by the San Samuele parish priest, and his grandmother agrees: *He condemned my studied curls and the delicate fragrance of my pomade: he told me that the devil held me by the hair.* Friar Casanova, never at a loss for words, replies that there are a hundred clergy roaming the streets of Venice with three times more powder on their hair than he, who uses but a touch of it, and they apply a pomade perfumed with ambergris that would make a woman in labor faint, while his has the fragrance of jasmine and brings him compliments from all quarters. We know the sequel; when his young protégé is asleep, Tosello mercilessly cuts off his pretty hair.

At nineteen, after being sent away from Rome by Cardinal Acquaviva, he decides to exchange his cassock for a martial outfit, and he has one made in Bologna: *On reflecting that it no longer seemed likely I could make my fortune in an ecclesiastical capacity, I decided to dress as a soldier in an invented uniform.*

He asks for a good tailor, chooses among fabric samples, and orders a white uniform with a blue vest, a gold-and-silver shoulder knot, and a sword knot of the same colors. He is now ready to "impersonate a disciple of Mars" and impress the whole city. He enjoys playing the impostor, assuming the false identity of an officer. He moves from his obscure inn to a quality hotel, Al Pellegrino, and makes an appearance at the Gran Caffè with what he feels is appropriate haughtiness; then he strolls under the arcades and along the promenade. He arrives in Venice a short time later with the intention of embarking for Constantinople in his country's service. When he goes to visit Abbot Grimani, the latter is surprised to see him in military attire and disbelieves his account of his peregrinations. *I could bear insults when I practiced the profession of humility, but today I practice the profession of honor,* he replies in outrage.

Casanova likes to play with appearances. For him, life is a perpetual carnival. When he wears a military disguise, he puffs out his chest; when he is pressed by circumstance—once he wanted to enter Rimini incognito because he had lost his passport—he skillfully assumes the look of a nobody: it is raining, Giacomo is wearing silk stockings; he needs a carriage, he stops in a chapel doorway to wait for the rain to stop, suddenly he sees forty laden mules pass by; he puts his hand on one of them and, walking slowly by its side, enters the city of Rimini. *With my hair under a nightcap, my hat turned down, my nice cane hidden under my reversed redingote, I looked like a nobody.*

If he wants to appear to be of modest means, he puts away his diamonds, when he has any, in his casket and introduces himself with no sign of wealth. When he is less well off, he is eager to maintain the bearing of a gentleman, but regrets it. At forty-six, he feels he has aged. More and more often, women prefer his younger rivals. His thinks of study more than of love. Since leaving England, he takes delight in the *Iliad* for an hour or two every day. He considers translating it from Greek into Italian stanzas.

On leaving Rome I had seven or eight hundred Roman scudi and jewelry that included watches, snuffboxes, and pretty rings, none particularly valuable, which did me more harm than good, for they made people think I was rich, and ambition compelled me to spend in a way that would show that they were not wrong. Knowledge of this truth made me take the wise decision of appearing in Florence in simple attire and with no display of wealth.

On April 24, 1760, Casanova pawns some personal effects having a value of eighty louis d'or at the Zurich shopkeeper J. Escher's, under the name of Chevalier de Seingalt. The pawnbroker's document has come down to us:

I the undersigned promise that as soon as I am given eighty French louis d'or by order of M. le Chr. de Seingalt, I will give to the person who disburses the money a blue coat jacket lined with ermine with a white embroidered satin waistcoat and trousers, plus a coat jacket, waistcoat, and trousers in four-color velvet, a guipure muff, a varnished toothpick case with gold decorations, two muslin shirts trimmed with narrow lace cuffs, a pair of English lace cuffs, a ring bearing a seal of arms, a Hercules seal, another Galba seal, another representing a Roman chariot, a two-sided seal representing two heads, another seal having a compass on one side and a head on the other. A small gold gusset, a gold charm representing two legs, a charm representing three towers, a rock-crystal flask mounted in gold and enameled, a rock-

crystal candy box mounted in gold, a gold box, a knife with a gold and steel blade, an amethyst needle surrounded with small carats, a gold screwdriver. All these effects are held by me.

This is the way Giacomo Girolamo Casanova appeared—Arcadian shepherd under the pseudonym of Eupolemo Pantaxeno, cabalist under the name of Paralis or Paralisée Galtinarde, traveler under the name of Count Kasanow de Farussi or Chevalier de Seingalt, Venetian.

EIGHT

Happiness Regained

CASANOVA, PHILOSOPHER

(We are in a castle in Bohemia, in a room two stories above the stables, in the building at the entrance to the castle's main courtyard, opposite the church. The furnishings include a bed with a toile canopy, a chest of drawers, a writing desk covered with a shiny cloth, a black night table, a big armchair, a music stand, a set of majolica writing implements, and a mirror.)

Casanova daydreams as he sits in front of the window, pen in hand. He reflects on the pain of aging. He foresees his impending death, a thought that grieves him, for he loves life with all his heart and is deeply attached to the life of the senses. True, he can reassure himself, he still has a ravenous appetite; but he is no longer the garden deity, the joyful and generous lover, fertilizing his fair mistresses with words and presents. It is only thanks to his numerous literary works and his correspondence with several wise men that he is still the gentleman with encyclopedic curiosity who used to hold forth in courts and salons—on theology and medicine, taxes and the lottery, cotton growing and mining, the arts and princely genealogies, reform of the Gregorian calendar and literary criticism.

Confined to his room, alone in front of his worktable for hours every day, Casanova copies and recopies his last manuscript, tirelessly. He polishes his work in his neat, precise handwriting, complicating the densely written pages with infinite variants. His former ardor and feverishness guide his hand and flow from his lively pen onto the paper, full of deletions and changes. With a patience he did not know he had, he sometimes reworks his prose as much as fourteen times. He has dreams of immortality in literary Europe. *Forty-two volumes of my opuscules have demonstrated to Italy that I am not a toad in Apollo's quagmire*, he proudly proclaims.

The indefatigable adventurer can no longer sit at the gaming table for entire nights at a time—he is short on money and ruining himself to publish his writings—or make speeches in blasphemous verse in the cafés of his lost homeland, or seduce a beautiful unknown woman by dancing the furlane twelve times in a row without losing his breath. The elderly Giacomo no longer wears a mask on his face. The carnival came to a halt at the castle gate.

The past wasted and crumbled away; nothing is left of it, or so little—scattered notes taken as the years went by, a few rough drafts of letters, and the weariness of constantly retelling the same heroic episodes of his life. His petulance, his escapades, his mad lavishness, everything has escaped from the great kaleidoscope of time, like thousands of glass fragments scattered on the ground, lost forever, purloined from the whirlwind of life.

Can it be that the child of Venice has already become an old man? How did the metamorphosis occur? Leaping from one moment of pure present to another direct sense-impression, Giacomo Casanova never ceased making light of time passing, of time lasting; he rejected it, denied it, with constancy and obstinacy. He maintained this illusion of omnipotence as long as he could. Now he is furious, despondent, and thinks he is going mad: old age is odious to him. Faced with confinement, madness, and despair, he knows but a single remedy, a single recourse: philosophy.

Interior dialogues, during which he sought to calm his ardors by reverting to his inner self, were familiar to him long before he deepened them through writing. He knows that a person who is strong enough to refrain from taking any steps until he has reached composure has attained wisdom. Hence, in a moment particularly damaging to his self-esteem, when he finds he is impotent in the arms of the beautiful Véronique, he resorts to reflection in order to regain some serenity:

Unable to fall asleep I tried to console myself with physico-metaphysical analyses pleading in favor of my senses so I would have strong reason for complaining only of myself. When I had finished I felt satisfied. Satisfied to find myself guilty! Strange satisfaction, but the only one which can bring cheer to a philosopher overcome by misfortune.

In choosing between fate and freedom, Casanova rejects the path of tragedy. To reconcile the power of personal will with the force of destiny, he makes himself responsible for his misfortunes and attributes his good fortune to Providence. The reverse would be unbearable. He cannot conceive that Fortune, which has taken on the magical silhouette of the mother figure seen on the night following the witchcraft in Murano, might be harmful or intentionally evil to him. He refuses to believe in the idea of a malevolent destiny. If fortune exists, it can only be good. Life's setbacks, failures, limits set on unbridled desire, disappointments fall within the province of individual freedom. Casanova stands by his existence, fully in harmony with it:

No unhappy thing has ever happened to me in my life that was not my own fault, and I attribute nearly all the good fortune I have had to coincidences; which in truth is a bit unjust and humiliating; but such is man. I would go mad, I believe, if in my soliloquies I would find I am unhappy without its being my own fault, for I would not know where to find fault unless I were to admit I am stupid. I know I am not stupid.

Casanova reconciles fatalism and freedom all the more easily for being unafraid of suffering and accepting responsibility for his own suffering when it occurs. He blames no one, certainly not some decree of heaven, for his errors and disappointments. He prefers to believe he is the protégé-son of a benevolent, motherly Providence, and a man free to go astray and make mistakes.

Though throughout his life he has proclaimed his freedom energetically, on getting old he questions, in a rare moment of avowed discouragement, what he has always claimed as his most prized possession and wonders suddenly if it is not simply an illusion, a phantom:

It is an unquestionable fact that a noble soul will never believe it might not be free. And yet who is free in this hell which we call the world? No one. Only the philosopher can be free, but due to sacrifices that may not be worth the phantom freedom.

Yet the idea of being reduced to a plaything of destiny is too painful for him to accept. Casanova is a man of action. His experience of imprisonment under the lead roofs of the Ducal Palace and his extraordinary, spectacular escape through sheer will taught him that man is required to try the impossible. The prospects of someone who is strong enough to take responsibility for his desires always remain wide open.

We are the authors of our so-called destiny . . . If the fatalists are obliged, by their own system, to consider as necessary, a parte ante [a priori], the concatenation of all events, nothing remains of man's moral freedom; and in that case he is neither worthy nor blameworthy. I cannot in good conscience think of myself as a machine.

Old age and bitterness fail to undermine his fundamental optimism. To the melancholy that overcomes him sometimes, when the castle is shrouded in fog and the flunkies escalate their harassment of him, he opposes a pronounced taste for happiness:

Those who say that life is merely a collection of misfortunes really mean that life itself is a misfortune. If it is a misfortune, then death is a joy. Those people do not write in good health, though their purses may be bulging with gold, or with contentment in their souls, having just had Cecilias and Marinas in their arms and being assured of having others in the future. They are a race of pessimists (excuse me, my dear French language) that can have existed only among roguish philosophers and mischievous or atrabilious theologians. If pleasure exists, and if we can enjoy it only in life, then life is a joy. Of course, misfortunes also exist; I am certainly in a position to know. But the very existence of these misfortunes proves that the quantity of good is greater. I very much like being in a dark room and seeing light through a window that looks out on a wide expanse.

True, the elderly Casanova no longer holds Marinas and Cecilias in his arms, but the voluptuous reminiscence of those happy moments now gone forever remains intact in his mind. Only death can make him lose those dear recollections. His familiar enemy has not won the game yet. As an old gambler accustomed to betting on chance, in a last double or quits he plays the card of resurrecting the past. He makes his adventurous youth march across the stage of memory. Through the magic of a writing which restores the grain of life, the exiled Venetian revives his past happiness.

Throughout his account of his life, Casanova sees himself as a free man, the master of his history, and if he admits that some things escape him, the judgment is nonetheless favorable. He makes no claim to wisdom, much less to morality. He knows he is the victim of his senses and his passions. His only rule of conduct, if it is one, has been always to go where the wind blew him.

This is his way of interpreting the Stoics' *Sequere Deum*. He does not believe in the schooling based on sermons, precepts, and tales given him by his educators. The theory of morals, he writes with irony, is of no more usefulness to the life of man than the *benefit someone gets scanning the index of a book before reading it; when he has read it, all he knows is the subject matter.* Good stems from evil just as misfortune arises from prudence and moderation. Misfortunes and joys are not distributed according to merits and errors; they escape the logic of moralists.

In a long page where he discusses the ways of Fortune, Casanova admits he is superstitious, even though the thought humiliates him. It seems natural to him that a divinity whom we call blind *should do with a man who submits to her whims the same thing a little child does when he pushes an ivory globe up and down a billiard table just so he can laugh when it falls into the pocket.* On the other hand, he opposes the idea that Fortune proceeds with a man *the way an expert billiard player proceeds with a ball, calculating the force, speed, distance, and levelness of reaction.* The man who lives for the moment, who throws himself avidly into a life of the senses, cannot tolerate the idea that fate may be an expert geometrician. Yet he has to admit that, at certain crucial moments in his life, chance circumstances seem to take on the appearance of divine fortune, sometimes favorable, sometimes unfavorable. As though this female destiny wanted to impress upon him that his will, far from proclaiming him free, was merely an instrument which she used to do with him *whatever she pleased.* Is she right, or is he? Facing Providence, is he an innocent little child or an expert player? What does she want from me? is the question he seems to ask all his life, and though it is addressed to the blindfolded goddess, the shadow of the distant and enigmatic Zanetta looms nearby. For Casanova, if God exists, She is female.

He prefers to acknowledge his escapades and waywardness without blushing or making confession. Worse yet: he likes to stray from the straight and narrow. In setting down the "history of my life" he is not writing confessions, nor is he repenting; he is asserting the right to his way of life. In a letter of February 20, 1792, to Johann Ferdinand Opiz, he writes:

The more the work progresses, the more I am convinced that it deserves to be burned . . . The cynicism I have introduced into it is excessive and oversteps the limits which propriety has set on indiscretion. But you would not believe how much it amuses me. I have realized, without blushing, that I love myself more than anyone . . . I tell all, sparing no pains, and yet, as a man of honor, I cannot entitle my memoirs Confessions, for I am repentant about nothing, and without repentance, as

*you know, absolution is impossible. You will think I am boasting? Not
at all. I narrate openly to make myself laugh.*

Laughter prevails, as always with him, over the morality of the
fearful and foolish, over the censorious authority figure who is
upset at the slightest coarse word, over the self-righteous who
fear the offensive truth and insolent freedom. Quite determined
not to publish the history of his life during his lifetime, the
elderly man laughs at the last good joke he reserves for posterity.

ACT II, SCENE 10

The scene takes place in Prague, at the Villa Bertramka, the
house of the soprano Josepha Duschek and her husband. It is
October 1787. Mozart, among joyful and agitated friends, puts
off completing his *Don Giovanni*. Lorenzo Da Ponte, the author
of the libretto, has just been summoned back to Vienna by Emperor Joseph II. The rehearsals are not going well, the words
and the music still need work, and the overture has yet to be
composed. The friendly group locks Mozart up in his room to
force him to complete the missing parts of the score. One evening, a guest passing through town, a Freemason like Mozart
and, like him, a Chevalier in the Papal Order of the Golden
Spur, joins the pleasant company. He recounts some episodes
from his adventurous life and sets some dialogue down on paper.
Two days later, on October 29, 1787, he attends the first performance of the opera.

Among the thousands of manuscript pages found at the Dux

castle after Casanova's death are two interchangeable variants, in rough draft, of scene 10, Act II, of *Don Giovanni*. In the first, Casanova portrays Leporello not as a coward trembling with terror but as an impudent, cocky character despite his fear:

LEPORELLO [*caught wearing Don Giovanni's costume*]: Indecisive, upset, unmasked, betrayed. Cannot justify myself. Implore forgiveness.

DONNA ELVIRA, DON OTTAVIO, MASETTO, ZERLINA: Impossible to forgive you!

LEPORELLO: My calamitous fate depends on you alone. My trembling heart awaits mercy from you.

ZERLINA: I'll eat your guts.

MASETTO: Devour your brain.

DON OTTAVIO: Pilloried and hanged.

DONNA ELVIRA: You must be pulled down a peg or two.

ALL FOUR *(together)*: Loathsome traitor!

LEPORELLO: On you alone . . .

ALL FOUR *(together)*: To the scaffold!

LEPORELLO: Woe is me: what a horrible death!

ALL FOUR *(together)*: To the galleys!

LEPORELLO: Rowing, exhaustion, a terribly hard life!

ALL FOUR *(together)*: Go sweep up the square!

LEPORELLO: I am of an illustrious race!

ALL FOUR *(together)*: Then let him know hard labor!

LEPORELLO: Oh, no, my lords, have mercy on me!

ALL FOUR *(together)*: What should we do about this deceitful impostor?

LEPORELLO: On you alone . . . (*He runs away.*)

In the second variant, Casanova, under the guise of Leporello, accuses women of being responsible for Don Giovanni's evil deeds:

LEPORELLO: Don Giovanni alone forced this disguise on me. He is the sole cause of so many sorrows. I deserve forgiveness. I myself am not guilty. The blame lies entirely with the female sex for bewitching his mind and enslaving his heart. Oh, seducing sex! Source of pain! Let a poor innocent person go in peace. I am not a rebel, I would never want to offend you and I will prove to you as much: it is he who exchanged suits, he who took my clothes to beat Masetto with a stick. With Donna Elvira I only obeyed orders, such was his will. What I say is true. Don Giovanni alone deserves your anger. I will go punish the unworthy one. Let me go. (*He runs away.*)

Did Mozart use the suggestions of his Venetian guest to put the finishing touches on Da Ponte's libretto?

DON GIACOMO

In his Bohemian retreat, Casanova hesitates for a long time before writing the three thousand seven hundred or so pages of the manuscript for his *Histoire de Jacques Casanova de Seingalt, Vénitien, écrite par lui-même à Dux, en Bohême.* During his last stay in Venice, in 1780, he published, in Italian, the story of his famous duel with the Polish nobleman Franciszek Branicki, and, seven years later, in Prague and in French, an account of his escape from "the prisons of the Republic of Venice which are called The Leads." He does not consider writing about other episodes in his life, in spite of his friends' insistence. He prefers to lose himself in some mathematical problems, and he attempts the *Solution to the Delos Problem*, then tries his hand at the *Corollary to the Duplication of the Hexahedron* and at the *Geometrical Demonstration of the Duplication of the Cube*. He moves heaven and earth in order to have his calculations recognized by the scholarly authorities. *The Soliloquy of a Thinker*, a work in which he takes on Cagliostro and the adventurers of his day, occupies him for a time. Then he begins a lengthy critique of the works of Bernardin de Saint-Pierre. He works on his *History of Unrest in Poland*, of which he has already published three volumes; then he writes eighteen philosophical dialogues, *The Philosopher and the Theologian*, tries his hand at plays and poems, and writes a *Critical Essay on Morals, the Sciences, and the Arts* and *Musings on the Mean Measurement of Time According to the Gregorian Reform*.

In a letter of April 15, 1785, to his friend Count Max Lamberg, Casanova describes the preparation of a long utopian novel for which he expects to reap glory:

Three years ago in Venice, displeased with everything, I suddenly had the fantasy of setting myself up as a creature of a new world, of a new human race, a new code of civil laws, a good religion, another way of providing food and lodgings, of living together and engendering fellow creatures, and I saw myself obtaining the approval of the whole world, everyone feeling obliged to say, after reading my work, Oh! happy world ... At the end of this work, which will be divided into two volumes in 8°, each 500 pages long, I will say as Ovid did about his Metamorphoses: *Here is a work that will vault me to immortality. I have written two-thirds, but I am making brisk progress and I will hand it in in a year.*

The writing of this bulky novel takes him two years. *Icosa-méron, or, The History of Edouard and Elisabeth Who Spent Eighty-one Years among the Megamicres, Aboriginal Inhabitants of the Protocosm Inside our Globe* finds only one hundred and fifty-six subscribers for the three hundred and fifty copies which Casanova has printed in Prague. He loses a great deal of money, but his literary verve is unquashed.

In the spring of 1789, Casanova falls gravely ill. After several weeks of an affliction that plunges him into a state of extreme languor, he consults an Irish physician living in Dux, Doctor James Columb O'Reilly, who orders absolute rest and, specifically, the suspension of his mathematical research. Knowing his patient's lively temperament and fear of boredom, he suggests an entertainment that he considers more restful: writing his reminiscences. In a letter of May 17, Doctor O'Reilly prescribes for Casanova: "For several months you must give up gloomy studies which tire the brain, and sex; for the time being you must be lazy, and, as a kind of relief, you might review the happy days spent in Venice and other parts of the world. I beg you, preserve as much of your life as you can for the public good."

The patient follows the prescription. He writes from morn to night, he writes in his sleep, he dreams about writing. In March 1791, the manuscript is two-thirds finished. By July 1792, he has added a description of his life to the year 1772, but he is enjoying the occupation less than when he started. A year later, he has reached "the age of fifty" in his narrative, which is where he wants to stop. Now everyday life overshadows the rest; it is not very happy: his last remaining friends die; he is distressed by the French Revolution; and he has dreadful problems with the steward of the castle, Georg Feldkirchner, to whom he writes

unsent letters that comfort him about all the pettiness, harassment, and humiliation he has to bear.

To be hit with a stick, find one's effigy smeared with filth in
the lavatory, see one's dog ill-treated, be mocked, insulted, sus-
pected—this is too much turpitude, too much impertinence. Casanova complains to the lord of the castle and wins his case, but
with a three-year delay. In the meantime, he endures, he is silent, he is furious. To prevent losing face, he writes his memoirs,
as well as twenty-one *Letters Written to Mr. Faulkircher* [sic] *by His
Best Friend Jacques Casanova de Seingalt January 10, 1792.*

*In the ordinary course of things, Mr. Faulkircher, there should have
been nothing in common between you and me at the Dux castle, where
I was employed as a librarian, and you as a steward; but these days
the extraordinary is so in style it can almost be counted on.*

He stresses everything that sets him apart from this vulgar
Austrian sub-lieutenant who became a soldier at the age when
he was learning to read. The angry Casanova takes pride in
having been "polite as a result of the education provided by
literature and good company, where man learns morality and the
rules of honorable conduct." Condescendingly, he reminds the
vile majordomo that they do not belong in the same world:

*You were never able, therefore, to become cultivated through a knowledge
of the sciences, which extend the sphere of intelligence, or become more
refined through the company of learned people, or ennoble your mind
with instructive reading, or educate yourself in the rules of honorable
conduct and the morality of social proprieties, as I have, though I am
poor and of humble birth. I pity you for this as much as I congratulate
myself, while thanking fate and fortune for having provided me with
these precious advantages that place me so much higher than you.*

Superiority is of little weight when one is alone against everyone in the absence of the master of the castle. On Sunday, December 11, 1791, at ten in the morning, Casanova is attacked in the streets of Dux by a minion of Feldkirchner's, who strikes him repeatedly with a stick. Nothing could have been easier: Casanova was old, unarmed, without even a cane, and could put up no resistance. To escape from his assailant, he had to run to the closest house.

Justice must be done, and it will be. Since he cannot put him to the sword or break his skull, as he would have in his youth, Casanova takes revenge with his pen. The only freedom he has left is writing. In letter XIX, his shortest, he writes to this man ridden with malevolent envy, rancor, and ambitious ignorance:

You are an ass who does not know his place; as such, you envy me; as an envious person, you hate me; whoever hates is an enemy; as an enemy, you slander me; and as a slanderer, you deserve to have your tongue cut out; for a severed tongue is not even worthy to serve as a dish towel.

Writing these reprimands gradually makes the elderly solitary exile recover tranquillity, he who has never enjoyed playing the part of victim or persecuted.

In 1793, Count Joseph Karl Emmanuel von Waldstein dismisses Georg Feldkirchner and his acolyte. Casanova regains his vitality and joie de vivre; he finishes the narrative of his life. In the summer of 1794, Prince Charles Joseph de Ligne, with whom he has become friends, wants to read the manuscript. Casanova works on it again and gives him a corrected, revised version of the first volumes. The Prince strongly encourages him to pursue the work and publish it. *You felt so good about not being castrated, why do you want your works to be?* He congratulates Casanova: *One-third of this charming second volume, my dear friend, made me laugh, one-third gave me an erection, one-third gave me food for thought. The first two make you fervently loved, and the last makes you admired. You outdo Montaigne, there is no greater compliment in my opinion.*

On April 27, 1797, Casanova requests the Cabinet Minister at the court of Saxony, Count Camillo Marcolini de Fano, to sponsor the publication of his memoirs, which he entitles *History of My Life to the Year 1797*. He then rewrites the preface, but the amount of time he has left to live is too short for him to finish. Revision of the existing pages brings him from his birth to the summer of 1774 in Trieste. The narrative stops with his meeting Irene, an actress he has known since childhood, whom he loved in Milan, neglected in Genoa, and was useful to in Avignon. In Trieste Irene introduces him to her husband, an actor who plays Scapino, the commedia dell'arte's deceitful and clever manservant, and her nine-year-old daughter, who has a gift for the dance and does not rebuff his caresses. The *History of My Life* ends abruptly at this sentence, with its whiff of incest: *At the beginning of Lent she left with the whole troupe, and three years later I saw her in Padua, where I became much more tenderly acquainted with her daughter.*

VENICE FOREVER LOST

In Trieste, Casanova is awaiting the pardon of the Venetian State Inquisitors. He writes a comedy for the theater of San Pietro, *La Forza della vera amicizia*, and a cantata for three voices, *La Felicità di Trieste*, performed on October 13, 1774. He tries to be of service to his country in various ways so he can return to Venice after his eighteen-year exile. Several weeks after his reunion with Irene, he receives from the hands of the Venetian Consul, his friend Marco de Monti, the safe-conduct he had so ardently wanted. De Monti describes his reaction: "He read it, he reread it, he kissed it many times, and after a short interval of concentration and silence, he burst into a torrent of tears."

Casanova starts making his way to Venice on September 10, 1774, and reaches his beloved city on November 15. He stays there for eight years, during which he never stops writing: adaptations of novels, a theater journal, the translation of the *Iliad* into Italian. He launches a French company at the Sant'Angelo theater, meets Lorenzo Da Ponte, and maintains an amorous relationship with Francesca Buschini, a modest seamstress who lives in a narrow house in Barberia delle Tole, near San Giustina. He sees himself as a "tall man brimming with kindness, intelligence, and courage." It is in his native city that he learns of his mother's death on November 29, 1776.

Under the name of Antonio Pratolini, he becomes a secret agent (*confidente*) of the Venetian Inquisition, first unofficially, then officially. His patrician friends do not seem to see this as dishonorable. For fifteen ducats a month, he reports on the quarrel between two rival noblemen, on the words of a lawyer at the court, on the nuisance caused by those who sit in a circle, occupying more than two-thirds of the Calle Larga at San Marco. He also informs Their Excellencies of his own altercation with the porter at the San Luca theater who had claimed that two grains were missing from the weight of the zecchino he gave to him. Coming from him, it is piquant to read that the ecclesiastical tribunals are too permissive in annulling marriages, and that this should be regarded as a paramount disorder, a criminal libertinism:

If Your Excellencies in your wisdom do not hasten to remedy this evil, it can give rise to the greatest dangers for society: the extinction of respected families, the confusion of kinships, genealogical murkiness, ambiguous inheritances, the squandering of property, the unjust presentation of children falsely legitimized, and finally the ruin and revenge of legitimate children who, through a combination of ambition and avarice, have become bastards. Extreme license in conversations, the independence of women, the indifference of men are sources of great evil, which avarice and impiety succeed in making legal. Young people entering society see these as coolly permitted by custom, from which there results a general corruption of education which will easily take root unless caution is exercised.

On November 16, 1781, Casanova warns the Inquisitors that at San Moisè, at the bottom of the Pescheria, where the Grand Canal joins the Calle del Ridotto, there is a painting academy where men and women pose nude in a variety of attitudes under the gaze of young draftsmen who are barely twelve or thirteen years old. In his denunciation of December 22, Casanova draws up a list of impious or licentious books. With a touch of irony he notes that these can be found everywhere, particularly in the libraries of patricians, who are sufficiently enlightened and intelligent for their morals to remain unaffected. A lengthy enumeration follows that includes works by Voltaire, Rousseau, Helvetius, La Mettrie, Lucian, Machiavelli, and Aretino, alongside books by Crébillon the younger and Spinoza! No doubt agent Antonio Pratolini has dreams of seeing his own real name added to this infamous list.

In August 1782, after a financial disagreement with the Marchese Spinola and the Grimani brothers, he feels wronged and humiliated. He avenges himself in a biting, impertinent satire in the form of a mythological roman à clef, *Ne amori ne donne, ovvero la stalla ripulita [Neither Loves nor Women, or, The Cleaned Stable]*, with a plot derived from the twelve labors of Hercules and the Augean stables cleaned by Alcidice. In it, he makes a veiled claim to being the illegitimate son of Michele Grimani, whom he singles out as illegitimate as well. This work costs him a second, permanent disgrace at the hands of the Inquisitors. He is forced to go into exile. He takes a last look at his divine Venice on June 16, 1783. He will never see it again.

To Madame de Pompadour, who asked him during his first Paris stay, in 1757, following his escape from prison, if he came from Venice, from down there, he had answered proudly: *Venice, madame, is not down there; it is up there.* Leaving Venice marks a downfall.

Casanova roams the roads of Europe for a position, for employment with some nobleman, ambassador, or patron. He feels old, lucid, and helpless. *I am fifty-eight; I cannot go around on foot: winter arrives suddenly. And whenever I consider becoming an adventurer again, I start laughing when I look at myself in the mirror.*

Casanova goes to his brother Francesco's in Paris, by way of Bolzano, Innsbruck, Augsburg, Frankfurt, Aachen, Spa, The Hague, Rotterdam, and Antwerp. Francesco, a recognized painter of battle scenes, accepted as a member of the Royal Academy of Painting and Sculpture in May 1763 for his painting *Combat de cavalerie*, now lives at the Louvre, where Giacomo stays with him for about three months. He meets an illustrious guest, Benjamin Franklin, who invites him to attend the opening session of the Academy of Sciences on November 28, 1783. On that day a report is presented on the experiments of the Montgolfier brothers, and Casanova briefly considers going up in a balloon.

After Paris, he goes to Vienna, where he leaves his brother, now the protégé of Prince Kaunitz, and travels once again: to Dresden, Berlin, Prague. In Vienna, in February 1784, Casanova enters the service of Signor Foscarini, Ambassador of Venice. It is at his dinner table, one evening, that Count Waldstein, a Freemason like himself, seduced by Casanova's volubility, his talent for storytelling, and his erudition in the occult, suggests he become the librarian at his castle in Bohemia. Casanova turns the offer down. He cannot yet reconcile himself to it. At the ambassador's death, when he finds no other position, he considers retiring from society and becoming a monk at the convent in Einsiedeln; then he applies in vain for employment at the Academy in Berlin. In September 1785, having no other means of support, the man from nowhere settles into his last castle.

PLEASURE IS NOT A SIN

At the point where Casanova's astounding life of adventures seems to break off, a final round is played, not on the stage of the world, but in the secluded room of a "writing sage." He who had been all action becomes all reminiscence, he who had been aware only of the present moment finds his fulfillment in the past. He who did not want to submit to any kind of calculation or premeditated plan retires from life to sample one of its most perilous experiences, one of its most mysterious alchemies: that of writing, which transforms the remarkable existence of an eighteenth-century Venetian into a literary masterpiece.

The impromptu man, the man of no importance, gives his own story consideration; he no longer evades it. He throws himself into it and lays public claim to it. He whose only schooling was life itself and his teachers the women he loved decides to write in order to establish the basis of his chosen existence: pleasure, pleasure without sin, pleasure without shame or guilt. Free, unburdened love without transgression, joyful and reciprocal. Love without drama or suffering, love that predates sin. Neither angel nor beast, simply human, nobly human, and ready to share with consorts the true pleasure of living: *Only human beings are capable of real pleasure for, endowed as they are with the faculty of reason, they anticipate it, seek it, fashion it, and reason about it after having enjoyed it.*

Animal nature, Casanova explains, must fulfill three instinctual needs in order to perpetuate itself: feed itself, reproduce itself, and destroy its enemy. These three sensations—hunger, appetite for coitus, and hatred of the enemy—bring habitual, crude satisfactions. And, he continues:

Man shares the same condition as animals when he engages in those three propensities without the interference of reason. When the human mind makes its contribution, these three satisfactions become pleasure, pleasure, and pleasure: an inexplicable sensation, which makes us savor what we call happiness . . . The voluptuous man who reasons disdains greediness, bawdiness, and the brutal revenge arising from the first impulse of anger; he is an epicure; he falls in love; but he will want to enjoy the object of his love only if he is certain of being loved; and when he is insulted, he can take revenge only after having coldly devised the best way to enjoy his revenge . . . We endure hunger in order to better savor ragouts; we put off the pleasure of love in order to make it more intense; and we postpone revenge in order to make it deadlier.

Long before writing these lines, Giacomo Casanova, at eighteen, had had lengthy philosophical conversations with Yusuf Ali, a Turkish wise man whom he met in Constantinople, one of the few tolerant and humane father figures the memoirist describes. This symbolic father, whom Casanova unambivalently respected, suggested that he transcend immediate gratifications for deeper sensual pleasures:

—*True pleasures are those that affect only the soul, completely independent of the senses,* said the wise Yusuf.

—*I cannot, my dear Yusuf, imagine pleasures that my soul could enjoy without the mediation of my senses,* the young man replied.

—*Listen to me. When you fill your pipe, do you feel pleasure?*

—*Yes.*

—*To which of your senses do you attribute it, if not to your soul?* . . .

—*What you say is quite true; but you will forgive me if I find that several pleasures affecting my senses deserve greater preference than those that affect only my soul.*

—*Forty years ago I thought as you do. Forty years from now, if you attain wisdom, you will think as I do. Pleasures, my dear son, stir the passions and trouble the soul; hence you must see that they cannot properly be called pleasures.*

—*You surprise me.*

—*The happiest of men is not always the most voluptuous but the one who knows how to choose the greatest voluptuous pleasures; and the greatest voluptuous pleasures, I repeat, can only be those which do not stir up the passions but increase peace of mind.*

Fifty years later, the impetuous young man has become wise; he has discovered that pleasure can only be savored during the calm intervals which we grant ourselves between the voluptuous moments. Real happiness stems from the recollection of pleasure:

Pleasure is the present enjoyment of the senses; it is complete satisfaction given in everything they long for; and when the senses are exhausted or tired and want rest, either as a respite or for renewal, pleasure becomes imagination; it enjoys reflecting on the happiness which its tranquillity procures.

THE CULT OF MEMORY

Not content with having led a full life, Casanova was presumptuous enough to aspire to renew it, and characteristically intemperate enough to do so as often as his "old soul" allows him to remember it: *Remembering the pleasures I experienced, I renew them and laugh at the pains I have endured, which I no longer feel.*

Now, at the end of his life, he whose memory awakened late in childhood and who claims that living is remembering, makes the act of preserving past states of consciousness the guiding principle behind his work and behind felicity. Ephemeral pleasure is followed by a reflective period of happiness. After hotheadedness and lighthearted eagerness, going from one enjoyment to another, comes the slow progression of thought, the reasoned and calm reconstitution of the past. Allegretto is followed by the adagio of happiness relived. Embracing the Epicurean idea of consciousness at rest, the sage of Dux praises the sensual enjoyment that deepens with the happiness of reliving life's moments through memory:

By putting between pleasures the calm that must follow each of them after enjoyment, we are given the time to recognize the reality of our happy state. Man can be happy only when he recognizes that he is happy, and he can recognize his state only when he is calm.

In this castle life, so remote from the social life he loved, he must confront solitude, isolation, exile, poverty, humiliation, and the decrepitude of age. True, he has known other confinements, but here, in Dux, he no longer has the recourse of running away, as from the prison in Venice, with the help of a bolt converted into an instrument of freedom. There is no escaping old age and death. An unbearable imprisonment to which he cannot resign himself without rebelling. He likes himself and misses his youth. He knows he is at the edge of the abyss. *I feel the approach of death*, he confesses, *but I want it to happen against my will: my consent would smack of suicide.* If, at sixty, he has had to accept Count Waldstein's offer to come and take up the appointment of librarian in the isolated castle of Dux, he has done so with feelings of rage and compulsory gratitude. *You are the only man in the world to have thought of putting an end to my travels in the beginning of September 1785 by entrusting me with your beautiful library*, he writes to his protector in the preface to his utopian novel, *Icosaméron*. He finally gives in to the temptation of immobility, which had never ceased to fascinate him even as it repelled him, but it is too soon, no doubt, for he would have preferred to suspend the implacable march of time.

Since he can no longer fight with his body or command himself to *Jump, Marquis!* the aged Casanova clashes swords with his pen. Since he must resign himself to this Bohemian exile devoid of glory, he escapes through writing. Once again writing is his revenge, allowing him to retake possession of the freedom to impose his own vision of the world.

With the onset of age, a painful disparity emerges between desire and its fulfillment. Casanova believes that the start of his existence "in his capacity of thinking being" coincided with the awakening of his memory, at the age of eight and four months, and he dates the end of the first act of his life to when he was thirty-eight years old and mortified by La Charpillon. A thirty-year feast of the senses! Thirty years of life instead of the death that had been predicted! But after the London misadventure, Casanova no longer had the same haughtiness or self-assurance; the ordeal literally made him fall ill. Though he does not let himself lose heart so easily and he pursues his adventures when he regains his health, from this time on, his self-image is different. He cannot believe in his infallible seductiveness. He could have omitted this unhappy episode out of vanity—for who likes to admit having been the puppet of a worthless girl, a small-time socialite?—but no doubt telling the story provides a sort of therapy, an initiatory trial marking the passage from youth to adulthood. Having arrived "midway on the journey of this life," he knows he is embarking on his inexorable descent to death.

He traces his second turning point to 1783, when Venice forced him to go into permanent exile at the age of fifty-eight. In his impotent rage he calls Venice "the ungrateful bosom of my stepmother." Now, instead of being a mature man, he is entering old age. Two years of wandering leads him to accept Count Waldstein's hospitality. At sixty-four, he begins to write the *History of My Life.*

Imperceptibly, as the pages accumulate, the writing of his adventures—told with the intensity, color, and authenticity of the immediate present—makes the distance between the past, which reemerges with lifelike illusion, and his present-day reality more and more vivid and painful. In renouncing youth, he has regained it. A privileged spectator, Casanova sets the carousel of his life spinning again, but the merry-go-round music is increasingly grating. He becomes aware of the irreversible march of time. While at the beginning of his narrative he invites the reader to share the progress of the adventurer's experiences, some thousand-odd pages later the main character and the writer become two different persons. Casanova, now, sees himself in action and gauges the distance that separates him from the person he once was and no longer is. Thanks to the merciless test of truth that is the writing of his life, he confronts what he has always denied—suffering, fragility, bereavement.

Revisiting the spot where, ten years earlier, he had had to part with the woman who was the greatest love of his life, Giacomo Casanova notes the changes that have come over him against his will, and though memory restores his tender and witty Henriette as she was then, he cannot say as much for himself. Soul-searching, he must record the sad changes he feels he has undergone:

Comparing myself to myself, I felt I was less worthy of possessing her than in those days. I still knew how to love, but I found I no longer had the delicacy I had then, or the feelings that justified a frenzy of the senses, or the same kindliness, or a certain probity; and what terrified me was, I no longer had the same vigor. Yet it seemed that the mere memory of Henriette restored it to me entirely.

The betrayal of his body affects him more than anything else. Until then, his self-confidence depended completely on his vigorous health, his athleticism, his acute awareness of being alive. At thirty-six, the restrictions of middle age worry him:

I was therefore in dire straits, and what distressed me most was having to admit to myself that I was feeling the first signs of despondency, a common result of age; I no longer had the carefree confidence conferred by youth and the feeling of strength, and yet experience had not matured me enough to mend my ways.

Though Casanova refuses to consider his autobiography as a kind of confession, Rousseau's shadow hovers over his thoughts, even if by default. As he strolls around the gardens of the Villa Ludovisi, he meditates melancholically on the twists and turns of life. Dark thoughts assail him. The specter of death stands before him, and though he was never a coward, he lacks the strength to treat it with cold-blooded resignation. The idea that all things come to an end horrifies him. In order to mitigate his somber mood, he reflects on the fact that he made all the women he loved (except La Corticelli) happy. For Casanova, beyond despair, the living memory of pleasure always endures, of pleasure received and pleasure given. And this pleasure, given to the women with whom he was in love, he cherishes all the more now that he is an old man who no longer masters it.

How many thoughts when I found myself in the spot where twenty-seven years earlier I had been with Donna Lucrezia! I saw the place, and I found it more beautiful, whereas I was not the same, but diminished in all my faculties, except in experience, which I abused and which compensated for nothing, except in making me more entitled to reason. Shabby gain! Reasoning led me to sadness, the pitiless mother of the dreadful idea of death which I lacked the strength to contemplate like a Stoic.

A hatred of old age and the impotence that ensues occupies more and more space as the account of his life progresses. Soon he will prefer to relinquish the pen rather than spell out his decline in greater detail.

I felt I had grown old . . . I found that a long session was not followed by the soundest sleep and that my appetite at the table, which had been sharpened by love in earlier times, was now dulled by it, just as it was after enjoying sexual pleasure. Aside from that, I found that the fair sex was no longer interested in me at first sight, I had to talk, rivals were preferred to me . . . When someone said of me, He is getting on in age, I had to admit it, but this truth annoyed me.

On self-examination, the adventurer becomes convinced that he should consider a good retirement, but this wise course of action is not easy to take. He still has hopes. Yet he suffers new rebuffs. Living in Ancona again, and falling in love with Lia, one of his last loves, he gauges the insurmountable difference that separates him from his youth. He finds he is a "completely different person":

Being forty-seven I knew I was at the age which is scorned by Fortune, and that was enough to sadden me, since without the blind goddess's favor, no one in the world can be happy . . . It is as he declines that the man who has spent his life in pleasures makes these gloomy reflections, which have no bearing in the full flower of youth, when he need not foresee anything and the present occupies him completely, and a permanent, forever rosy horizon makes his life happy and sustains such a happy illusion in his mind that he laughs at the philosopher who dares tell him that behind this charming horizon there is old age, wretchedness, repentance—always belated—and death.

After this melancholic digression, Casanova candidly confides his present distress to the reader: *If such were my reflections twenty-six years ago, it is easy to imagine the ones that obsess me today when I am alone.*

When he formulates this sentence, he is a man of seventy-three with only a few months to live, yet he feels young in spirit, and writing diverts him from boredom and melancholy. At the end of his life, Casanova remains free and happy: still the same "master of his hand" who had challenged the surgeons of the King of Poland.

AN INSOLENT LEGACY

In making his life into a narrative, Casanova accomplishes a metamorphosis, an internal transformation. Through this personal reexamination, this tardy apprehension of his actions and emotions, he transmutes ephemera into duration, esthetics into ethics, action into wisdom.

The man of the pure present ceases to avoid time, his implacable enemy. He now sees that he has a past, a present, and an all too brief future. This perception of the duration of things inevitably includes loss and suffering. With time, the pain of the irreparable is buried. Throughout his life Casanova has always tried to escape time's arrow, endeavored to place himself above the common laws of mankind, and retain, at whatever cost, a feeling of fusion in otherness, but now he finally confronts the reality of the world. Through this transmutation he achieves not just a deepened sense of self but also a moral meditation on existence.

Voluptuousness becomes memory. The unending repetition of his experiences is transcended by writing. The very act of writing allows this transcendence of self. Casanova enjoys the moment, and once it slips away, he enjoys remembering the moment, a moment that is enhanced by the precious feeling of transience. His pleasure in living is perpetuated as literary pleasure.

Of his adventurous life, everything has faded away. He has retained nothing, kept nothing, saved nothing. He possesses nothing other than his own person. This irascible and prickly old man, gradually growing bitter, fashions a work out of the narrative of his life. He directs himself onstage, renders his memories theatrical, and thus, unwitting but filled with hope, attains immortality. The *History of My Life* marks his official birth as a legendary character, and it is also his literary testament.

Adventurer, traveler, eternal lover, forever in quest of sensual pleasure and experience of the present, Casanova revels in the resurrection of the past, which allows him to escape the despair of old age and the melancholy of a scattered, splintered life, consumed in the moment that no longer is. Now, before the large open book of his recollections, pen in hand, primed to capture the faintest thrill of former happiness, he celebrates the quest for pleasure at the altar of memory. Not content with having made voluptuous pleasure the principle of life, the writer from Venice tells us that true happiness is the one offered by reminiscence. Memory not only takes the place of voluptuous pleasure but renews it. Beyond pleasure, there is still happiness—such is the insolent legacy of Giacomo Casanova.

Notes

The quotations from *Histoire de ma vie* are taken from the unabridged edition of the original manuscript published by Brockhaus-Plon in 1960 and reissued in 1993 by Robert Laffont in its "Bouquins" series. (Willard R. Trask's English translation of this edition, originally published by Harcourt, Brace & World in 1966–71, has recently been reissued in paperback by the Johns Hopkins University Press.) *Histoire de ma vie* is in twelve volumes and is divided into chapters. The source for each quotation refers to the original text, as follows: the first (Arabic) numeral refers to the volume number; the second (Roman) numeral refers to the chapter number; and the third (Arabic) numeral refers to the page number in the "Bouquins" edition.

For example : 12, II, 893 indicates that the quoted passage is in volume 12, chapter II, page 893.

ONE

The Last Castle

For this chapter I am greatly indebted to the essay by George Poulet, *Etudes sur le temps*, 4, Paris, Presses-Pocket, 1990 (chapter V on Casanova).

THE PRESENT MOMENT AND MEMORY

I have always believed . . . 4, XIII, 877.

On Casanova's relationship with Voltaire, see, among other letters, the one
dated 1766 to the actor Soulé, "Correspondance inédite de Jacques Casanova (1760–1766), *Pages casanoviennes*, Paris, 1925, pp. 34–47. "For me
(granted the hypothesis that all our mysteries, religions, and divine rev-
elations are pure inventions), I would say that there are some truths that
must not be uttered . . . Voltaire is all the more an imbecile that with all
his intellect he does not know that with the publication of his so-called
discoveries he harms the social economy and the very humanity which
he so loudly insists he is the protector of by setting himself up as the
preacher and apostle of libertinage."

Jump, Marquis! . . . 7, II, 471.

This is how God . . . 4, XIII, 887.

THE VOLUPTUOUSNESS OF LIVING,
THE VOLUPTUOUSNESS OF WRITING

height of taste . . . 1, Preface, 7.

sorcerer, forger, thief . . . 9, IV, 76

THE WRITER AND HIS DOUBLE

a polite man owes . . . Letter XXI in *Lettres écrites au sieur Faulkircher par son
meilleur ami Jacques Casanova de Seingalt le 10 janvier 1792*, Caen,
L'Echoppe, 1988, p. 71. The text was reissued under the title *Lettres à
un majordome*, Paris, Seuil, 1994.

I wrote a short petition . . . 1, VII, 118.

The effect of my petition . . . 1, VII, 118.

But two days after . . . 1, VII, 119.

Admit that if . . . 11, I, 612.

It was my first literary exploit . . . 1, II, 30.

It was on that fatal day . . . 9, XI, 221.

This is what Love did to me . . . 9, XII, 247.

Since you like games . . . 2, VIII, 386.
What compelled me to play . . . 2, VIII, 408.

LIFE IS THEATER

Cospetto! . . . This sentence of Casanova's, related by the Prince de Ligne, is cited in "Casanova seen by the Prince de Ligne," in *Histoire de ma vie*, 3, 1164.
We men, though devoid . . . *Lana Caprina, lettre d'un lycanthrope*, French translation in *Pages casanoviennes*, V, 1925, p. 36.
Do not ask me how . . . 8, VIII, 853.
In the morning, on waking . . . 9, XIII, 285.
I felt I had aged . . . 12, IV, 938.
Try as I might . . . 12, VII, 978.
I felt I was . . . 12, VIII, 987.
Just tell me how much . . . 6, II, 259.

CATALOGUE

Volume 2 of the "Bouquins" edition of *Histoire de ma vie* includes "Loterie grammaticale," "Les impôts sur les produits de première nécessité," "Projet pour réaliser à Venise la teinture écarlate des cotons," "Sur la colonisation de la Sierra Morena," and "Projet pour établir une fabrique de savon à Varsovie."

THE TIME OF HAPPINESS

Nothing is more bitter . . . 11, IV, 672.
You will forget . . . 3, V, 521.
most honorable . . . 9, IV, 68.
Nothing, my old friend . . . 11, VI, 731–32.
Oh, dearest friend, you . . . Letter by Cecilie von Roggendorf of June 25, 1797, "La dernière amie de Jacques Casanova (1797–1798)," *Pages casanoviennes*, 1926, p. 32.

Real love . . . In "Examen des études de la nature et de *Paul et Virginie* de Bernardin de Saint-Pierre," in *Histoire de ma vie*, 2, 1132.

For information concerning the fate of the manuscript of *Histoire de ma vie*, see Helmut Watzlawick, "Biographie d'un manuscrit," in *Europe*, May 1987, pp. 28–40, retold in *Histoire de ma vie*, 1, xv-xxviii.

TWO

The Child from Venice

Casanova recounts his childhood memories in the first three chapters of *Histoire de ma vie*.

THREE

The Curtain Rises

THE OMNIPOTENCE OF WOMEN

The following books discuss Casanova's relationships with the most important figures in his childhood: Octave Mannoni, *Clefs pour l'Imaginaire ou l'Autre Scène*, Paris, Seuil, 1969, pp. 24–32; François Roustang, *Le Bal masqué de Giacomo Casanova*, Paris, Minuit, 1984; Chantal Thomas, *Casanova: Un voyage libertin*, Paris, Denoël, 1985; Marie-Françoise Luna, "Casanova et ses dieux," *Europe*, no. 697, May 1987, pp. 59–67.

Some things . . . 1, I, 18.

CASANOVA'S MOTHER

In the most brilliant company . . . 1, IX, 171.

"FAREWELL, VENICE!"

He will set you on the road . . . 1, VI, 101.
Surrendering to fate . . . 1, VII, 134.
Without a good library . . . 1, VIII, 165.
Your family . . . 1, IX, 169.

WHAT IS A FATHER?

I was an interesting scatterbrain . . . 1, IX, 179.
The State Inquisitors . . . 1, I, 21.
Which I might still have . . . 1, III, 55.
Where can they be found? . . . 1, IV, 57.

A "YOUNG FRIAR OF NO IMPORTANCE"

In my capacity . . . 1, IV, 58–59.

LAUGHTER AND GUILT

Sequere Deum . . . Seneca, *Happiness*, XV, 5.
Sitting side by side . . . 1, VI, 103.
You struck me . . . 1, VI, 103.
I have never done . . . 3, XI, 637.
The meeting with Pope Benedict XIV is related in 1, X, 199–201.

THE RED SUIT OF FORTUNE

I kept a modest silence . . . 2, VII, 378.
Deceit is a vice . . . 1, VIII, 160.
Whoever you are . . . 2, VII, 383.
Sufficiently wealthy . . . 2, VIII, 384.
Prudence requires . . . 4, XI, 857–58.

IN WEDDING ATTIRE

I ripped up . . . 4, XVI, 951.
I then turned and looked . . . 4, XVI, 953.

FOUR

The Stratagems of Voluptuousness

THE PLEASURE OF WOMEN

when we find ourselves . . . 9, I, 15.

SHIELDED FROM HATRED

The very sound . . . 5, VII, 129.
I stood there transfixed . . . 9, VI, 116.
My dear and tender . . . 9, I, 1.
You were born . . . 9, I, 6.
Your submissiveness . . . 7, IV, 518.
I did not make a mistake . . . 7, IV, 521.
I adored them . . . 10, I, 309.
I have been dominated . . . 2, II, 245.
little garment . . . 7, I, 463.

SEX AND CONVERSATION

at least two-thirds . . . 6, V, 307.

THE PROMISE OF IMMORTALITY

We separated . . . 10, VII, 439.
fortunate soul . . . 12, IV–V, 934.

THREATENING FIGURES

I want you to dress me up . . . 1, V, 92.
Despite her, the stains . . . 1, V, 92.
My dear friend . . . 2, VI, 361.
Always like this, my dear friend . . . 2, V, 354.
Being very young . . . 2, IV, 311.
It is the plan of a monster . . . 9, XI, 221.

"THE DUPE OF WOMEN"

It was in this dreadful state . . . 1, III, 50.
The professional seducer . . . 12, V, 941.
bitterness compared to which . . . 2, V, 346.
Yet, despite such good schooling . . . 1, III, 40.

THE SAGE OF DUX

I loved, I was loved . . . 8, X, 909.

if I need to die . . . Casanova's letter to Elise von der Recke of April 17, 1797, in *Lettere di donne a Giacomo Casanova*, Milan, Aldo Rava, 1912, p. 305.

Concerning the impression Casanova made on Lorenzo Da Ponte's wife, see his *Mémoires et livrets*, Paris, Livre de Poche, 1980, p. 197.

I wish you to be my guide . . . Henriette de Schuckmann's letter of February 13, 1796, in *Histoire de ma vie*, 3, 1157.

to assure you of the esteem . . . Cecilie von Roggendorf's letter of April 20, 1727, in "La dernière amie de Jacques Casanova," p. 18.

UNDER A STORMY SKY

This episode is related in 1, V, 96–99.

LOVE AS MAGICIAN, OR, THE PHALLIC CHALLENGE

My philosophical system which I thought . . . 3, I, 466.
She no longer seemed . . . 3, I, 467.
According to her, not only . . . 5, VI, 97.
This false confidence . . . 5, V, 96.
make her soul enter . . . 5, VI, 98.
The undine, caressing me . . . 9, III, 50–51.
Her reasoning was very sound . . . 9, III, 53.
most extraordinary . . . 9, IV, 79.
without charlatanism no science . . . 6, II, 250.

THE FIRST LOVE QUARTET

There were four of us . . . 1, V, 82.
Little by little I uncurled her . . . 1, V, 89–90.
until, affecting . . . 1, V, 90.
This love, which was my first . . . 1, VII, 134.
You are in love with me . . . 2, I, 242–43.
It is a kind of long . . . 2, II, 248.
This is how I spent that day . . . 7, VII, 579.

FIVE

Gardens of Love

UNDER THE SIGN OF THE SERPENT

I will therefore have the honor . . . 1, IX, 172.
Do not be afraid . . . 1, IX, 194.
In spite of her intelligence . . . 1, IX, 194.
After several detours, we entered . . . 1, X, 196.
Mind your sister . . . 1, X, 204–5.

THE FACE OF HAPPINESS

See Helmut Watzlawick, "*Fata viam invenient:* Sur les traces d'Henriette," in *L'Intermédiaire des casanovistes*, VI, 1989, reprintd in *Histoire de ma vie*, 1, 1070–85.

With an empty heart . . . 3, I, 471.

If you tell me to accompany you to Parma . . . 3, II, 490.

People who believe . . . 3, III, 501.

Who is this Henriette . . . 3, IV, 510.

Let us simply prepare ourselves . . . 3, V, 517.

No, I have not forgotten her . . . 3, V, 521.

It is I, my only friend . . . 3, V, 522.

I considered I was justly . . . 3, V, 525.

THE LIBERTINE NUN

See Pierre Gruet, "M.M. et les anges de Murano," in *Histoire de ma vie*, 1, 1063–69.

A nun who has seen . . . 4, I, 714.

So much boldness . . . 4, II, 721.

Aside from M.M.'s birth . . . 4, II, 732.

I have lost all confidence . . . 4, III, 745.

It is unbelievable . . . 4, III, 745.

a commoner to whom a king . . . 4, VII, 789.

All three of us—intoxicated . . . 4, VII, 796.

LOVE LETTERS TO THE ADORED VENETIAN

Silvia's daughter . . . 5, III, 58.

The friendship and esteem . . . 5, IV, 65–66.

I will reply . . . Manon Balletti's letters to Casanova have been published in *Lettere di donne a Giacomo Casanova*, and selections translated into French by Maynial, in *Lettres de femmes à Jacques Casanova* (1912); some of these are included in *Histoire de ma vie*, 1, 1085–99. The letter of February 7, 1760, was published in *Mémoires*, Paris, La Pléiade, 1959, II, 1139.

I was fêted . . . 5, VIII, 141–42.
But Manon Balletti . . . 5, X, 191.

AN UNEXPECTED TURN OF EVENTS IN A
CHINESE ROOM

The love she had inspired in me . . . 7, X, 631.
Donna Lucrezia! . . . 7, X, 635.
She was content to be . . . 7, X, 640.
But the moment which . . . 7, X, 640.

A CHANCE MISHAP

She was lying . . . 9, IV, 63.
You are a strange person . . . 9, IV, 65.
My heart was pounding . . . 9, IV, 68.

SUCH LASTING FIDELITY

But if you return . . . 11, VI, 731. (The beginning of this letter is quoted in the first chapter herein.)

PARADISE ON EARTH

There were all the greatest . . . 11, X, 839–40.
But is our daughter . . . 11, X, 840.
We went and sat down . . . 11, X, 842.
Determined not to consummate . . . 11, X, 842.
Whether because of nature or education . . . 12, III, 910.
the boy's resemblance . . . 12, III, 911.
I laughed to myself . . . 10, II, 323.
Concerning gardens of love, see Catherine Laroze, *Une histoire sensuelle des jardins*, Paris, Olivier Orban, 1990.

SIX

On the World's Stage

The indexes to the Brockhaus-Plon and "Bouquins" editions enable us to retrace many aspects of Casanova's life. For this chapter I made use of the following entries: cosmetics, household and furnishings, culinary specialties and spices, means of transport and postal service, habits and customs. The different places where Casanova stayed are also in the index as well as names of inns, theaters, churches, embassies, gardens, etc.

To travel agreeably . . . In Marie-Françoise Luna, "Casanova, lecteur des guides touristiques," *L'Intermédiaire des casanovistes*, I, 1984, pp. 3–7.

Protect yourselves, mortals . . . 6, IV, 299.

I breathed more freely . . . 11, V, 708.

Tired and reeling . . . 10, X, 517.

LOGBOOK

His coat was indeed . . . 1, VIII, 150.

I had bought a carriage . . . 9, V, 97.

Having put a good mattress . . . 10, VII, 439.

Because of the sandy . . . 10, III, 341.

Uneven, stony . . . 10, XII, 566.

I admired the beauty . . . 9, VII, 127.

I was accustomed . . . 7, XI, 642.

THE SIGHTS

Poor Spaniards! . . . 11, IV, 677.

I saw that everything . . . 11, IV, 675.

A view of this city . . . 2, IV, 280.

twenty-four minutes . . . 10, V, 382.

eighteen hours . . . 10, V, 382.

In a week . . . 10, VI, 413.

to have seen all the sights . . . 11, X, 851.

Villainous spies . . . 3, XII, 641.
one must live like the Romans . . . 9, VII, 147.
The island called England . . . 9, VII, 127.
I told you my name . . . 9, VIII, 155.
But I want to know their names . . . 9, X, 203.
In the case of spectacles . . . 9, XII, 268.

A FEW DAYS IN THE TRAVELER'S LIFE

more to see the actresses . . . 7, VII, 570.
Not knowing where to go . . . 3, XII, 641.
You see my father . . . 7, VII, 573.
I saw that in this house . . . 7, VIII, 599.
with the goal of making . . . 7, VIII, 602.
It is rubbish . . . 7, IX, 619.

THE THEATER OF THE WORLD

I did not want to command respect . . . 7, VII, 569.

THE TEMPTATION OF IMMOBILITY

I could not resolve . . . 2, IV, 297.
It was not love for Manon . . . 5, VII, 136.
I could have lived happily . . . 7, XI, 644.
I thought I saw . . . 6, IV, 295–96.
I spent a week . . . 10, III, 388.

THE CARNIVAL OF THE IMPOSSIBLE

His refined witticisms . . . In *Confutazione della storia del governo veneto d'Amelot de la Houssaye*, Amsterdam, 1769, 3 vols., III, 287, quoted in Philippe Monnier, *Venise au XVIIIe siècle*, Paris, Perrin, 1906, reissued 1981, pp. 256–57.
But, monsieur, how am I . . . 3, VIII, 568.

NOTES

People go masked . . . 7, XI, 646.
The devil, death . . . 11, VI, 724.
I decided to go masked as Pierrot . . . 4, V, 769.
To the sound of applause . . . 4, V, 770.
In complete freedom . . . 4, V, 770.

PORTRAIT GALLERY

In spite of her wrinkles . . . 2, X, 451.
I found her above . . . 3, VIII, 560–61.
You are in France . . . 3, VIII, 578.
The appearance of each of the three . . . 3, VIII, 572.
Theater foyers . . . 5, V, 78–79.

A MAN OF THE THEATER

Throughout the carnival . . . 2, V, 340.
Seeing myself reduced . . . 2, VI, 369.
Nevertheless, I received . . . 3, X, 607.
The only thing I did . . . 3, XI, 636.
I wrote it in Italian . . . 5, IX, 170, note 2.
We will be presenting . . . 7, V, 536.

EPILOGUE ON TIPTOES

You were the first . . . 10, IV, 357.
the just reward . . . 10, IV, 360.

SEVEN

The Backstage of the Body

"THE COUNTRY IN EQUILIBRIUM"

My empty stomach ... 6, I, 243.
anger kills ... 10, X, 516.
Do not be afraid ... 4, IV, 760.
Tell, but do not call ... 2, V, 336.
It is a figure ... 1, VII, 127.
And without that relief ... 8, IV, 775.
After making punch ... 4, IV, 758–59.

THE INVALID IN SPITE OF HIMSELF, AND THE IMAGINARY DOCTOR

You are a very handsome ... 10, IV, 353.
Is it possible, sire ... 10, IV, 353.
My great treasure ... 2, II, 251.
You are afraid of nothing ... Francesca Buschini's letter, in
   Histoire de ma vie, 3, 1137.
In the morning, when I wake up ... 9, XIII, 285.
I could not refrain from scrutinizing ... 7, II, 471.
You have robbed me ... 10, IX, 493.
I succeeded very well and equally ... 3, XI, 637.
not to want something ... 1, VIII, 139. (On love diseases, see Jean-Didier
   Vincent, *Casanova: La contagion du plaisir,* Paris, Odile Jacob, 1990.)
Before knowing Melulla ... 2, VI, 365.
To judge a man ... 10, III, 329.

CHANGES IN HUMOR

Casanova ascribes the four temperaments to himself: 1, Preface, 5.
See the *Nouvelle revue de psychanalyse,* "L'humeur et son changement," 32,

autumn 1985, particularly the essays by Laurence Kahn, Jackie Pigeaud, Pascal Quignard, and Jean Starobinski.

I found I was so astonished . . . 2, IX, 418.

In adjusting my nutrition . . . 1, Preface, 5.

My vocation was to study . . . 1, III, 52.

This physician, thinking . . . 3, XII, 648–49.

"I WAS THE MASTER OF MY HAND"

The duel with Branicki is related in *Histoire de ma vie*, 10, VIII.

LOVE AS DOCTOR

Death by laughing . . . 1, IX, 167.

I licked her wound . . . 2, V, 355.

Now I had become the physician . . . 2, VII, 378.

You possess a treasure . . . 2, VII, 379.

I congratulate myself . . . 2, VII, 381.

You practice . . . 10, X, 533.

You are free to believe . . . In "Lettres d'un physicien ubiquiste adressées au docteur O'Reilly, médecin irlandais," in *Histoire de ma vie*, 3, 1215–24.

THE PLAY OF APPEARANCES

When their uterus . . . *Lana Caprina*, p. 30.

The pleasure I have felt . . . 11, III, 651.

After all this inquiry . . . 11, III, 651.

He condemned my studied . . . 1, IV, 59.

On reflecting that it no longer . . . 2, III, 260.

I could bear . . . 2, III, 269.

With my hair . . . 2, II, 257.

On leaving Rome . . . 12, IV, 938.

I the undersigned . . . 6, III, 291, note 1.

EIGHT

Happiness Regained

CASANOVA, PHILOSOPHER

Forty-two volumes . . . Quoted by Raoul Vèze, "Jacques Casanova à Dux: La composition des *Mémoires*," *Mémoires*, Paris, La Sirène, vol. XII, p. x.

Unable to fall asleep . . . 7, VI, 562–63.

No unhappy thing has . . . 7, VI, 563.

It is an unquestionable fact . . . 10, X, 516.

We are the authors . . . 7, VIII, 591–92.

Those who say that life . . . 2, I, 238.

benefit someone gets . . . 1, III, 52.

should do with a man . . . 11, II, 614.

The more the work progresses . . . Letter to Opiz of February 20, 1792, quoted in Raoul Vèze, "Jacques Casanova à Dux: La composition des *Mémoires*," pp. xx–xxi.

ACT II, SCENE 10

Concerning the links between Casanova and Mozart's *Don Giovanni*, see F.-L. Mars, "Casanova et Don Giovanni," Paris, Le Cerf-Volant, no. 34, April 1961, reprinted in *Histoire de ma vie*, 3, 1152–56; J. Rives Childs, *Casanova*, Paris, Pauvert, 1983, pp. 421–22; Félicien Marceau, *Casanova ou l'anti-Don Juan*, Paris, Gallimard, 1985 (new edition); and Macchia Giovanni, "Casanova et le Don Juan de Mozart," *Le Théâtre de la dissimulation*, Paris, Le Promeneur, 1993.

DON GIACOMO

Three years ago . . . Letter to Max Lamberg of April 15, 1785, quoted by Raoul Vèze, "Jacques Casanova à Dux: La composition des *Mémoires*," p. xi.

For several months . . . Letter written by Doctor O'Reilly, *ibid.*, p. xvii.

*In the ordinary course . . . polite as a result . . . You were never able . . . You are
an ass . . .* In *Lettres écrites au sieur Faulkirchner par son meilleur ami Jacques
Casanova de Seingalt le 10 janvier, 1792.*
At the beginning of Lent . . . 12, X, 1053.

VENICE FOREVER LOST

If Your Excellencies . . . In Giovanni Comisso, *Les Agents secrets de Venise au
XVIIIe siècle,* Paris, Grasset, 1944, p. 145.
Venice, madame . . . 3, IX, 586.
I am fifty-eight . . . Letter of September 22, 1782, quoted by J. Rives Childs,
Casanova, p. 412.

PLEASURE IS NOT A SIN

See Gérard Lahouati, "Le fantôme Liberté: Cohérences et discordances
dans l'*Histoire de ma vie,*" *L'Intermédiaire des casanovistes,* 1988, pp. 1–8.
Only human beings . . . 4, II, 732.
Man shares the same condition . . . 4, II, 732–33.
True pleasures . . . 2, IV, 287–89.
Pleasure is the present enjoyment . . . 3, X, 618.

THE CULT OF MEMORY

Remembering the pleasures . . . 1, Preface, 4.
By putting between pleasures . . . 3, IV, 507.
I feel the approach of death . . . Preface of 1791, p. 1218.
You are the only man . . . Quoted in Raoul Vèze, "Jacques Casanova à Dux:
La composition des *Mémoires,*" XII, p. ix.
the ungrateful bosom . . . 12, IX, 1012.
Comparing myself to myself . . . 6, IX, 399.
I was therefore in dire straits . . . 8, I, 716.
How many thoughts . . . 12, IV–V, 927.
I felt I had grown old . . . 12, IV, 938.
Being forty-seven . . . If such were my reflections . . . 12, VIII, 987.

AN INSOLENT LEGACY

Casanova's life has inspired a great number of writers, including, among others, Apollinaire, Balzac, Hesse, Hofmannsthal, Márai, Schnitzler, Szentkuthy, and Zweig.

Index